A Survey of Russian Literature, with Selections

BY

ISABEL F. HAPGOOD

AUTHOR OF

"RUSSIAN RAMBLES," AND "THE EPIC SONGS OF RUSSIA"

NEW YORK   CHAUTAUQUA   SPRINGFIELD   CHICAGO

The Chautauqua Press

MCMII

891
1d.

1

The Lakeside Press, Chicago, Ill., U. S. A.
R. R. Donnelley & Sons Company

5025

CONTENTS

iii

PREFACE.

In this volume I have given exclusively the views of Russian critics upon their literature, and hereby acknowledge my entire indebtedness to them.

The limits of the work, and the lack of general knowledge on the subject, rendered it impossible for me to attempt any comparisons with foreign literatures.

Isabel F. Hapgood.

New York, June 6, 1902.

RUSSIAN LITERATURE

CHAPTER I

THE ANCIENT PERIOD, FROM THE EARLIEST TIMES TO THE INTRODUCTION OF CHRISTIANITY IN 988.

Whether Russia had any literature, or even a distinctive alphabet, previous to the end of the tenth century, is not known.

In the year 988, Vladímir, Grand Prince of Kíeff, accepted Christianity for himself and his nation, from Byzantium, and baptized Russia wholesale. Hence his characteristic title in history, "Prince-Saint-equal-to-the-Apostles." His grandmother, Olga, had already been converted to the Greek Church late in life, and had established churches and priests in Kíeff, it is said. Prince Vladímir could have been baptized at home, but he preferred to make the Greek form of Christianity his state religion in a more decided manner; to adopt the gospel of peace to an accompaniment of martial deeds. Accordingly he compelled the Emperors of Byzantium, by force, to send the Patriarch of Constantinople to baptize him, and their sister to become his wife. He then ordered his subjects to present themselves forthwith for baptism. Finding that their idols did not punish Vladímir for destroying them, and that even great Perún the Thunderer did not resent being flung into the Dniépr, the people quietly and promptly obeyed. As their old religion had no temples for them to cling to, and nothing approaching a priestly class (except the *volkhvýe*, or wizards) to encourage them in opposition, the nation became Christian in a day, to all appearances. We shall see, however, that in many cases, as in other lands converted from heathendom, the old gods were merely baptized with new names, in company with their worshipers.

Together with the religion which he imported from Byzantium, "Prince-Saint" Vladímir naturally imported, also, priests, architects, artists for the holy pictures (*ikóni*), as well as the traditional style of painting them, ecclesiastical vestments and vessels, and—most precious of all— the Slavonic translation of the holy Scriptures and of the Church Service books. These books, however, were not written in Greek, but in the tongue of a cognate Slavonic race, which was comprehensible to the Russians. Thus were the first firm foundations of Christianity, education, and literature simultaneously laid in the cradle of the present vast Russian empire, appropriately called "Little Russia," of which Kíeff was the capital; although even then they were not confined to that section of the country, but were promptly extended, by identical methods, to old Nóvgorod—"Lord Nóvgorod the Great," the cradle of the dynasty of Rúrik, founder of the line of sovereign Russian princes

Whence came these Slavonic translations of the Scriptures, the Church Services, and other books, and the preachers in the vernacular for the infant Russian nation? The books had been translated about one hundred and twenty-five years previously, for the benefit of a small Sla-

vonic tribe, the Moravians. This tribe had been baptized
by German ecclesiastics, whose books and speech, in the
Latin tongue, were wholly incomprehensible to their converts. For fifty years Latin had been used, and naturally
Christianity had made but little progress. Then the
Moravian Prince Róstıslaff appealed to Michael, emperor
of Byzantium, to send him preachers capable of making
themselves understood. The emperor had in his domin-
ions many Slavonians; hence the application, on the
assumption that there must be, among the Greek priests,
many who were acquainted with the languages of the Slavonic tribes. In answer to this appeal, the Emperor
Michael dispatched to Moravia two learned monks, Kyríll
and Methódy, together with several other ecclesiastics, in
the year 863.

Kyríll and Methódy were the sons of a grandee, who
resided in the chief town of Macedonia, which was surrounded by Slavonic colonies. The elder brother, Methódy, had been a military man, and the governor of a
province containing Slavonians. The younger, Kyríll,
had received a brilliant education at the imperial court, in
company with the Emperor Michael, and had been a pupil
of the celebrated Photius (afterwards Patriarch), and
librarian of St. Sophia, after becoming a monk. Later
on, the brothers had led the life of itinerant missionaries,
and had devoted themselves to preaching the Gospel to
Jews and Mohammedans. Thus they were in every way
eminently qualified for their new task.

The Slavonians in the Byzantine empire, and the cognate tribes who dwelt nearer the Danube, like the Moravians, had long been in sore need of a Slavonic translation
of the Scriptures and the Church books, since they under-

stood neither Greek nor Latin; and for the lack of such a translation many relapsed into heathendom. Kyríll first busied himself with inventing an alphabet which should accurately reproduce all the varied sounds of the Slavonic tongues. Tradition asserts that he accomplished this task in the year 855, founding it upon the Greek alphabet, appropriating from the Hebrew, Armenian, and Coptic characters for the sounds which the Greek characters did not represent, and devising new ones for the nasal sounds. The characters in this alphabet were thirty-eight in number. Kyríll, with the aid of his brother Methódy, then proceeded to make his translations of the Church Service books. The Bulgarians became Christians in the year 861, and these books were adopted by them. But the greatest activity of the brothers was during the four and a half years beginning with the year 862, when they translated the holy Scriptures, taught the Slavonians their new system of reading and writing, and struggled with heathendom and with the German priests of the Roman Church. These German ecclesiastics are said to have sent petition after petition to Rome, to Pope Nicholas I., demonstrating that the Word of God ought to be preached in three tongues only—Hebrew, Greek, and Latin—"because the inscription on the Cross had been written by Pilate in those tongues only." Pope Nicholas summoned the brothers to Rome; but Pope Adrian II., who was reigning in his stead when they arrived there, received them cordially, granted them permission to continue their preaching and divine services in the Slavonic language, and even consecrated Methódy bishop of Pannonia; after which Methódy returned to Moravia, but Kyríll, exhausted by his labors, withdrew to a monastery near Rome, and died there in 869.

The language into which Kyríll and Methódy translated was probably the vernacular of the Slavonian tribes dwelling between the Balkans and the Danube. But as the system invented by Kyríll took deepest root in Bulgaria (whither, in 886, a year after Methódy's death, his disciples were banished from Moravia), the language preserved in the ancient transcripts of the holy Scriptures came in time to be called "Ancient Bulgarian." In this connection, it must be noted that this does not indicate the language of the Bulgarians, but merely the language of the Slavonians who lived in Bulgaria. The Bulgarians themselves did not belong to the Slavonic, nor even to the Indo-European race, but were of Ural-Altaic extraction; that is to say, they belonged to the family now represented in Europe by the Finns, Turks, Hungarians, Tatars, and Samoyéds. In the seventh century, this people, which had inhabited the country lying between the Volga and the Don, in southeastern Russia, became divided: one section moved northward, and settled on the Káma River, a tributary of the Volga; the other section moved westward, and made their appearance on the Danube, at the close of the seventh century. There they subdued a considerable portion of the Slavonic inhabitants, being a warlike race; but the Slavonians, who were more advanced in agriculture and more industrious than the Bulgarians, effected a peaceful conquest over the latter in the course of the two succeeding centuries, so that the Bulgarians abandoned their own language and customs, and became completely merged with the Slavonians, to whom they had given their name.

When the Slavonic translations of the Scriptures and the Church Service books were brought to Russia from

Bulgaria and Byzantium, the language in which they were written received the name of "Church Slavonic," because it differed materially from the Russian vernacular, and was used exclusively for the church services. Moreover, as in the early days of Russian literature the majority of writers belonged to the ecclesiastical class, the literary or book language was gradually evolved from a mixture of Church Slavonic and ancient Russian; and in this language all literature was written until the "civil," or secular, alphabet and language were introduced by Peter the Great, at the beginning of the eighteenth century. Books were written in "Kyríllian" characters until the sixteenth century, and the first printed books (which date from that century) were in the same characters. The most ancient manuscripts, written previous to the fourteenth century, are very beautiful, each letter being set separately, and the capital letters often assuming the form of fantastic beasts and birds, or of flowers, or gilded. The oldest manuscript of Russian work preserved dates from the middle of the eleventh century—a magnificent parchment copy of the Gospels, made by Deacon Grigory for Ostromír, the burgomaster of Nóvgorod (1056-1057), and hence known as "the Ostromír Gospels."

But before we deal with the written and strictly speaking literary works of Russia, we must make acquaintance with the oral products of the people's genius, which antedate it, or at all events, contain traces of such hoary antiquity that history knows nothing definite concerning them, although they deserve precedence for their originality. Such are the *skázki*, or tales, the poetical folk-lore, the epic songs, the religious ballads. The fairy tales, while possessing analogies with those of other lands, have their characteristic national features. While less striking and original than, for example, the exquisite Esthonian legends, they are of great interest in the study of comparative folk-lore. More important is the poetical folk-lore of Russia, concerning which neither tradition nor history can give us any clue in the matter of derivation or date. One thing seems reasonably certain: it largely consists of the relics of an extensive system of sorcery, in the form of fragmentary spells, exorcisms, incantations, and epic lays, or *bylíny*.

Song accompanies every action of the Russian peasant, from the cradle to the grave: the choral dances of spring, summer, and autumn, the games of the young people in their winter assemblies, marriages, funerals, and every phase of life, the sowing and the harvest, and so forth. The kazák songs, robber songs, soldiers' songs, and historical songs are all descendants or imitators of the ancient poetry of Russia. They are the remains of the third—the Moscow or imperial—cycle of the epic songs, which deals with really historical characters and events. The Moscow cycle is preceded by the cycles of Vladímir, or Kíeff, and of Nóvgorod. Still more ancient must be the foundations of the marriage songs, rooted in the customs of the ancient Slavonians.

The Slavonians do not remember the date of their arrival in Europe. Tradition says that they first dwelt, after this arrival, along the Danube, whence a hostile force compelled them to emigrate to the northeast. At last Nóvgorod and Kíeff were built; and the Russians, the descendants of these eastern Slavonians, naturally inherited the religion which must at one time, like the language, have been common to all the Slavonic races. This religion, like that of all Aryan races, was founded on reverence paid to the forces of nature and to the spirits of the dead. Their gods and goddesses represented the forces of nature. Thus Ládo and Láda, who are frequently mentioned in these ancient songs, are probably the sun-god, and the goddess of spring and of love, respectively. Ládo, also, is mentioned as the god of marriage, mirth, pleasure, and general happiness, to whom those about to marry offered sacrifices; and much the same is said of the goddess Láda. Moreover, in the Russian folk-songs, *ládo* and *láda* are used, respectively, for lover, bridegroom, husband, and for mistress, bride, wife; and *lad*, in Russian, signifies peace, union, harmony. Nestor, the famous old Russian chronicler (he died in 1114), states that in ancient heathen times, marriage customs varied somewhat among the various Slavonian tribes in the vicinity of the Dniéster; but brides were always seized or purchased. This purchase of the bride is supposed to be represented in the game and choral song (*khorovód*), called "The Sowing of the Millet." The singers form two choirs, which face each other and exchange remarks. The song belongs to the vernal rites, hence the reference to Ládo, which is repeated after every line—*Did-Ládo*, meaning (in Lithuanian) Great Ládo:

First Chorus: We have sown, we have sown millet, Oï, Did-Ládo, we have sown!

Second Chorus: But we will trample it, Oï, Did-Ládo, we will trample it.

First Chorus: But wherewith will ye trample it?

Second Chorus: Horses will we turn into it.

First Chorus: But we will catch the horses.

Second Chorus: Wherewith will ye catch them?

First Chorus: With a silken rein.

Second Chorus: But we will ransom the horses.
First Chorus: Wherewith will ye ransom them?
Second Chorus: We will give a hundred rubles.
First Chorus: A thousand is not what we want.
Second Chorus: What is it then, that ye want?
First Chorus: What we want is a maiden.

Thereupon, one of the girls of the second choir goes over to the first, both sides singing together: "Our band has lost," and "Our band has gained." The game ends when all the girls have gone over to one side.

The funeral wails are also very ancient. While at the present day a very talented wailer improvises a new plaint, which her associates take up and perpetuate, the ancient forms are generally used.

From the side of the East,
The wild winds have arisen,
With the roaring thunders
And the lightnings fiery.
On my father's grave
A star hath fallen,
Hath fallen from heaven.
Split open, O dart of the thunder!
Damp Mother Earth,
Fall thou apart, O Mother Earth!
On all four sides,
Split open, O coffin planks,
Unfold, O white shroud,
Fall away, O white hands
From over the bold heart,
And become parted, O ye sweet lips.
Turn thyself, O mine own father
Into a bright, swift-winged falcon;
Fly away to the blue sea, to the Caspian Sea,
Wash off, O mine own father,
From thy white face the mold.

> Come flying, O my father
> To thine own home, to the lofty térem.*
> Listen, O my father,
> To our songs of sadness!

The Christmas and New-Year carols offer additional illustrations of the ancient heathen customs, and mythic or ritual poetry.   The festival which was almost universally celebrated at Christmas-tide, in ancient heathen times, seems to have referred to the renewed life attributed to the sun after the winter solstice.   The Christian church turned this festival, so far as possible, into a celebration of the birth of Christ.   Among the Slavonians this festival was called *Kolyáda;* and the sun—a female deity—was supposed to array herself in holiday robes and head-dress, when the gloom of the long nights began to yield to the cheerful lights of the lengthening days, to seat herself in her chariot, and drive her steeds briskly towards summer. She, like the festival, was called Kolyáda; and in some places the people used to dress up a maiden in white and carry her about in a sledge from house to house, while the *kolyádki,* or carols, were sung by the train of young people who attended her, and received presents in return.   One of the *kolyádki* runs as follows:

> Kolyáda!   Kolyáda!
> Kolyáda has arrived!
> On the Eve of the Nativity,
> We went about, we sought Holy Kolyáda;
> Through all the courts, in all the alleys.
> We found Kolyáda in Peter's Court.
> Round Peter's Court there is an iron fence,
> In the midst of the Court there are three rooms;
> In the first room is the bright Moon;

* A Tatár word, signifying "tower"; used to mean the part of the house where the women were secluded, in Oriental fashion.

In the second room is the red Sun;
And in the third room are the many Stars.

A Christian turn is given to many of them, just as the Mermen bear a special Biblical name in some places, and are called "Pharaohs"; for like the seals on the coast of Iceland, they are supposed to be the remnants of Pharaoh's host, which was drowned in the Red Sea. One of the most prominent and interesting of these Christianized carols is the *Sláva*, or Glory Song. Extracts from it have been decoratively and most appropriately used on the artistic programmes connected with the coronation of the Emperor Nicholas II. This Glory Song is used in the following manner: The young people assemble together to deduce omens from the words that are sung, while trinkets belonging to each person present are drawn at random from a cloth-covered bowl, in which they have been deposited. This is the first song of the series:

Glory to God in Heaven, Glory!
To our Lord* on this earth, Glory!
May our Lord never grow old, Glory!
May his bright robes never be spoiled, Glory!
May his good steeds never be worn out, Glory!
May his trusty servants never falter, Glory!
May the right throughout Russia, Glory!
Be fairer than the bright sun, Glory!
May the Tzar's golden treasury, Glory!
Be forever full to the brim, Glory!
May the great rivers, Glory!
Bear their renown to the sea, Glory!
The little streams to the mill, Glory!
But this song we sing to the Grain, Glory!
To the Grain we sing, the Grain we honor, Glory!

* Lord, in the original, is Gosudàr, the word which, with a capital, is applied especially to the emperor.

For the old folks to enjoy, Glory!
For the young folks to hear, Glory! *

Another curious old song, connected with the grain, is sung at the New-Year. Boys go about from house to house, scattering grain of different sorts, chiefly oats, and singing:

In the forest, in the pine forest,
There stood a pine-tree,
Green and shaggy.
O, Ovsén! O, Ovsén!
The Boyárs came,
Cut down the pine,
Sawed it into planks,
Built a bridge,
Covered it with cloth,
Fastened it with nails,
O, Ovsén! O, Ovsén!
Who, who will go
Along that bridge?
Ovsén will go there,
And the New-Year,
O, Ovsén! O, Ovsén!

Ovsén, whose name is derived from Ovés (oats, pronounced *avyós*), like the Teutonic Sun-god, is supposed to ride a pig or a boar. Hence sacrifices of pigs' trotters, and other pork products, were offered to the gods at the New-Year, and such dishes are still preferred in Russia at that season. It must be remembered that the New-Year fell on March 1st in Russia until 1348; then the civil New-Year was transferred to September 1st, and January 1st was instituted as the New-Year by Peter the Great only in the year 1700.

* The dramatist Ostróvsky has made effective use of this game, and the more prophetic couplets of the song, in his famous play: "Poverty is not a Vice." Other national customs and songs are used in his play.

The highest stage of development reached by popular song is the heroic epos—the rhythmic story of the deeds of national heroes, either historical or mythical. In many countries these epics were committed to writing at a very early date. In western Europe this took place in the Middle Ages, and they are known to the modern world in that form only, their memory having completely died out among the people. But Russia presents the striking phenomenon of a country where epic song, handed down wholly by oral tradition for nearly a thousand years, is not only flourishing at the present day in certain districts, but even extending into fresh fields.

It is only within the last sixty years that the Russians have become generally aware that their country possesses this wonderfully rich treasure of epic, religious, and ceremonial songs. In some cases, the epic lay and the religious ballad are curiously combined, as in "The One and Forty Pilgrims," which is generally classed with the epic songs, however. But while the singing of the epic songs is not a profession, the singing of the religious ballads is of a professional character, and is used as a means of livelihood by the *kalyéki perekhózhie*, literally, wandering cripples, otherwise known as wandering psalm-singers. These *stikhí*, or religious ballads, are even more remarkable than the epic songs in some respects, and practically nothing concerning them is accessible in English.

In all countries where the Roman Church reigned supreme in early times, it did its best to consign all popular religious poetry to oblivion. But about the seventeenth century it determined to turn such fragments as had survived this procedure to its own profit. Accordingly they were written over in conformity with its particular tenets, for the purpose of inculcating its doctrines. Both courses were equally fatal to the preservation of anything truly national. Incongruousness was the inevitable result.

The Greek, or rather the Russo-Greek, Church adopted precisely the opposite course: it never interfered, in the slightest degree, with popular poetry, either secular or religious. Christianity, therefore, merely enlarged the field of subjects. The result is, that the Slavonic peoples (including even, to some extent, the Roman Catholic Poles) possess a mass of religious poetry, the like of which, either in kind or in quantity, is not to be found in all western Europe.

It is well to note, at this point, that the word *stikh* (derived from an ancient Greek word) is incorporated into the modern Russian word for poetry, *stikhotvorénie*— verse-making, literally rendered—and it has now become plain that Lomonósoff, the father of Russian Literature, who was the first secular Russian poet, and polished the ancient tongue into the beginning of the modern literary language, about the middle of the eighteenth century, did not originate his verse-measures, but derived them from the common people, the peasants, whence he himself sprang. Modern Russian verse, therefore, is thus traced back directly, in its most national traits, to these religious ballads. It is impossible to give any adequate account of them here, and it is especially difficult to convey an adequate idea of the genuine poetry and happy phrasing which are often interwoven with absurdities approaching the grotesque.

The ballads to which we shall briefly refer are full of illustrations of the manner in which old pagan gods became Christian deities, so to speak, of the newly baptized nation.

For example: Perún the Thunder-god became, in popular superstition, "St. Ilyá" (or Elijah), and the day dedicated to him, July 20th (old style), is called "Ilyá the
Thunder-bringer." Elijah's fiery chariot, the lightning,
rumbling across the sky, brings a thunder-storm on or very
near that date; and although Perún's name is forgotten in
Russia proper, he still remains, under his new title, the
patron of the husbandman, as he was in heathen times.
In the epic songs of the Vladímir cycle, as well as in the
semi-religious and religious ballads, he figures as the
strongest and most popular hero, under the name of "Ilyá
Múrometz (Ilyá of Múrom), the Old Kazák," and his
characteristic feats, as well as those attributed to his
"heroic steed, Cloud-fall," are supposed, by the school of
Russian writers who regard all these poems as cosmic
myths, rather than as historical poems, to preserve the
hero's mythological significance as the Thunder-god
Perún.

He plays a similar part in the very numerous religious
ballads on the Last Judgment. St. Michael acts as the
judge. Some "sinful souls" commit the gross error of
attempting to bribe him: whereupon, Michael shouts,
"Ilyá the Prophet! Anakh! Take ye guns with great
thunder! Move ye the Pharaoh mountains of stone!
Let me not hear from these sinners, neither a whine nor a
whimper!"

In Lithuania the Thunder-god's ancient name is still
extant in its original form of Perkun; the Virgin Mary is
called, "Lady Mary Perkunatele" (or "The Mother of
Thunder"), according to a Polish tradition; and in the
Russian government of Vilna, the 2d of February is dedicated to "All-Holy Mary the Thunderer." It is evidently

in this character that she plays a part similar to that of St. Michael and Ilyá the Prophet combined, as above mentioned, in another ballad of the Last Judgment. She appears in this ballad to be the sole inhabitant of heaven, judge and executioner. With her "thundering voice" she condemns to outer darkness all who have not paid her proper respect, promising to bury them under "damp mother earth and burning stones." To the just, that is, to those who have paid her due homage, she says: "Come, take the thrones, the golden crowns, the imperishable robes which I have prepared for you; and if this seem little to you, ye shall work your will in heaven."

St. Yegóry the Brave—our St. George—possesses many of the attributes of Perún. He is, however, a purely mythical character, and the extremely ancient religious poems relating to him present the most amusing mixture of Christianity and Greek mythology, as in the following example:

In the year 8008 (the old Russian reckoning, like the Jewish, began with the creation of the world), the kingdoms of Sodom, Komor (Gomorrah), and Arabia met their doom. Sodom dropped through the earth, Komor was destroyed by fire, and Arabia was afflicted by a sea-monster which demanded a human victim every day. This victim was selected by lot; and one day the lot fell upon the king; but at the suggestion of the queen, who hated her daughter, Elizabeth the Fair, the girl was sent in his place, under the pretext that she was going to meet her bridegroom. Yegóry the Brave comes to her assistance, as Perseus did to the assistance of Andromeda, but lies down for a nap while awaiting the arrival of the dragon. The beast approaches; Elizabeth dares not awaken Yegóry, but a "burning tear" from her right eye arouses him. He attacks the dragon with his spear, and his "heroic steed" (which is sometimes a white mule) tramples on it, after the fashion with which we are familiar in art. Then he binds Elizabeth's sash, which is "five and forty ells in length," about the dragon's jaws, and bids the maiden have three churches built in honor of her deliverance: one to St. Nicholas and the Holy Trinity, one to the All-Holy Birth-giver of God, and one to Yegóry the Brave. Elizabeth the Fair then returns to town, leading the tamed dragon by her sash, to the terror of the inhabitants and to the disgust of her mother. The three churches are duly built, and Christianity is promptly adopted as the state religion of Arabia. In another ballad, Yegóry is imprisoned for thirty years in a pit under the ground, because he will not accept the "Latin-Mussulman faith."

Among the most ancient religious ballads, properly speaking, are: "The Dove Book," "The Merciful Woman of Compassion" (or "The Alleluia Woman"), "The Wanderings of the All-Holy Birth-giver of God," in addition to the songs about Yegóry the Brave, already mentioned. The groundwork of "The Dove Book" is of very ancient heathen origin, and almost identical with the oldest religious songs of the Greeks. The book itself is somewhat suggestive of the "little book" in Revelation. "The Dove Book" falls from Alatýr, the "burning white stone on the Island of Buyán," the heathen Paradise, which corresponds to our Fortunate Isles of the Blest, in the Western Sea, but lies far towards sunrise, in the "Ocean Sea." The heathen significance of this stone is not known, but it is cleverly explained in "The Dove Book" as the stone whereon Christ stood when he preached to his disciples.   This "little book," "forty fathoms long and twenty wide," was written by St. John the Evangelist, and no man can read it.   The prophet Isaiah deciphered only three pages of it in as many years.   But the "Most Wise Tzar David" undertakes to give, from memory, the book's answers to various questions put to him by Tzar Vladímir, as spokesman of a throng of emperors and princes.   A great deal of curious information is conveyed—all very poetically expressed—including some odd facts in natural history, such as: that the ostrich is the mother of birds, and that she lives, feeds, and rears her young on the blue sea, drowning mariners and sinking ships.   Whenever she (or the whale on which the earth rests) moves, an earthquake ensues.   There are several versions of this ballad.   The following abridged extracts, from one version, will show its style.   Among the questions put to "the Most Wise Tzar David" by Prince Vladímir are some touching "the works of God, and our life; our life of holy Russia, our life in the free world; how the free light came to us; why our sun is red; why our stars are thickly sown; why our nights are dark; what causes our red dawns; why we have fine, drizzling rains; whence cometh our intellect; why our bones are strong"; and so forth.

Tzar David replies: "Our free white light began at God's decree; the sun is red from the reflection of God's face, of the face of Christ, the King of Heaven; the younger light, the moon, from his bosom cometh; the myriad stars are from his vesture; the dark nights are the Lord's thoughts; the red dawns come from the Lord's eyes; the stormy winds from the Holy Spirit; our intellects from Christ himself, the King of Heaven; our thoughts from the clouds of heaven; our world of people from Adam; our strong bones from the stones; our bodies from the damp earth; our blood from the Black Sea." In answer to other questions, Tzar David explains that "the Jordan is the mother of all rivers, because Jesus Christ was baptized in it; the cypress is the mother of all trees, because Christ was crucified on it; the ocean is the mother of all seas, because in the middle of the ocean-sea rose up a cathedral church, the goal of all pilgrimages, the cathedral of St. Clement, the pope of Rome; from this cathedral the Queen of Heaven came forth, bathed herself in the ocean-sea, prayed to God in the cathedral," which is a very unusual touch of Romanism.

The ancient religious ballads have no rhyme; and, unlike the epic songs, no fixed rhythm. The presence of either rhyme or rhythm is an indication of comparatively recent origin or of reconstruction in the sixteenth century.

"The Merciful Woman of Compassion," or "The Alleluia Woman," dates from the most ancient Christian tradition, and is a model of simplicity and beauty. It is allied to the English ballad of "The Flight into Egypt" (which also occurs among the Christmas carols of the Slavonians of the Carpathian Mountains), in which the Virgin Mary works a miracle with the peasant's grain, in order to save Christ from the Jews in pursuit. The Virgin comes to the "Alleluia Woman," with the infant Christ in her arms, saying: "Cast thy child into the oven, and take Christ the Lord in thy lap. His enemies, the Jews, are hastening hither; they seek to kill Christ the Lord with sharp spears." The Alleluia Woman obeys, without an instant's hesitation. When the Jews arrive, immediately afterwards, and inquire if Christ has passed that way, she says she has thrown him into the oven. The Jews are convinced of the truth of her statement, by the sight of a child's hand amid the flames; whereupon they dance for joy, and depart, after fastening an iron plate over the oven door. Christ vanishes from the arms of the merciful woman; she remembers her own child and begins to weep. Then Christ's voice assures her that he is well and happy. On opening the oven door, she beholds her baby playing with the flowers in a rich green meadow, reading the Gospels, or rolling an apple on a platter, and comforted by angels.

"The Wanderings of the All-Holy Birth-giver of God," another very ancient ballad, represents the Virgin Mother wandering among the mountains in search of Christ. She encounters three Jews; and in answer to her query, "Accursed Jews, what have ye done with Christ?" they inform her that they have just crucified him on Mount Zion. She hastens thither, and swoons on arriving. When she recovers, she makes her lament, and her *plakh*, or wail, beginning: "O, my dear son, why didst thou not obey thy mother?" Christ comforts her, telling her that he shall rise again, and bidding her: "Do not weep and spoil thy beauty." A form of the ballad which is common in Little Russia reverses the situation. It is the Jews who inquire of Mary what she has done with her son. "Into the river I flung him," she promptly replies. They drain the river, and find him not. Again they ask, "Under the mountains I buried him." They dig up the mountains, and find him not. At last they discover a church, and in it three coffins. Over the Holy Virgin's, the birds are warbling or flowers are blossoming; over

John the Baptist's, lights are burning; over Christ's, angels are singing.

As might be expected, the Holy Virgin is a very popular subject of song. In numerous ballads she delivers a temperance lecture to St. Vasíly the Great on his drunkenness, putting to him various questions, such as, "Who sleeps through matins? Who walks and riots during the liturgy?" [St. Vasíly being the author of a liturgy which is used on certain important occasions during the church year.] "Who has unwashed hands? Who is a murderer?" and so on, through a long list of peccadilloes and crimes. The answer to each question is, "The drunkard." Poor St. Vasíly dashes his head against a stone, and threatens to put an end to himself on the spot, if his one lapse in five and twenty years be not forgiven. Accordingly the Holy Virgin steps down from her throne, gives him her hand, and informs him that the Lord has three mansions: one is the House of David, where the Last Judgment will take place; through the second flows a river of fire, the destination of wizards, drunkards, and the like; and the third is Paradise, the home of the elect. The imagery in the very numerous and ancient poems on the Last Judgment, by the way, is purely heathen in character. The ferryman over the river of fire sometimes acts as the judge, and the punishments to which sinners are condemned by him recall those mentioned in the Æneid, and in Dante's Divina Commedia, the frescoes on the walls of churches bearing out the same idea.

Adam and Eve naturally receive a share of the minstrel's attention, and "Adam's Wail" before the gates of Paradise is often very touching. In a ballad from White Russia, Adam begs the Lord to permit him to revisit

Paradise. The Lord accordingly gives orders to "St. Peter-Paul" to admit Adam to Paradise, to have the song of the Cherubim sung for him, and so forth; but not to allow him to remain. In the midst of Paradise Adam beholds his coffin and wails before it: "O, my coffin, coffin, my true home! Take me, O my coffin, as a mother her own child, to thy white arms, to thy ruddy face, to thy warm heart!" But "St. Peter-Paul" soon catches sight of him, and tells him that he has no business to be strolling about and spying out Paradise; his place is on Zion's hill, where he will be shown books of magic, and of life, and things in general.

There is a great mass of poetry devoted to Joseph; and a lament to "Mother Desert," uttered as he is being led away into captivity by the merchants to whom his brethren have sold him, soon becomes the groundwork for variations in which the Scripture story is entirely forgotten. In these Joseph is always a "Tzarévitch," or king's son, his father being sometimes David, sometimes "the Tzar of India," or of "the Idolaters' Land," or some such country. He is confined in a tower, because the sooth-sayers have foretold that he will become a Christian (or because he is already a Christian he shuts himself up). One day he is permitted to ride about the town, and although all old people have been ordered to keep out of sight, he espies one aged cripple, and thus learns that his father has grossly deceived him, in asserting that no one ever becomes old or ill in his kingdom. He forthwith becomes a Christian, and flees to the desert. Then comes his wail to "Mother Desert Most Fair," as she stands "afar off in the valley": "O Desert fair, receive me to thy depths, as a mother her own child, and a pastor his faithful sheep, into thy voiceless quiet, beloved mother mine!" "Mother Desert" proceeds to remonstrate with her "beloved child": "Who is to rule," she says, "over thy kingdom, thy palaces of white stone, thy young bride? When spring cometh, all the lakes will be aflood, all the trees will be clothed with verdure, heavenly birds will warble therein with voices angelic: in the desert thou wilt have none of this; thy food will be fir-bark, thy drink marsh-water." Nevertheless, "Joseph Tzarévitch" persists in his intention, and Mother Desert receives him at last. Most versions of this ballad are full of genuine poetry, but a few are rather ludicrous: for example, "Mother Desert" asks Joseph, "How canst thou leave thy sweet viands and soft feather-beds to come to me?"

Of David, strange to say, we find very little mention, save in the "Dove Book," or as the father of Joseph, or of some other equally preposterous person.

Among the ballads on themes drawn from the New Testament, those relating to the birth of Christ, and the visit of the Wise Men; to John the Baptist, and to Lazarus, are the most numerous. The Three Wise Men sometimes bring queer gifts. One ballad represents them as being Lithuanians, and only two in number, who bring Christ offerings of *botvínya*—a savory and popular dish, in the form of a soup served cold, with ice, and composed of small beer brewed from sour, black, rye bread, slightly thickened with strained spinach, in which float cubes of fresh cucumber, the green tops of young onions, cold boiled fish, horseradish, bacon, sugar, shrimps, any cold vegetables on hand, and whatever else occurs to the cook. Joseph stands by the window, holding a bowl and a spoon, and stares at the gift. "Queer people, you Lithuanians," he remarks. "Christ doesn't eat *botvínya*. He eats only rolls with milk and honey (or rolls and butter)." In one case, the Three Wise Men appear as three buffaloes bringing gifts; in another as "the fine rain, the red sun, and the bright moon," showing that nature worship can assume a very fair semblance of Christianity.

Christ's baptism is sometimes represented by his mother bathing him in the river; and this is thought to stand for the weary sun which is bathed every night in the ocean. A "Legend of the Sun," whose counterpart can be found in other lands, represents the sun as being attended by flaming birds, who dip their wings in the ocean at night and sprinkle him, and by angels who carry his imperial robe and crown to the Lord's throne every night, and clothe him again in them every morning, while the cock proclaims the "resurrection of all things." In the Christmas carols, angels perform the same offices, and the flaming phœnix-birds are omitted.

The Apostle Peter's timid and disputatious character seems to be well understood by the people. One day, according to a ballad, he gets into a dispute with the Lord, as to which is the larger, heaven or earth. "The earth," declares St. Peter; "Heaven," maintains the Lord. "But let us not quarrel. Call down two or three angels to measure heaven and earth with a silken cord. So was it done; and lo! St. Peter was right, and the Lord was wrong! Heaven is the smaller, because it is all level, while the earth has hills and valleys!"

On another occasion, "all the saints were sitting at table, except the Holy Spirit." "Peter, Peter, my servant," says the Lord, "go bring the Holy Spirit." Peter has not traversed half the road, when he encounters a wondrous marvel, a fearful fire. He trembles with fear and turns back. "Why hast thou not brought the Holy Spirit?" inquires the Lord. Peter explains. "Ho, Peter, that is no marvel! that is the Holy Spirit. Thou shouldst have brought it hither and placed it on the table. All the saints would have rejoiced that the Holy Spirit sat before them!"

The Lazarus ballads illustrate how the people turn Scriptural characters into living realities, by incorporating their own observations on human nature with the sacred text. According to them, Lazarus and Dives were two brothers, both named Lazarus; the younger rich, the elder poor. Poor Lazarus begs alms of his brother: "How dare you call me brother?" retorts rich Lazarus. "I have brothers like myself—princes, nobles, wealthy merchants, who fare sumptuously and dress richly. Even the church dignitaries visit me. Your brethren are the fierce dogs which lie under my table and gather up the fragments. I fear not God, I will buy off intrusive death, I will attain to the kingdom of heaven; and if I attain not thereunto, I will buy it!" Thereupon, he sets the dogs on his brother, spits in his eye, locks the gates, and goes back to his feasting. The dogs which are set upon poor Lazarus bring him their food, instead of rending him. After three efforts to move his brother to compassion, poor Lazarus entreats the Lord to let him die: "Send sudden death, Lord, winged but not merciful," he prays. "Send two threatening angels; let them take out my unclean soul through my side with a hook, my little soul through my ribs, with a spear and with iron hooks; let them place my soul under their left wing, and carry it to the nethermost hell, to burning pitch and the river of fire.

All my life have I suffered hunger and cold, and my whole body hath been full of pains. It is not for me, a poor cripple, to enter Paradise.'' (This is in accordance with the uncomfortable Russian belief that a man's rank and station in this life determine his fate in the other world.) But the Lord gives orders to have everything done in precisely the opposite way. Holy angels remove Lazarus's soul gently, through his "sugar mouth" (referring, possibly, to the Siberian belief that the soul is located in the windpipe) wrap it in a white cloth, and carry it to Abraham's bosom. After a while rich Lazarus is overtaken by misfortune and illness, and he, also, prays for speedy death, minutely specifying how his "large, clean soul," is to be handled and deposited in Abraham's bosom. He acknowledges that he has committed a few trivial sins, but mentions, with pride, in extenuation, that he has never worn anything but velvet and satin, and that he formerly possessed great store of "flowered garments." Again the Lord gives contrary orders, and rich Lazarus undergoes the treatment which his poor brother had indicated for his own soul. When rich Lazarus looks up from his torment and beholds poor Lazarus in Abraham's bosom, he addresses him as "Brother, my own brother." Here one version comes to a sudden end, and the collector who transcribed it, asked: "What?" "He repented," answered the peasant woman who sang it, "and called him 'brother' when he saw that he was well off." In other versions, a long conversation ensues, in the course of which poor Lazarus reminds rich Lazarus of numerous sins of omission and commission, and inquires, with great apparent solicitude, what has become of all his gold, silver, flowered garments, and so forth, and assures him that he would gladly give him not a drop but a whole bucketful of water were he permitted to do so.

But to the share of no saint does a greater number of songs (and festivals) fall than to that of John the Baptist. In addition to June 24th, which still bears the heathen name of *Kupálo*, in connection with St. John's Eve, and which is celebrated by the peasants in as thoroughly heathen a fashion as is the Christmas festival, in honor of the Sun-goddess, Kolyáda, he has three special days dedicated to him. Two of these deserve mention, because of a curious superstition attached to them. On St. John's Day, May 25th, the peasants set out their cabbages; but on the autumn St. John's Day, August 29th, they must carefully avoid all contact with cabbages, because it is the anniversary of the beheading of John; no knife must be taken in the hand on that day, and it is considered a great crime to cut anything, particularly anything round, resembling a head. If a cabbage be cut, blood will flow; if anything round be eaten—onions, for example—carbuncles will follow.

In concluding this brief sketch of the religious ballads of the Slavonians, I venture to quote at length, a masterpiece of the Wandering Cripples' art. It is a Montenegrin version of a legend which is common to all the Slavonic peoples, and contains, besides an interesting problem in ethics, an explanation of the present shape of the human foot. In some versions the emperor's crown is replaced, throughout, by "the bright sun," thus suggesting a mythological origin. It is called "The Emperor Diocletian and John the Baptist."

> Two foster brothers were drinking wine,
> On a sunny slope by the salt seaside;

One was the Emperor Diocletian,
The other, John the Baptist.
Then up spake John the Baptist
As they did drink the wine:
" Foster brother, come now, let us play.
Use thou thy crown; but I will take an apple."
Then up they jumped, began to play,
And St. John flung his apple.
Down in the depths of the sea it fell
And his warm tears trickled down.
But the emperor held this speech to him:
" Now weep not, dear my brother,
Only carry thou not my crown away
And I will fetch thy apple."
Then did John swear to him by God
That he would not steal the crown.
The emperor swam out into the sea,
But John flew up to heaven,
Presented himself before the Lord,
And held this speech to him:
" Eternal God, and All-Holy Father!
May I swear falsely by thee?
May I steal the emperor's crown?"
The Lord replied:
" O John, my faithful servant!
Thrice shalt thou swear falsely by me,
Only, by my name must thou not swear."
St. John flew back to the sunny slope,
And the emperor emerged from the sea.
Again they played; again John flung his apple;
Again it fell into the depths of the sea.
But Diocletian, the emperor, said to him:
" Now, fear thou not, dear brother,
Only carry thou my crown not away,
And I will fetch thy apple."
Then did John swear to him by God,
Thrice did he swear to him by God
That he would not steal his crown.

The emperor threw his crown under his cap,
Beside them left the bird of ill omen,
And plunged into the blue sea.
St. John froze over the sea,
With a twelve-fold ice-crust he froze it o'er,
Seized the golden crown, flew on high to heaven.
And the bird of ill omen began to caw.
The emperor, at the bottom of the sea, divined the cause,
Raced up, as for a wager,
Brake three of the ice-crusts with his head,
Then back turned he again, took a stone upon his head,
A little stone of three thousand pounds,
And brake the twelve-fold ice.
Then unfolded he his wings,
Set out in pursuit of John,
Caught up with him at the gate of heaven,
Seized him by his right foot,
And what he grasped, he tore away.
In tears came John before the Lord;
The bright sun brought he to heaven,
And John complained unto the Lord,
That the emperor had crippled him.
And the Lord said:
" Fear not, my faithful servant!
I will do the same to every man."
Such is the fact, and to God be the glory!

"Therefore," say the Servians, in conclusion of their version of this ballad, "God has made a hollow in the sole of every human being's foot."

The Epic Songs, properly speaking, are broadly divisible into three groups: the Cycle of Vladímir, or of Kíeff; that of Nóvgorod; and that of Moscow, or the Imperial Cycle, the whole being preceded by the songs of the elder heroes. With regard to the first two, and the Kíeff Cycle in particular, undoubtedly composed during the tenth, eleventh, and twelfth centuries, authorities on the origin of Russian

literature differ considerably. One authority maintains
that, although the Russian epics possess a family likeness
to the heroic legends of other Aryan races, the Russians
forgot them, and later on, appropriated them again from
Ural-Altaic sources, adding a few historical and geographical names, and psychical characteristics. But this view
as to the wholesale appropriation of Oriental myths has
not been established, and the authorities who combat it
demonstrate that the heroes are thoroughly Russian, and
that the pictures of manners and customs which they
present are extremely valuable for their accuracy. They
would seem, on the whole, to be a characteristic mixture
of natural phenomena (nature myths), personified as gods,
who became in course of time legendary heroes. Thus,
Prince Vladímir, "the Fair Red Sun," may be the Sun-
god, but he is also a historical personage, whatever may
be said as to many of the other characters in the epic lays
of the Vladímir cycle. "Sadkó, the rich Guest of Nóvgorod," also, in the song of that title, belonging to the
Nóvgorod cycle, was a prominent citizen of Nóvgorod,
who built a church in Nóvgorod, during the twelfth
century, and is referred to in the Chronicles for a space
of two hundred years. In fact, the Nóvgorod cycle
contains less of the personified phenomena of nature
than the cycle of the Elder Heroes, and the Kíeff cycle,
and more of the genuine historical element.

A regular tonic versification forms one of the indispensable properties of these epic poems; irregularity of
versification is a sign of decay, and a complete absence
of measure, that is to say, the prose form, is the last
stage of decay. The airs to which they are sung or
chanted are very simple, consisting of but few tones, yet

are extremely difficult to note down. The peasant bard modifies the one or two airs to which he chants his lays with astonishing skill, according to the testimony of Rýbnikoff, who made the first large collection of the songs, in the Olónetz government (1859), and Hilferding, who made a still more surprising collection (1870), to the north and east of Olónetz.

The lay of Sadkó, above mentioned, is perhaps the most famous—the one most frequently alluded to in Russian literature and art. Sadkó was a harper of "Lord Nóvgorod the Great." "No golden treasures did he possess. He went about to the magnificent feasts of the merchants and nobles, and made all merry with his playing." Once, for three days in succession, he was bidden to no worshipful feast, and in his sorrow he went and played all day long, upon the shore of Lake Ílmen. On the third day, the Water King appears to him, and thanks him for entertaining his guests in the depths. He directs Sadkó to return to Nóvgorod, and on the morrow, when he shall be bidden to a feast, and the banqueters begin the characteristic brags of their possessions, Sadkó must wager his "turbulent head" against the merchants' shop in the bazaar, with all the precious wares therein, that Lake Ílmen contains fishes with fins of gold. Sadkó wins the bet; for the Tzar Vodyanóy sends up the fish to be caught in the silken net. Thus did Sadkó become a rich guest (merchant of the first class) of Nóvgorod, built himself a palace of white stone, wondrously adorned, and became exceeding rich. He also held worshipful feasts, and out-bragged the braggers, declaring that he would buy all the wares in Nóvgorod, or forfeit thirty thousand in money. As he continues to buy, wares continue to flow into this

Venice of the North, and Sadkó decides that it is the part
of wisdom to pay his thirty thousand. He then builds
"thirty dark red ships and three," of the dragon type,
lades them with the wares of Nóvgorod, and sails out into
the open sea, via the river Vólkhoff, Lake Ládoga, and
the Nevá. After a while the ships stand still and will
not stir, though the waves dash and the breeze whistles
through the sails. Sadkó arrives at the conclusion that
the Sea King demands tribute, as they have now been sail-
ing the seas for twelve years, and have paid none. They
cast into the waves casks of red gold, pure silver, and fair
round pearls; but still the ships move not. Sadkó then
proposes that each man on board shall prepare for himself
a lot, and cast it into the sea, and the man whose lot sinks
shall consider himself the sacrifice which the Sea King
requires. Sadkó's lot persists in sinking, whether he
makes it of hop-flowers or of blue damaskeened steel, four
hundred pounds in weight; and all the other lots swim,
whether heavy or light. Accordingly Sadkó perceives
that he is the destined victim, and taking his harp, a holy
image of St. Nicholas (the patron of travelers), and bowls
of precious things with him, he has himself abandoned on
an oaken plank, while his ships sailed off, and "flew as
they had been black ravens." He sinks to the bottom,
and finds himself in the palace of the Sea King, who makes
him play, while he, the fair sea-maidens, and the other
sea-folk dance violently. But the Tzarítza warns Sadkó
to break his harp, for it is the waves dancing on the shore,
and creating terrible havoc. The Tzar Morskóy then
requests Sadkó to select a wife; and guided again by the
Tzarítza's advice, Sadkó selects the last of the nine hundred maidens who file before him—a small, black-visaged

maiden, named Tchernáva. Had he chosen otherwise, he is told, he would never again behold "the white world," but must "forever abide in the blue sea." After a great feast which the Sea King makes for him, Sadkó falls into a heavy sleep, and when he awakens from it, he finds himself on the bank of the Tchernáva River, and sees his dark red ships come speeding up the Vólkhoff River. Sadkó returns to his palace and his young wife, builds two churches, and roams no more, but thereafter takes his ease in his own town.

Between these cycles of epic songs and the Moscow, or Imperial Cycle there is a great gap. The pre-Tatár period is not represented, and the cycle proper begins with Iván the Terrible, and ends with the reign of Peter the Great. Epic marvels are not wholly lacking in the Moscow cycle, evidently copied from the earlier cycles. But these songs are inferior in force. Fantastic as are some of the adventures in these songs, there is always a solid historical foundation. Iván the Terrible, for instance, is credited with many deeds of his grandfather (his father being ignored), and is always represented in rather a favorable light. The conquest of Siberia, the capture of Kazán and Ástrakhan, the wars against Poland, and the Tatárs of Crimea, and so forth, are the principal points around which these songs are grouped. But the Peter the Great of the epics bears only a faint resemblance to the real Peter.

Perhaps the most famous hero of epic song in the seventeenth century is the bandit-chief of the Volga, Sténka Rázin, whose memory still lingers among the peasants of those regions. He was regarded as the champion of the people against the oppression of the nobles, and "Ilyá of Múrom, the Old Kazák" is represented as the captain of the brigands under him.   To Sténka, also, are attributed magic powers.   From the same period date also the two most popular dance-songs of the present day—the "Kamarýnskaya" and "Bárynya Sudárynya," its sequel.   The Kamarýnskaya was the district which then constituted the Ukráina, or border-marches, situated about where the government of Orél now is.   The two songs present a valuable historical picture of the coarse manners of the period on that lawless frontier; hence, only a few of the lines which still subsist of these poetical chronicles can be used to the irresistibly dashing music.

The power of composing epic songs has been supposed to have gradually died out, almost ceasing with the reign of Peter the Great, wholly ceasing with the war of 1812. But very recently an interesting experiment has been begun, based on the discovery of several new songs about the Emperor Alexander II., which are sung by the peasants over a wide range of country   All these songs are being written down with the greatest accuracy as to the peculiarities of pronunciation and accentuation.   If, in the future, variants make their appearance, containing an increasing infusion of the artistic and poetical elements, considerable light will be thrown upon the problem of the rise and growth of the ancient epic songs, and on the question of poetical inspiration among the peasants of the present epoch.   One of these ballads, written down in the Province of the Don, from the lips of a blind beggar, says that Alexander II., "burned with love, wished to give freedom to all, kept all under his wing, and freed them from punishment.   He reformed all the laws, heard the groans of the needy, and himself hastened to their aid." "So the wicked killed him," says the ballad, and proceeds to describe the occurrence, including the way in which "the black flag" was lowered on the palace, and "they sent a telegram about the eclipse of our sun." In the far northern government of Kostromá, on the Volga, two more ballads on the same subject have been taken down on the typewriter, so that the bard could readily correct them. The first, entitled "A Lay of Mourning for the Death of the Tzar Liberator," narrates how "a dreadful cloud of black, bloodthirsty ravens assembled, and invited to them the underground, subterranean rats, not to a feast-ball, not to a christening, but to undermine the roots of the olive-branch." Naturally this style demands that the emperor be designated as "the bright falcon, light winged, swift eyed." It describes the plot, and how the bombs were to be wrapped up in white cloths, and the conspirators were "to go for a stroll, as with watermelons." When the bombs burst, "the panes in the neighboring houses are shattered," and "the dark blue feathers" of the "bright falcon" are set on fire. "As there were no Kostromá peasants on hand to aid the emperor—no Komisároffs or Susánins," adds the ballad, with local pride (alluding to the legend of Ivan Susánin saving the first Románoff Tzar from the Poles in 1612, which forms the subject of the famous opera by Glínka, "Life for the Tzar"), "he laid himself down in the bosom of his mother (earth)." The second ballad is "The Monument-Not Made-with-Hands to the Tzar Liberator"—the compound adjective here referring to that in the title of a favorite *ikóna*, or Holy Picture, which corresponds to the one known in western Europe as the imprint of the Saviour's face on St. Veronica's kerchief. There are four stanzas, of six lines each, of which the third runs as follows:

He is our Liberator and our father!
And we will erect a monument of hearts
Whose cross, by its gleaming 'mid the clouds,
Shall transmit the memory to young children and the babes in
    arms,
And this shall be unto ages of ages
So long as the world and man shall exist!

In southwestern Russia, where the ancient epic songs of the Elder Heroes and the Kíeff Cycle originated, the memory of them has died out, owing to the devastation of southern Russia by the Tatárs in the thirteenth and fourteenth centuries, and the decay of its civilization under Lithuanian sway in the fourteenth and fifteenth centuries. In the sixteenth century the population of southern Russia reorganized itself in the forms of kazák communes, and fabricated for itself a fresh cycle of epic legends, which replaced those of Kíeff; and there the *kobzárs* (professional minstrels who accompany their songs on the *kábza*, a mandolin-like, twelve-stringed instrument) celebrate the deeds of a new race of kazák heroes. But in the lonely wildernesses of the northeast, whither the Tatár invasion drove the descendants of those who composed and sang the great epic songs, no more recent upheavals have brought forward heroes to replace the historic paladins, who there hold undisputed sway to the present time.

Of the songs still sung by the people, the following favorite (in the version from the Olónetz government) may serve as a sample. It is not rhymed in the original.

Akh! Little guelder-rose, with pinkish azure bloom,
And merry little company, where my dear one doth drink;
My darling will not drink, until for me he sends.
When I, a maiden, very young did dally,

Tending the ducks, the geese, the swans,
When I, a young maid, very young, along the stream-bank
    strolled,
I trampled down all sickly leaves and grass,
I plucked the tiny azure flowerets,
At the swift little rivulet I gazed;
Small was the hamlet there, four cots in all,
In every cot four windows small.
In every little window, a dear young crony sits.
Eh, cronies dear, you darlings, friends of mine,
Be ye my cronies, one another love, love me,
When into the garden green ye go, then take me, too;
When each a wreath ye twine, twine one for me;
When in the Danube's stream ye fling them, drop mine, too;
The garlands all upon the surface float, mine only hath sunk
    down.
All your dear lover-friends have homeward come, mine only
    cometh not.

QUESTIONS FOR REVIEW

1. How was Christianity introduced into Russia?
2. In what two important centers was it finally established?
3. How was the Greek Church able to supply these converts with a Slavonian translation of the Bible?
4. Who were Kyríll and Methódy? Describe their work.
5. Why was "Ancient Bulgarian" not the original language of the Bulgarians?
6. In what language was Russian literature written up to the time of Peter the Great?
7. Where, according to tradition, did the early Slavonians settle in Europe?
8. How are the forces of nature represented in the ancient marriage songs?
9. What custom is illustrated in "The Sowing of the Millet"?
10. What connection is there between the funeral wails of modern and of ancient Russia?

11. What was the festival of Kolyáda?

12. What Christian character has been given to the ancient " Glory Song"?

13. Why is pork commonly used at the Russian New-Year?

14. What different dates have been observed for the opening of the New-Year?

15. What remarkable fact is true of the preservation of the Russian epic songs?

16. How were the religious ballads brought before the people?

17. Describe some of the characteristics of these ballads.

18. Into what three groups do the epic songs naturally fall?

19. What is the Lay of Sadkó?

20. What are the favorite subjects of the songs of the " Imperial Cycle"?

21. What interesting discovery of modern epic songs has recently been made?

22. Why have the songs of the Kíeff Cycle died out in their own country?

BIBLIOGRAPHY

The Epic Songs of Russia. Isabel F. Hapgood.
Myths and Folk-Tales of Russians, Western Slavs, and Magyars. Jeremiah Curtin.
Cossack Fairy-Tales. R. Nisbet Bain.
Sixty Folk-Tales from Exclusively Slavonic Sources. A. H. Wratislaw.
Russian Fairy-Tales. R. Nisbet Bain.
Fairy-Tales of the Slav Peasants and Herdsmen. From the French of Alexander Chodsko.
Songs of the Russian People and Russian Folk-Tales. W. R. S. Ralston.
Slavonic Fairy-Tales. M. Gastner.
Slavonic Literature and its Relations to the Folk-Lore of Europe. M. Gastner.
Russian Folk-Songs as Sung by the People. Mme. Eugenie Lineff.

CHAPTER II

THE ANCIENT PERIOD, FROM THE INTRODUC-TION OF CHRISTIANITY TO THE TATÁR DO-MINION, 988-1224.

As soon as Prince Saint Vladímir introduced Chris-tianity into Russia, he and his sons began to busy them-selves with the problem of general education. Priests came from Greece and Bulgaria to spread the Gospel in Russia; but they thought only of disseminating Christianity, and were, moreover, not sufficiently numerous to grapple with educational problems. Accordingly, Vladímir founded schools in Kíeff, and ordered that the children of the best citizens should be taken from their unwilling parents, and handed over to these schools for instruction. His son, Yároslaff I. ("the wise"), pursued the same policy, in Kíeff and elsewhere—the schools being attached to the churches, and having for their chief object the preparation of ecclesiastics. The natural result was, that in ancient Russia, most people who could read and write were eccle-siastics or monks, and religious literature was that most highly prized. Even so-called worldly literature was strongly tinctured with religion. The first Russian liter-ary compositions took the form of exhortations, sermons, and messages addressed by the clergy to their flocks, and the first Russian authors were Ilarión, metropolitan of Kíeff (beginning in 1051), and Luká Zhidyáta, appointed bishop of Nóvgorod in 1036. The latter's "Exhortation to the Brethren" has come down to us, and is noteworthy for the simplicity of its language, and its conciseness of form. From Ilarión we have, "a Word Concerning the Law" (meaning, the Law of God), which deals with the opposing character of Judaism and Christianity. It proves not only that he was a cultivated man, capable of expressing himself clearly on complicated matters, but also that his hearers were capable of comprehending him. Other good writers of that period were: Feodósiy, elected in 1062, abbott of the Monastery of the Catacombs in Kíeff (which was fated to become one of the most important nurseries of enlightenment and literature in Russia); Nestor, who left a remarkable "Life of Feodósiy"; Nikifór, a Greek by birth, educated in Byzantium, who was metropolitan of Kíeff, 1104–1121; and Kyríll, bishop of Nóvgorod, 1171–1182.

Thus, it will be seen, events took their ordinary course in Russia as in other countries: learning was, for a long time, confined almost exclusively to the monasteries, which were the pioneers in education and culture elements, such as they were. Naturally the bulk of the literature for a long time consisted of commentaries on the Holy Scriptures, translations from the works of the fathers of the church (Eastern Catholic), homilies, pastoral letters, and the like. But in the monasteries, also, originated the invaluable Chronicles; for not only did men speedily begin to describe in writing those phenomena of life which impressed them as worthy of note, but ecclesiastics were in a position to learn all details of importance from authoritative sources, and were even, not infrequently, employed as diplomatic agents, or acted as secretaries to the ruling princes. The earliest and most celebrated among these ancient Russian historical works is the Chronicle of Nestor, a monk of the Catacombs Monastery in Kíeff (born about 1056), the reputed author of the document which bears his name. Modern scientists have proved that he did not write this Chronicle, the earliest copy of which dates from the fourteenth century, but its standing as a priceless monument of the twelfth century has never been impunged, since it is evident that the author gathered his information from contemporary eye-witnesses. The Chronicle begins by describing how Shem, Ham, and Japhet shared the earth between them after the flood, and gives a detailed list of the countries and peoples of the ancient world. It then states that, after the building of the Tower of Babel, God dispersed all the peoples into seventy-two tribes (or languages), the northern and western lands falling to the tribe of Japhet. Nestor derives the Slavonians from Japhet—describes their life, first on the banks of the Danube, then their colonization to the northeast as far as the River Ílmen (the ancient Nóvgorod), the Oká, in central Russia, and the tributaries of the Dniépr, delineating the manners and customs of the different Slavonic tribes, and bringing the narrative down to the year 1110, in the form of brief, complete stories. The style of the Chronicle is simple and direct. For example, he relates how, in the year 945, the Drevlyáns (or forest-folk) slew Ígor, prince of Kíeff, and his band of warriors, who were not numerous.

Then said the Drevlyáns, " Here we have slain the Russian Prince; let us now take his wife, Olga, for our Prince Malo; and we will take also Svyátoslaff (his son), and will deal with him as we see fit"; and the Drevlyáns dispatched their best men, twenty in number, in a boat, to Olga, and they landed

their boat near Borítcheff, and Olga was told that the Drevlyáns had arrived, and Olga summoned them to her. "Good
guests are come, I hear"; and the Drevlyáns said: "We are
come, Princess." And Olga said to them, "Tell me, why are ye
come hither?" Said the Drevlyáns: "The land of the Drevlyáns hath sent us," saying thus: 'We have slain thy husband,
for thy husband was like unto a wolf, he was ever preying and
robbing; but our own princes are good. Our Drevlyán land doth
flourish under their sway; wherefore, marry thou our Prince,
Malo'" for the Drevlyán Prince was named Malo. Olga said
to them: "Your speech pleaseth me, for my husband cannot be
raised from the dead; but I desire to show you honor, to-morrow, before my people; wherefore, to-day, go ye to your boat,
and lie down in the boat, exalting yourselves; and to-morrow I
will send for you, and ye must say: 'we will not ride on horses,
we will not walk afoot, but do ye carry us in our boat.'" Thus
did she dismiss them to the boat. Then Olga commanded a
great and deep pit to be digged in the courtyard of the palace,
outside the town. And the next morning, as Olga sat in her
palace, she sent for the guests, and Olga's people came to them,
saying: "Olga biddeth you to a great honor." But they said:
"We will not ride on horses, nor on oxen, neither will we walk
afoot, but do thou carry us in our boat." And the Kievlyáns
said: "We must, perforce, carry you; our prince is slain, and
our princess desireth to wed your prince," and they bore them
in the boat, and those men sat there and were filled with pride;
and they carried them to the courtyard, to Olga, and flung them
into the pit, together with their boat. And Olga, bending over
the pit, said unto them: "Is the honor to your taste?" and they
made answer: "It is worse than Ígor's death; and she commanded that they be buried alive, and they were so buried."

The narrative goes on to state that Olga sent word to
the Drevlyáns, that if they were in earnest, their distinguished men must be sent to woo her for their prince;
otherwise, the Kievlyáns would not let her go. Accordingly, they assembled their best men, the rulers, and sent

them for her. Olga had the bath heated and ordered them to bathe before presenting themselves to her, and when they began to wash, Olga had the bath-house set on fire, and burned them up. Then Olga sent again to the Drevlyáns, demanding that they collect a vast amount of hydromel in the town where her husband had been slain, that she might celebrate the ancient funeral feast, and weep over his grave. So they got the honey together, and brewed the hydromel (or mead), and Olga, taking with her a small body-guard, in light marching order, set out on the road and came to her husband's grave and wept over it; and commanded her people to erect a high mound over it; and when that was done, she ordered the funeral feast to be celebrated on its summit. Then the Drevlyáns sat down to drink, and Olga ordered her serving-boys to wait on them. And the Drevlyáns asked Olga where was the guard of honor which they had sent for her? And she told them that it was following with her husband's body-guard. But when the Drevlyáns were completely intoxicated, she ordered her serving-lads to drink in their honor, went aside, and commanded her men to slay the Drevlyáns, which was done, five hundred dying thus. Then Olga returned to Kíeff, and made ready an army against the remaining Drevlyáns. Such is one of the vivid pictures of ancient manners and customs which the chronicle of Nestor furnishes.

The descendants of Prince-Saint Vladímir were not only patrons of education, but collectors of books. One of them, in particular, Vladímir Monomáchus, is also noted as the author of the "Exhortation of Vladímir Monomáchus" (end of the eleventh century), which he wrote for his children, in the style of a pastoral address from an ecclesiastic to his flock—a style which, in Russia, as elsewhere, was the inevitable result of the first efforts at non-religious literature, in the eleventh and twelfth centuries. "Chiefest of all," he writes, among other things, "forget not the poor, and feed them according to your powers; give most of all to the orphans, and be ye yourselves the defenders of the widows, permitting not the mighty to destroy a human being. Slay ye not either the righteous or the guilty yourselves, neither command others to slay them. In discourse, whatsoever ye shall say, whether good or evil, swear ye not by God, neither cross ye yourselves; there is no need of it. . . . . Reverence the aged as your father, the young as brethren. In thy house be not slothful, but see to all thyself; put not thy trust in a steward, neither in a servant, that thy guests jeer not at thy house, nor at thy dinner. . . . . Love your wives, but give them no power over you. Forget not the good ye know, and what ye know not, as yet, that learn ye," and so forth.

The beginning of the twelfth century witnessed other notable attempts at secular literature. To the twelfth century, also, belongs Russia's single written epic song, "The Word (or lay) Concerning Ígor's Raid," which contains an extremely curious mixture of Christianity and heathen views. By a fortunate chance, this epic was preserved and was discovered, in 1795, by Count Músin-Púshkin, among a collection which he had purchased from a monastery. Unhappily, Count Músin-Púshkin's valuable library was burned during the conflagration of Moscow, in 1812. But the *Slóvo* had been twice published previous to that date, and had been examined by many learned paleographists, who decided that the chirography belonged to the end of the fourteenth century or the beginning of the fifteenth century.

Ígor Svyátoslavitch was the prince of Nóvgorod-Syéversk, who in 1185, made a raid against the Pólovtzy, or Plain-dwellers, and the Word begins thus:

> Shall we not begin our song, oh brothers,
> With the story of the feuds of old;
> Song of the valiant troop of Ígor,
> And of him, the son of Svyátoslaff,
> And sing them as men now do sing,
> Striving not in thought after Boyán.*
> Making this ballad, he was wont the Wizard,
> As a squirrel swift to flit about the forest,
> As a gray wolf o'er the clear plain to trot,
> And as an eagle 'neath the clouds to hover;
> When he recalleth ancient feuds of yore,
> Then, from out the flock of swans he sendeth
> In pursuit, ten falcons, swift of wing.

The whole expedition is described in this poetical style, in three hundred and eighty-four unrhymed lines, with a curious mingling of heathen beliefs and Christian views. God shows Ígor the road "to the land of Pólovetzk, to the Russian land," and on his return from captivity, Ígor rides to Kíeff to salute the Holy Birth-giver of God of Pirogóshtch, while the Pólovtzi are called "accursed," in contrast with the orthodox Russians. But the winds are called "the grandchildren of Stribog," and the Russian people are alluded to as "the grandsons of Dázhbog," both heathen divinities, and other mythical and obscure personages are introduced.

With this epic lay, the first period of Russian literature closes.

* Evidently an ancient epic bard.

QUESTIONS FOR REVIEW

1. How did Vladímir and his son provide for the education of their people?

2. What kind of literature naturally grew out of the learning of the monasteries?

3. What was the chronicle of Nestor? What special interest has it?

4. Quote some of the precepts from the "Exhortation of Monomáchus."

5. By what good fortune has "Ígor's Raid" been preserved?

6. What is the character of this Epic Song?

CHAPTER III

SECOND PERIOD, FROM THE TATÁR DOMINION
TO THE TIME OF IVÁN THE TERRIBLE, 1224–
1330.

During the Tatár Dominion, or yoke (1224–1370),
Kíeff lost its supremacy, and also ceased to be, as it had
been up to this time, the center of education and literature. The dispersive influence of the Tatár raids had the
effect of creating centers in the northeast, which were,
eventually, concentrated in Moscow; and in so far it
proved a blessing in disguise for Russia. The conditions
of life under the Tatár sway were such, that any one, man
or woman, who valued a peaceful existence, or existence
at all, was driven to seek refuge in monasteries. The inevitable consequence was, that a religious, even an æsthetic,
cast was imparted to what little literature was created.
One celebrated production, dating from about the middle
of the fourteenth century, will serve to give an idea of the
sort of thing on which men then exercised their minds and
pens. It is the Epistle of Archbishop Vasíly of Nóvgorod to Feódor, bishop of Tver, entitled, "Concerning
the Earthly Paradise," wherein the author discusses a
subject of contention which had arisen among the clergy
of the latter's diocese, as to "whether the earthly paradise planted by God for Adam doth still exist upon the
earth, or whether not the earthly but only an imaginary
paradise doth still exist." The worthy archbishop, with

divers arguments, defends his position, that the earthly
paradise does still exist in the East, and hell in the West:
which latter proposition is not surprising when we recall
the historical circumstances under which it was enounced.

The monks continued to be the leaders in the educational and literary army, and under the stress of circumstances, not only won immense political influence over the
life of the people, but also developed a new and special
type of literature—political sermons—which attained to
particular development in the fourteenth century.
Another curious phenomenon was presented by the narratives concerning various prominent personages, which
contain precious facts and expressions of contemporary
views. The authors always endeavored, after the time-
honored fashion of biographers, to exalt and adorn their
subjects; so that "decorated narratives," a most apt title
for that sort of literature in general, was the characteristic
name under which they came to be known. One peculiarity of all of these, it is worth noting, including that which
dealt with the decisive battle with the Tatárs on the field
of Kulikóvo, on the Don, in 1370, under Dmítry Donskóy
(Dmítry of the Don), Prince of Moscow, is, that they are
imitated, in style and language, from the famous "Word
Concerning Ígor's Raid."

Among the many purely secular tales of the fifteenth
and sixteenth centuries preserved in manuscript, not one
has anything in common with Russian national literature.
All are translations, or reconstructions of material derived
from widely divergent sources, such as the stories of Alexander of Macedon, of the Trojan War, and various Oriental tales. About the middle of the sixteenth century,
Makáry, metropolitan of Moscow, collected, in twelve

huge volumes, the Legends (or Spiritual Tales) of the Saints, under the title of Tchetyá Mináya—literally, Monthly Reading. It was finished in 1552, and contains thirteen hundred Lives of Saints.

QUESTIONS FOR REVIEW

1. What was the effect of the Tatár raids upon Kíeff?

2. What striking illustration have we of the weak religious literature of this time?

3. What were the "decorated narratives"? To what famous epic are they similar in style?

4. What foreign character have the secular tales of this period?

5. What famous collection of Legends of the Saints was made in the sixteenth century.

CHAPTER IV

THIRD PERIOD, FROM THE TIME OF IVÁN THE
TERRIBLE, 1530, TO THE MIDDLE OF THE
SEVENTEENTH CENTURY.

Political events had tended to concentrate absolute
power in the hands of the Grand Princes of Moscow,
beginning with Iván III. But no counterbalancing power
had arisen in Russian society; there was no independent
life, no respect for the individual, no public opinion to
counteract the abuse of power. In the beginning of the
sixteenth century, Russian society had reached the extreme
limits of development possible to it under its unfavorable
conditions. The time for the Russian Renaissance had
arrived. It is well to remember that at this time in other
parts of Europe also the spirit of despotism and intoler-
ance was holding individual liberty in check. This was
the age of Henry VIII., of Catherine de Medici, of the
Inquisition, and of the Massacre of St. Bartholomew.

In this century of transition, the sixteenth, the man
who exerted over the spirit of the age more influence than
any other was Maxím the Greek (1480–1556), a learned
scholar, a monk of Mt. Athos, educated chiefly in Italy.
He was invited to Russia by Grand Prince Vasíly Ivánovitch, for the purpose of cataloguing a rich store of Greek
manuscripts in the library of the Grand Prince. To his
influence is due one of the most noteworthy books of the
sixteenth century, the "Stogláva," or "Hundred Chap-

ters," a set of regulations adopted by the young Tzar Iván Vasílievitch (afterwards known as Iván the Terrible), the son of Vasíly, and by the most enlightened nobles of his time at a council held in 1551. Their object was to reform the decadent morals of the clergy, and various ecclesiastical and social disorders, and in particular, the absolute illiteracy arising from the lack of schools. Another famous work of the same century is the "Domostróy," or "House-Regulator," attributed to Pope (priest) Sylvester, the celebrated confessor and counselor of Iván the Terrible in his youth. In an introduction and sixty-three chapters Sylvester sets forth the principles which should regulate the life of every layman, the management of his household and family, his relations to his neighbors, his manners in church, his conduct towards his sovereign and the authorities, his duties towards his servants and subordinates, and so forth. The most curious part of the work deals with the minute details of domestic economy—one injunction being, that all men shall live in accordance with their means or their salary—and family relations, in the course of which the position of woman in Russia of the sixteenth century is clearly defined. This portion is also of interest as the forerunner of a whole series of articles in Russian literature on women, wherein the latter are depicted in the most absurd manner, the most gloomy colors—articles known as "About Evil Women"—and founded on an admiration for Byzantine asceticism. In his Household Regulations Sylvester thus defines the duties of woman:

"She goeth to church according to opportunity and the counsel of her husband. Husbands must instruct their wives with care and judicious chastisement. If a wife live not according to the precepts of her husband, her husband must reprove her in private, and after that he hath so reproved her, he must pardon her, and lay upon her his further injunctions; but they must not be wroth one with the other. . . . . And only when wife, son, or daughter accept not reproof shall he flog them with a whip, but he must not beat them in the presence of people, but in private; and he shall not strike them on the ear, or in the face, or under the heart with his fist, nor shall he kick them, or thrash them with a cudgel, or with any object of iron or wood. But if the fault be great, then, removing the offender's shirt, he shall beat him (or her) courteously with a whip," and so forth.

We have seen that Iván IV. (the Terrible) took the initiative in reforms. After the conquest of Kazán he established many churches in that territory and elsewhere in Russia, and purchased an immense quantity of manuscript service-books for their use, many of which turned out to be utterly useless, on account of the ignorance and carelessness of the copyists. This circumstance is said to have enforced upon Iván's attention the advisability of establishing printing-presses in Russia; though there is reason to believe that Maxím the Greek had, long before, suggested the idea to the Tzar. Accordingly, the erection of a printing-house was begun in 1543, but it was only in April, 1563, that printing could be begun, and in March, 1564, the first book was completed—The Acts of the Apostles. The first book printed in Slavonic, however, is the "Októikh," or "Book of the Eight Canonical Tones," containing the Hymns for Vespers, Matins, and kindred church services, which was printed in Cracow seventy years earlier; and thirty years earlier, Venice was produ-

cing printed books in the Slavonic languages, while even in
Lithuania and White Russia printed books were known
earlier than in Moscow. After printing a second book, the
"Book of Hours" (the Tchasoslóff)—also connected with
Vespers, Matins, kindred services, and the Liturgy, in
addition—in 1565, the printers, both Russians, were accused of heresy, of spoiling the book, and were compelled
to flee from Moscow. In 1568 other printers produced in
Moscow the Psalter, and other books. In 1580, in Ostróg,
Government of Volhýnia, in a printing-house founded by
Prince Konstantín Konstantínovitch Ostrózhsky, was
printed the famous Ostrózhky Bible, which was as handsome as any product of the contemporary press anywhere
in Europe.

Nevertheless, manuscripts continued to circulate side
by side with printed books, even during the reign of Peter
the Great.

During the reign of Iván the Terrible, secular literature
and authors from the highest classes of society again
made their appearance; in fact, they had never wholly
disappeared during the interval. Iván the Terrible himself headed the list, and Prince Andréi Mikháilovitch
Kúrbsky was almost his equal in rank, and more than his
equal in importance from a literary point of view. Iván
the Terrible's writings show the influence of his epoch,
his oppressed and agitated childhood, his defective education; and like his character, they are the perfectly
legitimate expression of all that had taken place in the
kingdom of Moscow.

The most striking characteristic of Iván's writings is
his malicious, biting irony, concealed beneath an external
aspect of calmness; and it is most noticeable in his prin-

cipal works, his "Correspondence with Prince Kúrbsky,"
and his "Epistle to Kozmá, Abbot of the Kiríllo-Byelózersk
Monastery." They display him as a very well-read man,
intimately acquainted with the Scriptures, and the translations from the Fathers of the Church, and the Russian
Chronicles, as well as with general history. Abbot
Kozmá had complained to the Tzar concerning the conduct of certain great nobles who had become inmates of
his monastery, some voluntarily, others by compulsion, as
exiles from court, and who were exerting a pernicious
influence over the monks. Iván seized the opportunity
thus presented to him, to pour out all the gall of his irony
on the monks, who had forsaken the lofty, spiritual traditions of the great holy men of Russia.

Of much greater importance, as illustrating Ivan's literary talent, is his "Correspondence with Prince Kúrbsky"
(1563–1579), a warrior of birth as good as Iván's own, a
former favorite of his, who, in 1563, probably in consequence of the profound change in Iván's conduct, which
had taken place, and weighed so heavily upon the remainder of his reign, fled to Iván's enemy, the King of Poland.
The abuses of confidence and power, with the final
treachery of Priest Sylvester (Iván's adviser in ecclesiastical affairs), and of Adasheff (his adviser in temporal
matters), had changed the Tzar from a mild, almost
benevolent, sovereign, into a raging despot. On arriving
in Poland, Prince Kúrbsky promptly wrote to Iván an-
nouncing his defection, and plainly stating the reasons
therefor. When Iván received this epistle—the first
in the celebrated and valuable historical correspondence
which ensued—he thrust his iron-shod staff through the
foot of the bearer, at the bottom of the Red (or Beauti-

ful) Staircase in the Kremlin, and leaning heavily upon it, had the letter read to him, the messenger making no sign of his suffering the while. Kúrbsky asserted the rights of the individual, as against the sovereign power, and accused Iván of misusing his power. Iván, on his side, asserted his omnipotent rights, ascribed to his own credit all the noteworthy events of his reign, accused Kúrbsky of treason, and demonstrated to the Prince (with abundant Scriptural quotations), that he had not only ruined his own soul, but also the souls of his ancestors—a truly Oriental point of view. "If thou art upright and pious," he writes, "why wert not thou willing to suffer at the hands of me, thy refractory sovereign lord, and receive from me the crown of life? . . . . Thou hast destroyed thy soul for the sake of thy body . . . . and hast waxed wroth not against a man, but against God."

Kúrbsky's letters reveal in him a far more cultivated man, with more sense of decency and self control, and even elegance of diction, than the Tzar. He even reproaches the latter, in one letter, for his ignorance of the proper way to write, and for his lack of culture, and tells him he ought to be ashamed of himself, comparing the Tzar's literary style with "the ravings of women," and accusing him of writing "barbarously."

In addition to these letters, Kúrbsky wrote a remarkable history of Iván the Terrible's reign, entitled, "A History of the Grand Principality of Moscow, Concerning the Deeds Which We Have Heard from Trustworthy Men, and Have also Beheld with Our Own Eyes." It is brought down to the year 1578. This history is important as the first work in Russian literature in which a completely successful attempt was made to write a fluent historical narrative (instead of setting forth facts in the style of the Chronicles), and link facts to preceding facts in logical sequence, deducing effects from causes.

To the reign of Iván the Terrible belong, also, "A History of the Kingdom of Kazán," by Priest Ioánn Glazátly; and the "Memoirs of Alexéi Adásheff"—the most ancient memoirs in the Russian language.

In the mean time, during this same sixteenth century, a new culture was springing up in southwestern Russia, and in western Russia, then under the rule of Poland, and under the influence of the Jesuits. Many Russians had joined the Roman Church, or the "Union" (1596), by which numerous eastern orthodox along the western frontier acknowledged the supremacy of the Pope of Rome, on condition of being allowed to retain their own rites and vernacular in the church services. In the end, they were gradually deprived of these, almost entireiy; and curiously enough, the solution of this problem has been found, within the last decade, in the United States, where the immigrant Uniates are returning by the thousand to the Russian Church. In order to counteract the education and the wiles of the Jesuits, philanthropic "Brotherhoods" were formed among the orthodox Christians of southwest Russia, and these brotherhoods founded schools in which instruction was given in the Greek, Slavonic, Latin, and Polish languages; and rhetoric, dialectics, poetics, theology, and many other branches were taught. One of these schools in Kíeff was presided over by Peter Moghíla (1597–1646), the famous son of the Voevóda of Wallachia, who was brilliantly educated on the Continent, and at one time had been in the military service of Poland. Thus he thoroughly understood the situation when, later on (1625), he became a monk in the Kíeff Catacombs Monastery, and eventually the archimandrite or abbot, and devoted his wealth and his life to the dissemination of education among his fellow-believers of the Orthodox Eastern Catholic Church. The influence of this man and of his Academy on Russia was immense. The earliest school-books were here composed. Peter Moghíla's own "Shorter Catechism" is still referred to. The Slavonic grammar and lexicon of Lavrénty Zizánie-Tustanóvsky and Melénty Smotrítzky continued in use until supplanted by those of Lomonósoff one hundred and fifty years later. The most important factor, next to the foundation of the famous Academy, was, that towards the middle of the seventeenth century learned Kievlyanins, like Simeón Polótzky, attained to the highest ecclesiastical rank in the country, and imported the new ideas in education, which had been evolved in Kíeff, to Moscow, where they prepared the first stable foundations for the future sweeping reforms of Peter the Great.

Literature continued to bear an ecclesiastical imprint; but there were some works of a different sort. One of the compositions which presents a picture of life in the seventeenth century—among the higher and governing classes only, it is true—is Grigory Kotoshíkin's "Concerning Russia in the Reign of Alexéi Mikháilovitch." Kotoshíkin was well qualified to deal with the subject, having been secretary in the foreign office, and attached to the service of Voevóda (field marshal), Prince Dolgo-rúky, in 1666–1667. Among other things, he points out that the "women of the kingdom of Moscow are illiterate," and deduces the conclusion that the chief cause of all contemporary troubles in the kingdom is excessive

ignorance.   He declares, "We must learn from foreigners, and send our children abroad for instruction"—precisely Peter the Great's policy, it will be observed.

Another writer, Yury Krizhánitz, must have exerted a
very considerable influence upon Peter the Great, as it is
known that the latter owned his work on "The Kingdom
of Russia in the Middle of the Seventeenth Century."
This book contains a discussion as to the proper means
for changing the condition of affairs then prevailing; as
to the degree in which foreign influence should be permitted; and precisely what measures should be adopted to
combat this or that social abuse or defect.   The programme of reforms, which he therein laid down, was, to
proceed from the highest source, by administrative process, and without regard to the opposition of the masses.
This programme Peter the Great carried out most effectually later on.

Battle was also waged with the old order of things in
the spiritual realm by the famous Patriarch Níkon (1605–
1681), who, as a peasant lad of twelve, ran away from
his father's house to a monastery.   Although compelled
by his parents to return home and to marry, he soon went
back and became a monk in a monastery in the White
Sea.   Eventually he rose not only to the highest ecclesiastical post in the kingdom, but became almost more
powerful than the Tzar himself.   He may be classed with
the great literary forces of the land, in that he caused the
correction of the Slavonic Church Service-books directly
from the Greek originals, and eliminated from them innumerable and gross errors, which the carelessness and ignorance of scribes and proof-readers had allowed to creep
into them.   The far-reaching effects of this necessary and

important step, the resulting schism in the church, which still endures, Níkon's quarrels with the Tzar Alexéi Mikháilovitch, Peter the Great's father, are familiar matters of history; as is also the fact that the power he won and the course he held were the decisive factors in Peter the Great's resolve to have no more Patriarchs, and to intrust the government of the church to a College, now the Most Holy Governing Synod.

When Níkon passed from power, lesser men took up the battle. Chief among these was Archimandrite Simeón Polótzky (already mentioned), who lived from 1626-1681, and was the first learned man to become tutor to a Tzarévitch. The spirit of the times no longer permitted the heir to the throne to be taught merely to read and write from the primer, the Psalter, and the "Book of Hours"; and Alexéi Mikháilovitch appointed Simeón Polótzky instructor to the Tzarévitch Feódor.

QUESTIONS FOR REVIEW

1. What unfavorable conditions do we find in Russian society at the beginning of the sixteenth century?

2. Who was Maxím the Greek, and what service did he render to his times?

3. What was the purpose of the "House-Regulator" of Pope Sylvester?

4. How does he define the duties of woman?

5. What early attempts at printing were made in Russia?

6. What qualities of Iván the Terrible may be seen in his writings?

7. Describe his correspondence with Prince Kúrbsky.

8. How do Kúrbsky's qualities compare with those of the Tzar, as shown in this correspondence?

9. Why is Kúrbsky's history of Moscow a remarkable work?

10. What great work was done by Moghíla and his Academy?

11. How did his influence prove very far-reaching?

12. What did other writers of this time say of the need for better education in Russia?

13. Describe the career of the famous Patriarch Níkon.

BIBLIOGRAPHY

History of Russia. Rambaud, Chapter XV., Iván the Terrible, also Chapters XVI.–XX.

The Story of Russia. W. R. Morfill.

CHAPTER V

FOURTH PERIOD, FROM THE MIDDLE OF THE
SEVENTEENTH CENTURY TO THE EPOCH
OF REFORM UNDER PETER THE GREAT.

Even in far-away, northeastern Russia a break is apparent in the middle of the sixteenth century; and during the
reign of Iván the Terrible, a new sort of historical composition came into vogue—the so-called "Stépennaya
Kníga," or "Book of Degrees" (or steps), wherein the
national history was set forth in order, according to the
Degrees of the Princely Houses in the lines of descent
from Rúrik to Iván the Terrible in twenty degrees. This
method found favor, and another degree was added in the
seventeenth century, bringing the history down to the death
of the Tzar Alexéi Mikháilovitch. During the seventeenth century many attempts were made at collections
and chronicles, the only one approaching fullness being
the "Chronicle of Níkon," so-called, probably, because it
was compiled by order of the Patriarch Níkon.

During the seventeenth century a fad also sprang up of
writing everything, even school-books, petitions, and
calendars in versified form, which was known as *vírshi*,
and imported from Poland to Moscow by Simeón Polótzky.
At that time, also, it was the fashion for school-boys to
act plays as a part of their regular course of study in the
schools in southwest Russia; and in particular, in Peter
Moghíla's Academy in Kíeff. Plays of a religious charac-

ter had, naturally, been imported from western Europe, through Poland, in the seventeenth century, but as early as the beginning of the sixteenth century certain church ceremonies in Russia were celebrated in a purely dramatic form, suggestive of the mystery plays in western Europe. The most curious and famous of these was that which represented the casting of the Three Holy Children into the Fiery Furnace, and their miraculous rescue from the flames by an angel. This was enacted on the Wednesday before Christmas, during Matins, in Moscow and other towns, the first performance, so far as is known, having been in the beginning of the sixteenth century, it being mentioned, in the year 1548, in the finance-books of the archiepiscopal residence of St. Sophia at Nóvgorod. The "furnace" was a circular structure of wood, on architectural lines, gayly painted with the figures of appropriate holy men; specimens have been preserved, one being in the Archeological Museum in St. Petersburg.

The second famous "Act" (for such was their title) was known under the name of "The Riding on the Foal of an Ass," and took place (beginning with the end of the sixteenth century) in Moscow and other towns, generally on Palm Sunday. It represented the triumphal entry of Christ into Jerusalem, and in Moscow it was performed in accordance with a special ritual by the Patriarch, in the presence of the Tzar himself; the Patriarch represented Christ, the Tzar led the ass upon which he was mounted. In other towns it was acted by the archbishops and the Voevódas. The third, and simplest, of these religious dramas, the "Act of the Last Judgment," generally took place on the Sunday preceding the Carnival.

In 1672 Tzar Alexéi Mikháilovitch ordered Johann

Gregory, the Lutheran pastor in Moscow, to arrange "comedy acts," and the first pieces acted before the Tzar on a private court stage were translations from the German—the "Act of Artaxerxes," the comedy "Judith," and so forth. But under the influence of southwestern Russia, as already mentioned, it was not long before a Russian mystery play, "St. Alexéi, the Man of God," founded on a Polish original, thoroughly imbued with Polish influence, was written in honor of Tzar Alexéi, and acted in public by students of Peter Moghíla's College in Kíeff. A whole series of mystery plays followed from the fruitful pen of Simeón Polótzky. Especially curious was his "Comedy of King Nebuchadnezzar, the Golden Calf, and the Three Youths Who Were Not Consumed in the Fiery Furnace." He wrote many other "comedies," two huge volumes of them.

Theatrical representations won instant favor with the Tzar and his court, and a theatrical school was promptly established in Moscow, even before the famous and very necessary Slavonic-Greco-Latin Academy, for "higher education," as it was then understood.

None of the school dramas—several of which Peter Moghíla himself is said to have written—have come down to us; neither are there any specimens now in existence of the spiritual dramas and dramatic dialogues from the early years of the seventeenth century. In addition to the dramas of Simeón Polótzky, of the last part of that century, we have the dramatic works of another ecclesiastical writer, St. Dmítry of Rostóff (1651–1709), six in all, including "The Birth of Christ," "The Penitent Sinner," "Esther and Ahashuerus," and so forth. They stand half-way between mysteries and religio-allegorical pieces, and begin with a prologue, in which one of the actors sketches the general outline of the piece, and explains its connection with contemporary affairs; and end with an epilogue, recited by another actor, which is a reinforcement and inculcation of the moral set forth in the play. St. Dmítry's plays were first acted in the "cross-chamber," or banquet-hall, of the episcopal residence in Rostóff, where he was the Metropolitan, by the pupils of the school he had founded. He cleverly introduced scenes from real life into the middle of his spiritual dramas.

Collections of short stories and anecdotes current in western Europe also made their way to Russia, via Poland; and freed from puritanical, religious, and conventional bonds, light satirical treatment of topics began to be met with in the seventeenth century, wherein, among other things ridiculed, are the law-courts, the interminable length of lawsuits, the covetousness and injustice of the judges, and so forth. Among such productions are: "The Tale of Judge Shemyák" (Herring), "The Description of the Judicial Action in the Suit Between the Pike and the Perch"; or, applying personal names to the contestants, "The Story of Yórsha Yórshoff (Perch, the son of Perch) and the Son of Shtchetínnikoff (the Bristly)." A similar production is "The Story of Kúra (the Cock) and Lisá (the Fox)." The first place among such works, for simplicity of style and truth of description, belongs to "The History of the Russian Nobleman, Frol Skovyéeff, and Anna, Daughter of Table-Decker Nárdin Nashtchókin." But many writers of that age could not take a satirical view of things, and depicted life as a permanent conflict between the powers of evil and good—wherein the Devil chiefly got the upper hand—and man's principal occupa-

tion therein, the saving of his soul. One of the best compositions of ancient Russian secular literature belongs to
this gloomy category, "The Tale of Góre-Zlostchástye;
How Góre-Zlostchástye Brought the Young Man to the
Monastic State," Góre-Zloshtchástye being, literally,
"Woe-Misfortune." Woe-Misfortune persecutes the
youth, who finds no safety from him, save on one road,
where, alone, he does not besiege him—the road to the
monastery.

It will be seen that the spirit of the age was deeply
influenced by the state of material things.

QUESTIONS FOR REVIEW

1. What kind of historical writing sprang up in northeastern Russia during the time of Iván the Terrible?
2. Describe the fashion of acting plays in the schools.
3. What were the "comedy acts" given before the Tzar?
4. For what is Dmítry of Rostóff to be remembered?
5. What kind of anecdotes and short stories came from
western Europe to Russia in the seventeenth century?
6. What picture of Russian life do they bring before us?

BIBLIOGRAPHY

History of Russia. Alfred Rambaud.
The Story of Russia. W. R. Morfill.

CHAPTER VI

FIFTH PERIOD, THE REIGN OF PETER THE GREAT (1689-1723).

The Fifth Period of Russian literature is that which comprises the reign of Peter the Great, with its reforms, scientific aims, and utter change of views upon nearly all conceivable practical and spiritual subjects. With the general historical aspects of that reign we cannot deal here. The culture which Peter I. introduced into Russia was purely utilitarian; and moreover, in precisely that degree which would further the attainment of his ends. But however imperatively his attention was engaged with other matters, he never neglected to maintain and add to the institutions of general education and special schools, and to order the translation of such works as were adapted to the requirements of his people, as he understood those requirements.

His views on the subject of literature were as peculiar as those on culture, and were guided by the same sternly practical considerations. But it must be said, that under him the printing-press first acquired in Russia its proper position of importance, and became the instrument for the quick, easy, and universal dissemination and exchange of thought, instead of serving merely as an indifferent substitute for manuscript copies. Not only were books printed, but also speeches and official poetry for special occasions; and at last the "Russian News" (January,

1703), the first Russian newspaper, keenly and carefully supervised by .Peter the Great himself, made its appearance.

At the end of the seventeenth century, only two typographical establishments existed in all Russia: one in the Kíeff Catacombs Monastery (which does an immense business in religious books, and cheap prints and paper *ikóni*, or holy pictures); the other in Moscow, in the "Printing-House." In 1711 the first typographical establishment appeared in St. Petersburg, and in 1720 there were already four in the new capital, in addition to new ones in Tchernígoff, Nóvgorod-Syéversk, and Nóvgorod; while another had been added in Moscow. Yet Peter the Great distrusted the literary activity of the monks—and with reason, since most of them opposed his reforms, while many deliberately plotted against him—and in 1700–1701 ordered that monks in the monasteries should be deprived of pens, ink, and paper.

His official, machine-made literature offers nothing of special interest. But one of the curious phenomena of the epoch was the peasant writer Iván Tikhonóvitch Posóshkoff (born about 1670), a well-to-do, even a rich, man for those days, very well read, and imbued with the spirit of reform. Out of pure love for his fatherland he began to write projects and books in which he endeavored to direct the attention of the government to many social defects, and to point out means for correcting them. One of the most interesting works of Peter the Great's period was Posóshkoff's written "Plan of Conduct" for his son (who was one of the first young Russians sent abroad, in 1708, for education), entitled, "A Father's Testamentary Exhortation." His "Book on Poverty and Wealth" is also noteworthy, inasmuch as it affords a complete survey of Russia under Peter the Great.

During this reign, the highly educated and eminently practical Little Russians acquired more power than ever. The most notable of them all was Feofán Prokópovitch, Archbishop of Nóvgorod (born in Kíeff, 1681), who had been brilliantly educated in Kíeff and Rome, and was the most celebrated of Peter the Great's colaborers, the most zealous and clever executor of his sovereign's will, who attained to the highest secular and ecclesiastical honors, and prolonged his influence and his labors into succeeding reigns. His sermons were considered so important that they were always printed immediately after their delivery, and forwarded to the Emperor abroad, or wherever he might chance to be. Like others at that period, he indulged in dramatic writing, for acting on the school stage; and at Peter the Great's request he drew up a set of "Ecclesiastical Regulations" for the Ecclesiastical College, and was appointed to be the head of the church government, though Stepán Yavórsky was made head of the Holy Governing Synod when it was established, in 1721.

Peter the Great's ideas were not only opposed but persecuted, after his death (1723), until the accession to the throne of his daughter Elizabeth, in 1741. It was a long time before literature was regarded seriously, on its own merits; before literary and scientific activity were looked upon as separate departments, or any importance was attributed to literature. Science usurped the first place, and literature was regarded as merely a useful accessory thereto. This view was held by all the first writers after Peter the Great's time: Kantemír, Tatíshtcheff, Tredia-

kóvsky, and even the gifted Lomonósoff, Russia's first
secular writers, in the present sense of that word.

The first of these, in order, Prince Antiókh Dmítrie-
vitch Kantemír, was born in 1708, and brought to Moscow
at the age of three by his father, the Hospodár of Molda-
via (after the disastrous campaign on the Pruth), who
assumed Russian citizenship. Prince Kantemír published
his first work, "A Symphony (concordance) of the
Psalter," at the age of eighteen, being at that time in the
military service, and a member of Feofán Prokópovitch's
circle, and his close friend. His father had left a will
by which he bequeathed his entire estate and about one
hundred thousand serfs to that one of his children who
should prove "the most successful in the sciences"; and
one of Prince Antiókh's brothers having married a daughter
of Prince D. M. Galítzyn, one of the most influential men
of the day, Peter the Great naturally adjudged him the
heir to the estate. This embittered Prince Antiókh
Kantemír, and he revealed his wrath against the Emperor
and his party in his first two notable satires, which
appeared about the time the Empress Anna Ioánnovna
ascended the throne (1730). Galítzyn was one of the
nobles who were ruined by this event, and Prince Kantemír recovered a portion of his rightful possessions. In
1731 his powerful protection secured him the appointment
of diplomatic resident in London. Thence he was, later
on, transferred to Paris, and never returned to Russia.
Before his departure to London, he wrote five satires,
several fables and epistles, none of which were printed,
however, though they won him great reputation in cultivated society, where they circulated in manuscript copies.
Satire was quite in the spirit of the age, and Kantemír

devoted himself to it.   He displayed much wit and keen
observation.   In all, he produced nine satires, four being
written during his sojourn abroad.   In Satire Second,
entitled, "Filarét and Evgény," or "On the Envy and
Pride of Cantankerous Nobles," he describes the arrogance of the nobility, and their pretensions to the highest
posts, without any personal exertion or merit, solely on
the merits of their ancestors; and here he appears as a
zealous advocate of Peter the Great's "Table of Ranks,"
intended to put a stop to precisely this state of affairs, by
making rank depend on personal services to the state.
The Third and Sixth Satires are curious in that they
clearly express the author's views on his own literary activity, and also on society and literature in general.   The
Sixth Satire, written in 1738, is the most important, as
showing Kantemír's own nature, both as a man and as a
writer.

One of the men most in sympathy with Peter the Great
was Vasíly Nikítitch Tatíshtcheff (1686–1750), who was
educated partly in Russia, partly abroad.   He applied
his brilliant talents and profound mind to the public service, first in the Artillery, then in the Department of Mines,
later on as Governor òf Ástrakhan.   In pursuance of a
general plan for useful literary labors, Tatíshtcheff collected materials for a geography, which he did not finish,
and for a history of Russia, which he worked out with
considerable fullness, in five volumes.   It was published
thirty years after his death, by command of Katherine II.
It is not history in the sense of that word at the present
day, but merely a very respectable preliminary study of
materials; and the author's expressions of opinion are
valuable features, as setting forth the spirit of the Epoch

of Reformation. He is generally mentioned as a historian, but far more important are his "Spiritual Testament" (Last Will) and "Exhortation to his son Evgráff" (1733), and "A Discussion between Two Friends as to the Advantages of Sciences and Schools" (probably written 1731–1736). The Testament consists of a general collection of rules concerning worldly wisdom, applied to contemporary needs and views, though his son was already grown up and in the government service, so that much of its contents are of general application only, and were introduced to round out the work, and for the edification of the rising generation. It is the last specimen of a class of works in which, as has been seen, Russian literature is rich.

The first Russian who devoted himself exclusively to literature was Vasíly Kiríllovitch Trediakóvsky (born at Ástrakhan in 1703), the son and grandson of priests, who was educated in Russia and abroad. When he decided, on his return from abroad in 1730, to adopt literature as a profession, the times were extremely unpropitious. He had, long before, during his student days in Moscow, written syllabic verses, an elegy on the death of Peter the Great, and a couple of dramas, which were acted by his fellow-students. In 1732 he became the court poet, or laureate and panegyrist, and wrote, to the order of the Empress Anna Ioánnovna, speeches and laudatory addresses, which he presented to the grandees, receiving in return various gifts in accordance with the custom of the epoch. But neither his official post nor his personal dignity prevented his receiving, also, violent and ignominious treatment at the hands of the powerful nobles. His "New and Brief Method of Composing Russian Verses" constituted an epoch in the history of Russian poetry, since therein was first set forth the theory of Russian tonic versification. But although he endeavored to create a distinct Russian style, and to put his own system into practice, he wrote worse than many of his contemporaries, and his poems were all below mediocrity; while not a single line of them supported the theory he announced. They enjoy as little consideration from his literary posterity as he enjoyed personally in the society of Anna Ioánnovna's day. Yet his work was very prominent in the transition period between the literature of the seventeenth century and the labors of Lomonósoff, and he undoubtedly rendered a great service to Russian culture by his translations, as an authority on literary theories and as a philologist.

The first writer of capital importance in modern Russian literature in general was the gifted peasant-academician Mikháil Vasílievitch Lomonósoff (1711–1755)—a combination of the scientific and literary man, such as was the fashion of the period in general, and almost necessarily so in Russia. Born in a village of the Archángel Government, near Kholmogóry on the White Sea, he was a fisherman, like his father, until the age of sixteen, having learned to read and write from a peasant neighbor. A tyrannical stepmother forced him to endure hunger and cold, and to do his modest studying and reading in desert spots. Accordingly, when he obtained from the village authorities the permission requisite for absenting himself for the space of ten months, he failed to return, and was inscribed among the "fugitives." In the Slavo-Greco-Latin Academy at Moscow, which he managed to enter, and where he remained for five years, he distanced all competitors (though he lived, as he said, "in incredible poverty," on three kopeks a day), devoting himself chiefly to the natural sciences. At the age of twenty-two he was sent abroad by the government to study metallurgy at Freiburg. There and elsewhere abroad, in England, France, and Holland, he remained for five years, studying various practical branches.

In 1742 he became assistant professor at the Academy of Science in St. Petersburg, at a wretched salary, and in 1748 professor, lecturing on physical geography, chemistry, natural history, poetry, and the Russian language. He also was indefatigable in translating scientific works from the French and German, in writing a work on mining, a rhetoric-book, and so forth. By 1757 he had written many odes, poetical epistles, idyls, and the like; verses on festival occasions and tragedies, to order; a Russian grammar; and had collected materials for a history, and planned extensive philological researches. Eager to benefit his country, and conscious that he was capable of doing so, he made practical application of many important improvements in architecture, navigation, mining, and manufacturing industries. For example: in 1750 he zealously engaged in the manufacture of glass (with the aid of the government), set up a glass-factory, and applied his chemical knowledge to colored glass for mosaics. The great mosaic pictures which glorify Peter the Great, and the vast, magnificent *ikóni* (holy pictures) which adorn the Cathedral of St. Isaac of Dalmatia, in St. Petersburg, are the products of those factories, which still exist and thrive.

It is impossible to narrate in detail all Lomonósoff's enterprises for the improvement of the economic condition of the masses, his government surveys of Russia, ethno-

graphical and geographical aims, and the like. His
administrative labors absorbed most of his time leaving
little for literary work. Like others of his day, he
regarded literature as an occupation for a man's leisure
hours, and even openly ridiculed those who busied themselves exclusively with it; though he ascribed to it great
subsidiary importance, as a convenient instrument for
introducing to society new ideas, and for expounding
divers truths, both abstract and scientific. Thus he
strove to furnish Russia with models of literary productions in all classes, and to improve the language of literature and science.   Nevertheless, although he rendered
great services in these directions, and is known as "the
Father of Russian Literature," he was far more important
as a scientific than as a literary man.   It is true that precisely the opposite view of him was held during the period
immediately succeeding him, and he became an authority
and a pattern for many Russian writers, who imitated his
pseudo-classical poetry, and even copied his language, as
the acme of literary perfection.   In reality, although he
acquired a certain technical skill, he was a very mediocre
poet; yet he was as an eagle among barnyard fowls, and
cleverly made use of the remarkable possibilities of the
Russian language as no other man did, although he borrowed his models from the pseudo-classical productions
then in vogue in foreign countries.   A few of his versified
efforts which have come down to us deserve the name of
poetry, by virtue of their lofty thoughts and strong, sincere feeling, expressed in graceful, melodious style.
Among the best of these are: "A Letter Concerning the
Utility of Glass," "Meditations Concerning the Grandeur
of God," and his triumphal ode, "On the Day of the

Accession to the Throne of the Empress Elizavéta Petróvna"—this last being the expression of the general rapture at the accession of Peter the Great's daughter.

The most important feature of all Lomonósoff's poetical productions is the fine, melodious language, which was a complete novelty at that time, together with smooth, regular versification. Not one of his contemporaries possessed so profound and varied a knowledge of the Russian popular and book languages, and this knowledge it was which enabled him to make such a wide choice between the ancient Church Slavonic, ancient Russian, the popular, and the bookish tongues.

In Peter the Great's Epoch of Reform, the modern "secular" or "civil" alphabet was substituted for the ancient Church Slavonic, and the modern Russian language, which Lomonósoff did so much to improve, began to assume shape, literature and science at last freeing themselves completely from ecclesiasticism and monasticism.

The first writer to divorce literature and science, like Lomonósoff, a talent of the transition period, between the Epoch of Reform and the brilliant era of Katherine II.—a product, in education and culture, of the Reform Epoch, though he strove to escape from its traditions—was Alexander Petróvitch Sumarókoff (1717–1777). Insignificant in comparison with Lomonósoff, the most complete contrast with the peasant-genius by his birth and social rank, which were of the highest, he was plainly the forerunner of a new era; and in the sense in which Feofán Prokópovitch is called "the first secular Russian writer," Sumarókoff must be described as "the first Russian literary man."

The Empress Anna Ioánnovna had had a troop of

Italian actors, early in her reign; and in 1735 a troop of actors and singers. The Empress Elizavéta Petróvna revived the theater, and during her reign there were even two troops of actors, one French, the other Italian, for ballet and opera-bouffe (1757), both subsidized by the court. Sometimes an audience was lacking at their performances, and on one occasion at least, Elizavéta Petróvna improved upon the Scripture parable; when an insufficient number of spectators presented themselves at the French comedy, she forthwith dispatched mounted messengers to numerous persons of rank and distinction, with a categorical demand to know why they had absented themselves, and a warning that henceforth a fine of fifty rubles would be exacted for such dereliction of duty.

A distinctive feature of Elizavéta's reign was the growth of closer relations with France, which at this period represented the highest culture of Europe. Dutch and German influences which had hitherto impressed themselves upon Russian society, now gave place to French ideas. Translations of the French classics of the brilliant age of Louis XIV. were made in Russian, and the new Academy of Fine Arts established by Elizavéta in St. Petersburg was put under the care of French masters. It was in her reign also that the University of Moscow was founded.

In 1746 Feódor Grigórievitch Vólkhoff, the son of a merchant, built in Yaroslávl (on the upper Volga), the first Russian theater, to hold about one thousand spectators. Five years later, the news of the fine performances of the actors and actresses of Vólkhoff's theater reached St. Petersburg, and the troop was ordered to appear before the court. Four years later still, the existence of the

Russian theater was assured, by imperial decree. Sumarókoff was appointed the director, having, evidently, for a
long time previously had full charge of all dramatic performances at court; and also, evidently, been expected to
furnish plays. His first tragedy, "Khóreff," dates from
1747. In the following year "Hamlet" appeared. Until
the arrival of the Vólkhoff troop, all his plays were acted
in St. Petersburg only, by the cadets and officers of the
"Nobles' Cadet Corps," where he himself had been educated. Towards the end of Elizavéta Petróvna's reign,
Sumarókoff acquired great renown, almost equaling that
of Lomonósoff in his literary services, and the admirers
of Russian literature of that day were divided into hostile
camps, which consisted of the friends and advocates of
these two writers, the Empress Elizabeth being at the
head of the first, the Empress Katherine II. (then Grand
Duchess) at the head of the second.

For about ten years (1759–1768), Sumarókoff pub-
lished a satirical journal, "The Industrious Bee," after
which he returned to his real field and wrote a tragedy,
"Výsheslaff," and the comedies, "A Dowry by Deceit,"
"The Usurer," "The Three Rival Brothers," "The
Malignant Man," and "Narcissus." In all he wrote
twenty-six plays, including the tragedies "Sínav and
Trúvor," "Aristona," and "Semira," before the establishment of the theater in St. Petersburg, in addition to
"Hóreff" and "Hamlet," "Dmítry the Pretender," and
"Mstíslaff." "Semira" was regarded as his masterpiece,
and among his comedies "Tressotinius" attracted the most
attention. All these, however, were merely weak imitations of the narrow form in which all French and pseudo-
classical dramas were molded, the unities of time, place,

and action exerting an embarrassing restriction on the action; and the heroes, although they professed to be Russians, with obscure historical names (like Sínav and Trúvor), or semi-mythical (like Khóreff), or genuinely historical (like Dmítry the Pretender), were the stereotyped declaimers of the bombastic, pseudo-classical drama.

Sumarókoff's dramatic work formed but a small part of his writings, which included a great mass of odes, eclogues, elegies, ballads, and so forth; and although he ranks as a dramatist, he is most important in his series of fables, epigrams, and epitaphs, which are permeated with biting satire on his own period, though the subjects are rather monotonous—the bad arrangement of the courts of justice, which permitted bribery and other abuses among lawyers, the injurious and oppressive state monopolies, attempts at senseless imitations of foreigners in language and customs, and ignorance concealed by external polish and culture. Coarse and imperfect as are these satires, they vividly reproduce the impressions of a contemporary gifted with keen observation and the ability to deal dispassionately with current events. As we shall see later on, this protest against the existing order of things continued, and blossomed forth in the succeeding—the sixth —period of literature in productions, which not only form the flower of the century, but also really belong to modern literature, and hold the public attention at the present day. This Sumarókoff's dramatic and other works do not do, and their place is rather in the archives of the preparatory school.

QUESTIONS FOR REVIEW

1. What was the general character of the reign of Peter the Great?

2. How important did the printing press become in his time?

3. Why did Peter the Great deprive the monks of pens, ink, and paper?

4. What interesting works were written by Posóshkoff?

5. Who was Feofán Prokópovitch?

6. Give an account of the life and writings of Kantemír.

7. What literary influence had Tatíshtcheff and Trediakóvsky?

8. Describe the early life of Lomónosoff.

9. Give an account of his many activities.

10. How did he regard literature, and what were his best works.

11. In what way did he exert a strong literary influence?

12. What attention did the Court give to theatrical representations at this time?

13. What new relations with Europe marked the reign of Elizavéta?

14. When and where was Vólkhoff's theater established?

15. What share had Sumarókoff in developing the Russian drama?

16. How did he protest against the abuses of his times?

BIBLIOGRAPHY

History of Russia. Alfred Rambaud. Vol. II., Chapter VI.
The Story of Russia. W. R. Morfill.
Specimens from the Russian Poets. Two volumes, Sir John Bowring, contain many specimens from Lomonósoff to Zhukóvsky inclusive.

CHAPTER VII

SIXTH PERIOD, THE REIGN OF KATHERINE II.
(1762–1796).

Under the brilliant sway of Katherine II. (1762–1796) literature and literary men in Russia first began to acquire legitimate respect and consideration in the highest circles— the educated minority, which ruled tastes and fashions. Wealthy patrons of literature had existed even in the Empress Elizabeth's day it is true; and a taste for the theater had been implanted or engendered, partly by force, as we have seen. Western ideas had made much progress in a normal way, through the close contact with western European nations, brought about by Elizabeth's great political genius, which had made St. Petersburg the diplomatic center and law-giver; and Katherine's own interest in literature before her accession to the throne had also had much to do with raising the standard and the respect in which literature and writers were held, and in preparing the ground for the new era. During her reign, life and literature may be said to have come into close contact for the first time. Katherine II. herself may be placed at the head of the writers of her day, in virtue not only of her rank and her encouragement of literature, at home and abroad, but because of her own writings. One of her comedies, "O, Ye Times! O, Ye Manners!" is still occasionally given on the stage. Her own Memoirs and her Correspondence with Voltaire, Diderot, and others, furnish invaluable pictures of contemporary views and manners. Her satires, comedies, and journalistic work and polemical articles are most important, however, because most original. In 1769 she began to publish a newspaper called "All Sorts of Things" (or "Varieties"), to which she personally contributed satirical articles attacking abuses—chiefly the lack of culture, and superficiality of education. It was extremely popular with the public, and imitators started up, which the Empress eventually suppressed, because of their virulent attacks on her own journal. She ceased journalistic work in 1774, and then introduced on the stage, in her comedies, the same types and aspects of Russian life which she had previously presented in her satirical articles.

Of the fourteen comedies, nine operas, and seven proverbs which she wrote, in whole or in part (she had the skeletons of some filled out with choruses and verses according to her own plans), up to 1790, eleven comedies, seven operas, and five proverbs have come down to us. The comedies are not particularly artistic, but they are important in a history of the national literature, as noteworthy efforts to present scenes and persons drawn from contemporary life—the first of that sort on the Russian stage—the most remarkable being the one already referred to, and "The Gambler's Name-day" (1772). The personages whom she copied straight from life are vivid; those whom she invented as ideals, as foils for contrast, are lifeless shadows. Her operas are not important. Towards the close of her literary activity she once more engaged in journalism, writing a series of satirical sketches, "Facts and Fiction" (published in 1783), for a new journal, issued on behalf of the Academy of Sciences by the

Princess Dáshkoff, the director of that academy, and chairman of the Russian Academy, founded in that year on the Princess's own plan.

This Princess Ekaterína Románovna Dáshkoff (born Vorontzóff, 1743–1810) was a brilliantly educated woman, with a pronounced taste for political intrigue, who had a great share in the conspiracy which disposed of Peter III., and placed Katherine II. on the throne. Katherine richly rewarded the Princess, but preserved her own independence and supremacy, which offended Princess Dáshkoff, the result being a coldness between the former intimate friends. This, in turn, obliged the Princess to leave the court and travel at home and abroad. During one trip abroad she received a diploma as doctor of laws, medicine, and theology from Edinburg University. Her Memoirs are famous, though not particularly frank, or in agreement with Katherine II.'s statements, naturally. The Empress never ceased to be suspicious of her, but twenty years later a truce was patched up between them, and Katherine appointed her to the offices above mentioned—never held before or since by a woman.

Princess Dáshkoff wrote much on educational subjects, and in the journal referred to above, she published not only her own articles and Katherine II.'s, but also the writings of many new and talented men, among them, Von Vízin and Derzhávin. This journal, "The Companion of the Friends of the Russian Language," speedily came to an end when the Princess-editor took umbrage at the ridicule heaped on some of her projects and speeches by the Empress and her courtiers.

If Katherine II. was the first to introduce real life on the Russian stage, Von Vízin was the first to do so in a manner sufficiently artistic to hold the stage, which is the case with his "Nédorosl," or "The Hobbledehoy." He is the representative of the Russian type, in its best aspects, during the reign of Katherine II., and offers a striking contrast to the majority of his educated fellow-countrymen of the day. They were slavish worshipers of French influences. He bore himself scornfully, even harshly, towards everything foreign, and always strove to counteract each foreign thing by something of native Russian origin.

Denís Ivánovitch Von Vízin (1744–1792), as his name suggests, was the descendant of an ancient German family, of knightly rank. An ancestor had been taken prisoner in the reign of Iván the Terrible, and had ended by settling in Russia and assuming Russian citizenship. The family became thoroughly Russified when they joined the Russian Church. Von Vízin was of a noble and independent character, to which he added a keen, fine mind, and a caustic tongue. His father, he tells us, in his "A Frank Confession of Deeds and Thoughts" (imitated from Rousseau's "Confession"), was also of an independent character in general, and in particular—contrary to the custom of the epoch—detested extortion and bribery, and never accepted gifts. "Sir!" he was accustomed to say to persons who asked favors of him in his official position, "a loaf of sugar affords no reason for condemning your opponent; please take it away and bring legal proof of your rights."

Denís Von Vízin received a thorough Russian education at home—which was unusual at that era of overwhelming foreign influence; and his inclination for literature having manifested itself in his early youth, while

still at the University School for Nobles, he made various
translations from foreign languages before entering the
Moscow University, at the age of fifteen.   During a visit
which he made to St. Petersburg, while still a student at
the University, he saw the theater for the first time, and
soon made acquaintance with F. G. Volkhoff (already
mentioned), and one of the actors.   These things exerted
a great influence upon him.   During a visit of the Court
to Moscow, in 1755, he was appointed translator to the
Foreign College (Office), with the inevitable military rank,
and went to live in the new capital.   After divers vicissi-
tudes of service, he wrote "The Brigadier," which he was
promptly asked to read before royalty and in society.   It
won for him great reputation with people who were capable of appreciating the first play which was genuinely
Russian in something more than externals.   It jeers at
ignorance coated over with an extremely thin veneer of
pretentious foreign culture.   The types in "The Brigadier" (written about 1747) had long been floating about
in literature, and as it were, awaiting a skillful pen which
should present them in full relief to the contemporary
public.   Von Vízin set forth these types on the stage in a
clearer, more vivid manner than all previous writers who
had dealt with them, as we have seen, in satires and
dramas, from Kantemír to Katherine II.   The characters,
as Von Vízin depicted them, were no longer abstract
monsters, agglomerations of evil qualities, but near relations to everybody.   Moreover, the drama was gay, playful—not even the moral was gloomy—with not a single
depressing line.

Totally different is "The Hobbledehoy" ("Nédorosl,"
1782), which is even more celebrated, and was written

towards the close of a long career in the service, filled
with varied and trying experiences—part of which arose
from the difficulties of the author's own noble character
in contact with a different type of men and from his
attacks on abuses of all sorts—after a profound study of
life in the middle and higher classes of Russian court and
diplomatic circles. The difference between "The Brigadier" and "The Hobbledehoy" is so great that they must
be read in the order of their production if the full value
of the impression created by the earlier play is to be appreciated. "The Hobbledehoy" was wholly unlike anything
which had been seen hitherto in Russian literature. Had
the authorities permitted Von Vízin to print his collection
of satires, he would have stood at the head of that branch
of literature in that epoch; as it was, this fine comedy
contains the fullest expression of his dissatisfaction at the
established order of things in general. The merits of the
play rest upon its queer characters from life, who are
startlingly real, and represent the genuine aims and ideas
of the time. The contrasting set of characters, whom he
introduced as the exponents of his ideals, do not express
any aims and ideas which then existed, but merely what
he personally would have liked to see. Katherine II.,
with whose comedies Von Vízin's have much in common,
always tried to offset her disagreeable real characters by
honorable, sensible types, also drawn from real life as
ideals. But Von Vízin's ideal characters are almost hostile in their bearing towards his characters drawn from
real life. Altogether, Von Vízin must be regarded as the
first independent, artistic writer in Russia, and therefore
epoch-making, just as Feofán Prokópovitch must be rated
as the first Russian secular writer, and Sumarókoff as the

first Russian literary man and publicist in the modern
meaning of the words. It is worth noting (because of a
tendency to that sort of thing in later Russian writers
down to the present day) that towards the end of his life
a stroke of paralysis, in 1785, and other unfortunate circumstances, threw Von Vízin into a gloomy religious state
of mind, under the influence of which he judged himself
and his works with extreme severity, and condemned them
with excessive harshness.

The general outline of "The Hobbledehoy" is as follows: Mrs. Prostakóff (Simpleton), a managing woman, of
ungovernable temper, has an only child, Mitrofán (the
Hobbledehoy), aged sixteen. She regards him as a
mere child, and spoils him accordingly. He is, in fact,
childish in every way, deserving his sobriquet, and is followed about everywhere by his old nurse, Eremyéevna.
Mr. Simpleton has very little to say, and that little, chiefly,
in support of his overbearing wife's assertions, and at her
explicit demand. She habitually addresses every one,
except her son, as "beast," and by other similar epithets.
She has taken into her house, about six months before the
play opens, Sophia, a fairly wealthy orphan, and a connection of hers by marriage, whom she ill-treats to a degree.
She is on the point of betrothing her to Skotínin (Beastly),
her brother, who frankly admits that he cares nothing for
the girl, and not very much for her estate, which adjoins
his own, but a very great deal for the extremely fine pigs
which are raised on it—a passion for pigs, which he pre-
fers to men, constituting his chief interest in life. Mr.
Beastly, who says that he never goes to law, no matter
what losses he may suffer, no matter how much his neighbors injure him, because he simply wrings the deficit out

of his peasants, and that ends it, declares that Sophia's
pigs, for which he expresses a "deadly longing," are so
huge that "there is not one of them which, stood up on
its hind legs, would not be a whole head taller than any
one of us," is eager for the match.   While this is under
discussion (Sophia being entirely ignorant of their inten-
tions), the young girl enters, and announces that she has
received good news: her uncle, who has been in Siberia
for several years in quest of fortune, and is supposed to
be dead, has written to inform her of his speedy arrival.
Mrs. Simpleton takes the view that he is dead, ought to
be dead; and roughly tells Sophia that the latter need not
try to frighten her into giving her her liberty, and asserts
that the letter must be from the officer who has been in
love with her, and whom she wishes to marry.   Sophia
offers her the letter, in proof of innocence, saying, "Read
it yourself."   "Read it myself!" cries Mrs. Simpleton;
"no, madam, thank God, I was not brought up in that
way.   I may receive letters, but I always order some one
else to read them," whereupon she orders her husband
to read it.   Her husband gives it up as too difficult, and
Mr. Beastly, on being asked, replies, "I!   I have never
read anything since I was born, my dear sister!   God has
delivered me from that boredom."   Právdin (Mr. Upright),
an official charged with inspecting the condition of the
peasants, also empowered to put under arrest cruel proprietors, and under guardianship of the state those who
have been ill-treated, enters and reads the letter to them.
When Mrs. Simpleton learns from it that Uncle Starodúm
(Oldidea) has a large income, and that Sophia is to inherit
it, she immediately overwhelms Sophia with flattery and
affection, and decides to marry her to her precious

"child," Mitrofán. This leads to violent quarrels during the rest of the play between her and her brother, who wants the pigs; and to violence from the latter to Mitrofán, who declares that he has long wished to marry, and intends to have Sophia. In the mean time a company of soldiers, on the march to Moscow, arrives, and is quartered in the village, while their commanding officer, Mílon, a friend of Mr. Upright, makes his appearance at the house, where to his surprise, he finds his lady-love, Sophia, who promptly explains to him the situation of affairs.

Mitrofán is still under teachers, consisting of Vrálman (Liar), a former gunner, who is supposed to be teaching him French and all the sciences; Tzýfirkin (Cipherer), a retired army-sergeant, who instructs him in arithmetic, and Kutéikin, who, as his name implies, is the son of a petty ecclesiastic, and teaches him reading and writing, talking always in ecclesiastical style, interlarded with old Church-Slavonic words and phrases. He is always doing "reviews," never advancing to new lessons, and threatens to drown himself if he be not allowed to wed Sophia at once. There is a most amusing lesson-scene. The teacher of arithmetic sets him a problem: three people walking along the road find three hundred rubles, which they divide equally between them; how much does each one get? Mitrofán does the sum on his slate: "Once three is three, once nothing is nothing, once nothing is nothing." But his mother exclaims, that if he finds such a sum, he must not divide it, but keep it all, and that arithmetic, which teaches such division, is a fool of a science. Another sum is worked out in equally absurd style, with equally intelligent comments from the mother. Kutéikin then takes his turn, and using a pointer, makes

Mitrofán repeat after him a ridiculously appropriate sentence from the Psalms, in the "Tchasoslóff," the "Book of Hours," or first reader. Vrálman enters, meddles with everybody, in a strong foreign accent, and puts an end to the lessons, as quite unnecessary for the precious boy; for which, and his arrogance (when Mrs. Simpleton and the Hobbledehoy have retired), the other teachers attack him with slate and book.

Meanwhile, Uncle Starodúm has arrived, and talks in long paragraphs and stilted language to Právdin and Sophia, expressing the ideal view of life, conduct, service to the state, and so forth. He, as well as Sophia, Právdin Mílon, are quite colorless. The Simpletons overwhelm Starodúm with stupid courtesies, and Mrs. S. gets Právdin to examine Mitrofán, in order to prove to Starodúm that her darling child is fit to be Sophia's husband. The examination is even more brilliant than the lesson. Mitrofán says that door, that is to say, the door to that room, is an adjective, because it is added, or affixed, to its place; but the door of the store-house is a noun, because it has been standing off its hinges for six weeks. Further examination reveals the fact, that Vrálman's instruction in history has impressed his pupil with the idea that the histories (stories) told by Khavrónya, the herd-girl, constitute that science. When asked about geography, the Hobbledehoy declares that he does not know what is meant, and his mother prompts him with "'Eography," after asking Právdin what he said. On inquiring further as to its meaning and its use, and on being informed that it is a description of the earth, and its first use is to aid people in finding their way about, she makes the famous speech, frequently quoted, "Akh, good gra-

cious! What are the cabmen for, then? That's their business. That's not a science for the nobility. All a noble
has to do is to say, 'Drive me to such a place!' and you're
driven whithersoever you wish. Believe me, my good sir,
everything that Mitrofán does not know is nonsense.''

Uncle Starodúm makes acquaintance with Mílon,
whose good qualities he has learned through an old friend,
and betroths him to Sophia. Mrs. Simpleton, on learning
of this, and that Starodúm and Sophia are to set out for
Moscow early the next morning, arranges to have Mitrofán
abduct Sophia at a still earlier hour, and marry her.
Sophia escapes; Mrs. Simpleton raves and threatens to
beat to death her servants who have failed to carry out
her plan. Právdin then announces that the government
has ordered him to take charge of the Simpletons' house
and villages, because of Mrs. S.'s notorious inhumanity.
Vrálman, whom Starodúm recognizes as a former coach-
man of his, mounts the box, and Starodúm, Sophia, and
Mílon set out for Moscow, virtue reigning triumphant,
and wickedness being properly punished—which, again,
is an ideal point of view.

But the man who, taken as a whole, above all others in
the eighteenth century, has depicted for us governmental,
social, and private life, is Gavríl Románovitch Derzhávin
(1743–1816). His memoirs and poetical chronicle furnish
the most brilliant, vivid, and valuable picture of the reign
of Katherine II. Moreover, in his own person, Derzhávin
offers a type of one of the most distinguished Russians of
the last half of the eighteenth century, in his literary and
official career. He presented a great contrast to his contemporary and friend, Von Vízin, in that, while the latter
was a noteworthy example of all the best sides in contem-

porary social life, with very few defects, Derzhávin was an example of all the defects of contemporary life, and of several distinctly personal merits, which sharply differentiated him from others in the same elevated spheres of court and official life. He was the son of a poor noble. His opportunities for education were extremely limited, and in 1762 he entered the military service as a common soldier, in the famous Preobrazhénsky (Transfiguration) infantry regiment of the Guards. As he had neither friends nor relatives in St. Petersburg, he lived in barracks, where with difficulty he followed his inclinations, and read all the Russian and German books he could obtain, scribbling verses at intervals. In 1777 he managed to obtain a small estate and the rank of bombardier-lieutenant, and left the service to become an usher in one department of the Senate, where he made many friends and acquaintances in high circles. Eventually he became governor of Olónetz, then of Tambóff. In 1779 he began "in a new style," among other compositions therein being an ode "To Felitza," meaning the Empress Katherine II. He continued to write verses, but published nothing under his own name until his famous ode, "God" and "The Murza's Vision," in 1785. We cannot here enter into his official career further than to say, that all his troubles arose from his own honesty, and from the combined hostile efforts of the persons whose dishonest practices he had opposed. Towards the end of Katherine's reign he became a privy councilor (a titular rank) and senator; that is to say, a member of the Supreme Judicial Court. Under Paul I. he was President of the Commerce College (Ministry of Commerce), and Imperial Treasurer. Under Alexander I. he was made Minister of Justice.

"Katherine's Bard," as he was called, like several of his predecessors, cherished an idea of fixing a style in Russian literature, his special aim being to confine it to the classical style, and to oppose the new school of Karamzín. In this he was upheld by I. I. Dmítrieff, who was looked upon as his successor. But after Derzhávin heard Púshkin read his verses, at the examination in the Tzárskoe Seló Lyceum (1815), he frankly admitted that the lad had already excelled all living writers of Russia; and he predicted that this school-boy would become the new and brilliant star.

Despite the burdens of his official life, Derzhávin wrote a great deal; towards the end of his life, much dramatic matter; yet he really belongs to the ranks of the lyric poets. He deserved all the fame he enjoyed, because he was the first poet who was so by inspiration, not merely by profession or ambition. Even in his most insignificant works of the stereotyped sort, with much sound and very little thought and feeling, the hand of a master is visible, and talent is perceptible; while many passages are remarkable for their poetic figures, melody of versification, and beauty and force of expression. No poet previous to Púshkin can be compared to him for talent, and for direct, independent inspiration. His poetry is chiefly the poetry of figures and events, of solemn, loudly trumpeted victories and feats, descriptions of banquets, festivals, noisy social life, and endless hymns of praise to the age of Katherine II. It is not very rich in inward contents or in ideas. But he possessed one surpassing merit: he, first of all among Russian poets, brought poetry down from its lofty, classical flights to the every-day life of his fatherland at that age, and to nature, and freed Russian poetry from that monotonous, stilted, tiresome, official form which had been introduced by Lomonósoff and copied by all the latter's followers. Derzhávin's language is powerful, picturesque, and expressive, but still harsh and uneven, the ordinary vernacular being mingled with Church-Slavonic, and frequently obscuring the meaning; also, and owing to his deficient education, he often had recourse to inelegant, tasteless forms. If we compare him with Lomonósoff and Sumarókoff, it is evident that Russian poetry had made a great stride in advance under him, both as to external and internal development, in that he not only brought it nearer to life, but also perfected its forms, to a considerable degree, and applied it to subjects to which his predecessors would never have dreamed of applying it. His famous ode "God" will best serve to illustrate his style:

GOD*

O Thou eternal One! whose presence bright
All space doth occupy, all motion guide;
Unchanged through time's all-devastating flight;
Thou only God! There is no God beside!
Being above all beings! Three in One!
Whom none can comprehend and none explore;
Who fill'st existence with *thyself* alone:
Embracing all,— supporting,— ruling o'er,—
Being whom we call GOD — and know no more!

*I take this translation from Sir John Bowring's "Specimens of the Russian Poets," rather than attempt a metrical translation myself. It is reasonably close to the original—as close as most metrical translations are —and gives the spirit extremely well. Sir John Bowring adds the following footnote: "This is the poem of which Golovnin says in his narrative, that it has been rendered into Japanese, by order of the emperor, and hung up, embroidered in gold, in the Temple of Jeddo. I learn from the periodicals that an honor somewhat similar has been done in China to the same poem. It has been translated into the Chinese and Tartar languages, written on a

In its sublime research, philosophy
May measure out the ocean deep, may count
The sands or the sun's rays — but God! for Thee
There is no weight nor measure: — none can mount
Up to Thy mysteries; Reason's brightest spark,
Though kindled by Thy light, in vain would try
To trace Thy counsels, infinite and dark:
And thought is lost ere thought can soar so high,
Even like past moments in eternity.
Thou from primeval nothingness didst call,
First chaos, then existence. Lord! on Thee
Eternity had its foundation; all
Sprung forth from Thee: — of light, joy, harmony,
Sole origin: — all life, all beauty Thine.
Thy word created all, and doth create;
Thy splendor fills all space with rays divine.
Thou wert, and art, and shalt be! Glorious! Great!
Light-giving, life-sustaining Potentate!

Thy chains the unmeasured universe surround:
Upheld by Thee, by Thee inspired with breath!
Thou the beginning with the end has bound,
And beautifully mingled life and death!
As sparks mount upwards from the fiery blaze,
So suns are born, so worlds spring forth from Thee;
And as the spangles in the sunny rays
Shine round the silver snow, the pageantry
Of heaven's bright army glitters in Thy praise.
A million torches lighted by Thy hand
Wander unwearied through the blue abyss:
They own Thy power, accomplish Thy command;
All gay with life, all eloquent with bliss.
What shall we call them? Piles of crystal light —

piece of rich silk, and suspended in the imperial palace at Pekin." There
are several editions of Sir John's book, the one here used being the second,
1821; but the author admits that in the first edition he stretched the poetic
license further than he had a right to do, in this first verse. The book is
now rare, but this statement will serve as a warning to those who may
happen upon the first edition.

A glorious company of golden streams —
Lamps of celestial ether burning bright —
Suns lighting systems with their joyous beams?
But Thou to these art as the noon to night.

Yes, as a drop of water in the sea,
All this magnificence in Thee is lost: —
What are ten thousand worlds compared to Thee?
And what am *I* then? Heaven's unnumber'd host,
Though multiplied by myriads, and array'd
in all the glory of sublimest thought;
Is but an atom in the balance weighed
Against Thy greatness; is a cypher brought
Against infinity! What am I, then? Naught!

Naught! But the effluence of Thy light divine,
Pervading worlds, hath reach'd my bosom, too;
Yes! In my spirit doth Thy spirit shine
As shines the sunbeam in a drop of dew.
Naught! But I live, and on hope's pinions fly
Eager towards Thy presence; for in Thee
I live, and breathe, and dwell; aspiring high,
Even to the throne of Thy divinity.
I am, O God! and surely *Thou* must be!

Thou art! directing, guiding all, Thou art!
Direct my understanding then to Thee:
Control my spirit, guide my wandering heart:
Though but an atom midst immensity,
Still I am something fashioned by Thy hand!
I hold a middle rank 'twixt heaven and earth,
On the last verge of mortal being stand,
Close to the realms where angels have their birth,
Just on the boundaries of the spirit-land!

The chain of being is complete in me:
In me is matter's last gradation lost,
And the next step is spirit — Deity!
I can command the lightning, and am dust!

A monarch, and a slave; a worm, a god!
Whence came I here, and how? so marvelously
Constructed and conceived? Unknown! This clod
Lives merely through some higher energy;
For from itself alone it could not be!

Creator, yes! Thy wisdom and thy word
Created me! Thou source of light and good!
Thou spirit of my spirit, and my Lord!
Thy light, Thy love, in their bright plenitude
Fill'd me with an immortal soul, to spring
O'er the abyss of death, and bade it wear
The garments of eternal day, and wing
Its heavenly flight beyond this little sphere,
Even to its source — to Thee — its author there.
O thoughts ineffable! O visions blest!
Though worthless our conceptions all of Thee,
Yet shall Thy shadowed image fill our breast,
And waft its homage to Thy Deity.
God! Thus alone my lowly thoughts can soar;
Thus seek Thy presence — Being wise and good!
Midst Thy vast works admire, obey, adore;
And when the tongue is eloquent no more,
The soul shall speak in tears of gratitude.

But the literary activity of Katherine II.'s reign was not confined to its two most brilliant representatives—Von Vízin and Derzhávin; many less prominent writers, belonging to different parties and branches of literature, were diligently at work. Naturally, there was as yet too little independent Russian literature to permit of the existence of criticism, or the establishment of a fixed standard of taste.

Among the worthy writers of the second class in that brilliant era, were Kheraskóff, Bogdanóvitch, Khémnitzer, and Kápnist.

Mikháil Matvyéevitch Kheraskóff (1733–1801), the author of the epic "The Rossiad," and of other less noteworthy works, was known during his lifetime only to the very restricted circle of his friends. In his convictions and views on literature he belonged to the epoch of Lomonósoff and Sumarókoff; by birth and education to the highest nobility. More faithfully than any other writer of his century does Kheraskóff represent the pseudo-classical style in Russian epic, lyric, and dramatic poetry, for he wrote all sorts of things, including sentimental novels. To the classical enthusiasts of his day he seemed the "Russian Homer," and his long poems, "The Rossiad" (1789) and "Vladímir" (1786), were confidently believed to be immortal, being the first tolerable specimens of the epic style in Russian literature. In twelve long cantos he celebrates the capture of Kazán by Iván the Terrible in "The Rossiad." "Vladímir" (eighteen cantos) celebrates the Christianizing of Russia by Prince-Saint Vladímir.

Ippolít Feodórovitch Bogdanóvitch (1743–1803), who was developed under the immediate supervision and patronage of Kheraskóff, belonged, by education and his comprehension of elegance and of poetry, to a later epoch—on the borderland between pseudo-classicism and the succeeding period, which was ruled by sentimentalism. His well-known poem, "Dúshenka" ("Dear Little Soul"), was the first light epic Russian poem, with simple, intelligible language, and with a jesting treatment of a gay, playful subject. This subject Bogdanóvitch borrowed from La Fontaine's novel, "The Loves of Psyche and Cupid," which, in turn, was borrowed from Apuleius.

The third writer of this group, Iván Ivánovitch Khémnitzer (1745–1784), the son of a German physician, was unknown during his lifetime; enjoyed no literary fame, and cared for none, regarding his capacities and productions as unworthy of notice. In 1779, at the instigation of his friends, he published a collection of his "Fables and Tales." At this time there existed not a single tolerable specimen of the fable in Russian; but by the time literary criticism did justice to Khémnitzer's work, Karamzín, and Dmítrieff had become the favorites of the public, and Khémnitzer's productions circulated chiefly among the lower classes, for whom his Fables are still published. His works certainly aided Dmítrieff and Krylóff in handling this new branch of poetical literature in Russia. His "The Metaphysician" still remains one of the greatest favorites among Russian fables for cultivated readers of all classes.

Briefly told, the contents of "The Metaphysician" are as follows: A father, who had heard that children were sent beyond sea to be educated, and that those so reared were more respected than those brought up at home, determined, being wealthy, to send his son thither. The son, despite his studies, from being stupid when he went, returned more stupid than before, having fallen into the clutches of educational quacks, of whom there is no lack. Aforetime, he had babbled stupidities simply, but now he began to expound such things in learned wise; aforetime, only the stupid had failed to understand him, now he was beyond the comprehension of the wise. The whole house, and town, and world were bored to death with his chatter. He was possessed with a mania for searching out the cause of everything. With his wits thus woolgathering as he walked, he one day suddenly tumbled into a pit.

His father, who chanced to be with him, rushed off to get a rope, wherewith to drag out "his household wisdom." Meanwhile, his thoughtful child, as he sat in the pit, reasoned with himself as to what might be the cause of his fall, and came to the conclusion that it was an earthquake; also, that his sudden flight into the pit might create an atmospheric pressure, from the earth and the pit, which would wipe out the seven planets. The father rushed up with a rope. "Here's a rope for you," says he, "catch hold of it. I'll drag you out; look out that you don't fall off!" "No, wait; don't pull me out yet; tell me first, what sort of a thing is a rope?" "Although the father was not learned, he was gifted by nature with common sense," winds up the fable.

Another, called "The Skinflint," runs thus:

" There was once a Skinflint, who had a vast amount of money.
    And, as he was wont to say, he had grown rich,
Not by crooked deeds. Not by stealing or ruining men.
No, he took his oath to that: That God had sent all this
        wealth to his house,
And that he feared not, in the least, to be convicted of in-
        justice towards his neighbor.
And to please the Lord for this, His mercy,
And to incline Him unto favors in time to come—
Or, possibly, just to soothe his conscience—
The Skinflint took it into his head to build a house for the
        poor.
The house was built, and almost finished. My Skinflint,
        gazing at it,
Beside himself with joy, cheers up and reasons with himself.
How great a service he to the poor hath rendered, in order-
        ing a refuge to be built for them!
Thus was my Skinflint inwardly exulting over his house.
Then one of his acquaintances chanced along.

The Skinflint said, with rapture, to his friend,
' I think a great lot of the poor can be housed here!'
' Of course, a great many can live here;
But you cannot get in all whom you've sent wandering
    homeless o'er the earth!'"

One of Khémnitzer's most intimate friends, and also
one of the most notable members of Derzhávin's circle
(being related to the latter through his wife), was Vasíly
Vasílievitch Kápnist (1757–1824), whose ancestors had
been members of an Italian family, the Counts Capnissi.
He owed his fame chiefly to his ode on "Slavery" (1783);
to another, "On the Extirpation in Russia of the Vocation
of Slave by the Empress Katherine II." (1786); and to
a whole series celebrating the conquests of the Russian
arms in Turkey and Italy. But far more important are
his elegies and short lyrics, many of which are really very
light and graceful; and his translations of "The Monument," from Horace, which was quite equal to Derzhávin's, or even Púshkin's. His masterpiece was the
comedy "Yábeda" (Calumny), which was written probably at the end of Katherine's reign, and was printed
under Paul I., in 1798. It contains a sharp condemnation
of the morals in the provincial courts of justice, and of the
incredible processes of chicanery and bribery through
which every business matter was forced to pass. The
types which Kápnist put on the stage, especially the petti-
fogger Právoloff, and the types of the presiding judge and
members of the bench, were very accurately drawn, and
can hardly fail to have been taken from life. Alarmed by
the numerous persecutions of literary men which took
place during the last years of Katherine II.'s reign, Kápnist
dared not publish his comedy until the accession of the

Emperor Paul I., when he dedicated it to the Emperor, and set forth in a poetical preface the entire harmlessness of his satire. But even this precaution was of no avail. The comedy created a tremendous uproar and outcry from officialdom in general; the Emperor was petitioned to prohibit the piece, and to administer severe punishment to the "unpatriotic" author. The Emperor is said to have taken the petition in good faith and to have ordered that Kápnist be dispatched forthwith to Siberia. But after dinner his wrath cooled (the petitioners had even declared that the comedy flagrantly jeered at the monarchical power), and he began to doubt the justice of his command. He ordered the piece to be played that very evening in the Hermitage Theater (in the Winter Palace). Only he and the Grand Duke Alexander (afterwards Alexander I.), were present at the performance. After the first act the Emperor, who had applauded incessantly, sent the first state courier he could put his hand on to bring Kápnist back on the instant. He richly rewarded the author on the latter's return, and showed him favor until he died. Another amusing testimony to the lifelikeness of Kápnist's types is narrated by an eye-witness. "I happened," says this witness, "in my early youth, to be present at a representation of 'Calumny' in a provincial capital; and when Khvatáïko (Grabber), sang,

> ' Take, there's no great art in that;
> Take whatever you can get;
> What are hands appended to us for
> If not that we may take, take, take? '

all the spectators began to applaud, and many of them, addressing the official who occupied the post corresponding to that of Grabber, shouted his name in unison, and cried, 'That's you! That's you!' "

Towards the end of Katherine II.'s reign, a new school, which numbered many young writers, arose. At the head of it, by reason of his ability as a journalist, literary man, poet, and savant, stood Nikolái Mikháilovitch Karamzín (1766–1826). Karamzín was descended from a Tatár princeling, Karamurza, who accepted Christianity in the days of the Tzars of Moscow. He did much to disseminate in society a discriminating taste in literature, and more accurate views in regard to it. During the first half of his sixty years' activity—that under Katherine II.—he was a poet and literary man; during the latter and most considerable part of his career—under Alexander I.—he was a historian. His first work to win him great renown was his "Letters of a Russian Traveler," written after a trip lasting a year and a half to Germany, Switzerland, France, and England, begun in 1789, and published in the "Moscow Journal," which he established in 1791. For the next twelve years Karamzín devoted himself exclusively to journalism and literature. It was his most brilliant literary period, and during it his labors were astonishing in quantity and varied in subject, as the taste of the majority of readers in that period demanded. During this period he was not only a journalist, but also a poet, literary man, and critic. His poetical compositions are rather shallow, and monotonous in form, but were highly esteemed by his contemporaries. They are interesting at the present day chiefly because of their historical and biographical details, as a chronicle of history, and of the heart of a profoundly sincere man. Their themes are, generally, the love of nature, of country life,

friendship; together with gentleness, sensibility, melancholy, scorn for rank and wealth, dreams of immortality
with posterity. His greatest successes with the public
were secured by "Poor Liza," and "Natálya, the Boyár's
Daughter," which served as much-admired models for
sentimentalism to succeeding generations. Sentimentality
was no novelty in Russia; it had come in with translations
from English novels, such as Richardson's "Clarissa
Harlowe," and the like; and imitations of them in Russia.
"Sensibility" was held to be the highest quality in human
nature, and a man's—much more a woman's—worth was
measured by the amount of "sensibility" he or she possessed. This new school paid scant heed to the observation and study of real life. An essential tenet in the cult
consisted of a glorification of the distant past, "the good
old times," adorned by fancy, as the ideal model for the
present; the worship of the poor but honest country folk,
the ideal of equality, freedom, happiness, and nearness to
nature.

Of this style, Karamzín's "Poor Liza" is the most
perfect and admired specimen. Liza, a poor country
lass, is "beautiful in body and soul," supremely gifted
with tenderness and sensibility. Erást, a wealthy noble,
possessed of exceptional brains and a kind heart, but weak
and trifling by nature, falls in love with her. He begins
to dream of the idyllic past, "in which people strolled,
care-free, through the meadows, bathed in crystal clear
pools, kissed like turtle-doves, reposed amid roses and
myrtle, and passed their days in happy idleness." So he
feels himself summoned to the embrace of nature, and
determines to abandon the high society, for a while at
least. He even goes so far as to assure Liza that it is

possible for him to marry her, despite the immense difference in their social stations; that "an innocent soul, gifted with sensibility, is the most important thing of all, and Liza will ever be the nearest of all persons to his heart." But he betrays her, involuntarily. When she becomes convinced of his treachery, she throws herself into a pond hard by, beneath the ancient oaks which but a short time before had witnessed their joys.

"Natálya, the Boyár's Daughter," is a glorification of a fanciful past, far removed from reality, in which "Russians were Russians"; and against this background, Karamzín sets a tale, even simpler and more innocent, of the love of Natálya and Alexéi, with whom Natálya falls in love, "in one minute, on beholding him for the first time, and without ever having heard a single word about him." These stories, and Karamzín's "Letters of a Russian Traveler," already referred to, had an astonishing success; people even learned them by heart, and the heroes of them became the favorite ideals of the young; while the pool where Liza was represented as having drowned herself (near the Simónoff Monastery, in the suburbs of Moscow) became the goal for the rambles of those who were also "gifted with sensibility." The appearance of these tales is said to have greatly increased the taste for reading in society, especially among women.

Although Karamzín did not possess the gift of artistic creation, and although the imaginative quality is very deficient in his works, his writings pleased people as the first successful attempts at light literature. In his assumption that people should write as they talked, Karamzín entirely departed from Lomonósoff's canons as to the three styles permissible, and thereby imparted the final

impulse to the separation of the Russian literary language
from the bookish, Church-Slavonic diction. His services
in the reformation and improvement of the Russian literary language were very important, despite the violent
opposition he encountered from the old conservative
literary party.*

When Alexander I. ascended the throne, in 1801,
Karamzín turned his attention to history. In 1802 he
founded the "European Messenger" (which is still the
leading monthly magazine of Russia), and began to publish in it historical articles which were, in effect, preparatory to his extended and famous "History of the Russian
Empire," published in 1818, fine in style, but not accurate, in the modern sense of historical work.

Karamzín's nearest followers, the representatives of
the sentimental tendency in literature, and of the writers
who laid the foundations for the new literary language and
style, were Dmítrieff and Ózeroff.

Iván Ivánovitch Dmítrieff (1760–1810), and Vladisláff
Alexándrovitch Ózeroff (1769–1816), both enjoyed great
fame in their day. Dmítrieff, while under the guidance
of Karamzín, making sentimentalism the ruling feature in
Russian epic and lyric poetry, perfected both the general
style of Russian verse, and the material of the light, poetical language. Ózeroff, under the same influence and
tendency, aided in the final banishment from the Russian
stage of pseudo-classical ideals and dramatic compositions
constructed according to theoretical rules. Dmítrieff's

* Karamzín's youngest daughter, by his second marriage, was alive when
I was in Russia,—a charming old lady. She gave me her own copy of her
"favorite book," a volume (in French) by Khomyakóff, very rare and
difficult to obtain; and in discussing literary matters, wound up thus:
"They may say what they will about the new men, but no one ever wrote
such a beautiful style as my dear papa!" I also knew some of Ózeroff's
relatives.

most prominent literary work was a translation of La Fontaine's Fables, and some satirical writings. Ózeroff, in 1798, put on the stage his first, and not entirely successful, tragedy, "Yáropolk and Olég." * His most important work, both from the literary and the historical points of view—although not so regarded by his contemporaries—was his drama "Fingal," founded on Ossian's Songs, and is a triumph of northern poetry and of the Russian tongue, rich in picturesqueness, daring, and melody. His contemporaries regarded "Dmítry Donskóy" as his masterpiece, although in reality it is one of the least noteworthy of his compositions, and it enjoyed a brilliant success.

But the most extreme and talented disciples of the Karamzín school were Vasíly Andréevitch Zhukóvsky (1783–1852) and Konstantín Nikoláevitch Bátiushkoff (1786–1855), who offer perfectly clear examples of the transition from the sentimental to the new romantic school, which began with Púshkin. Everything of Zhukóvsky's that was original, that is to say, not translated, was an imitation, either of the solemn, bombastic productions of the preceding poets of the rhetorical school, or of the tender, dreamy, melancholy works of the sentimental school, until he devoted himself to translations from the romantic German and English schools. He was not successful in his attempts to create original Russian work in the romantic vein; and his chief services to Russian literature (despite the great figure he played in it during his day) must be regarded as having consisted in giving romanticism a chance to establish itself firmly on Russian soil; and in having, by his splendid translations, among them Schiller's "Maid of Orleans," Byron's "The Pris-

* Pronounced Alyóg.

oner of Chillon," and de la Mott Fouqué's "Undine," brought Russian literature into close relations with a whole mass of literary models, enlarged the sphere of literary criticism, and definitively deprived pseudo-classical theories and models of all force and influence.

Zhukóvsky's own history and career were romantic. He was the son of a wealthy landed proprietor named Búnin, who already had eleven children; when his peasants, on setting out for Rumyántzoff's army as sutlers, asked their owner, "What shall we bring thee from the Turkish land, little father?" Búnin replied, in jest, "Bring me a couple of pretty Turkish lasses; you see my wife is growing old." The peasants took him at his word, and brought two young Turkish girls, who had been captured at the seige of Bender. The elder, Salkha, aged sixteen, first served as nurse to Búnin's daughters. In 1783, shortly after seven of his children had died within a short time of each other, she bore him a son, who was adopted by one of his friends, a member of the petty nobility, Búnin's daughter standing as godmother to the child, and his wife receiving it into the family, and rearing it like a son, in memory of her dead, only son. This baby was the future poet Zhukóvsky. When Búnin died, he bequeathed money to the child, and his widow and daughters gave him the best of educations. Zhukóvsky began to print bits of melancholy poetry while he was still at the university preparatory school. When he became closely acquainted with Karamzín (1803-1804), he came under the latter's influence so strongly that the stamp remained upon all the productions of the first half of his career, the favorite "Svyetlána" (Amaryllis), written in 1811, being a specimen. In 1812 Zhukóvsky served in the army, and wrote his poem "The Bard in the Camp of the Russian Warriors," * which brought him more fame than all his previous work, being adapted to the spirit of the time, and followed it up with other effusions, which made much more impression on his contemporaries than they have on later readers. But even in his most brilliant period, the great defect of Zhukóvsky's poetry was a total lack of coloring or close connection with the Russian soil, which he did not understand, and did not particularly love. His poetical "Epistle to Alexander I. after the Capture of Paris, in 1824," he sent in manuscript to the Emperor's mother, the Empress Márya Feódorovna. The result was, that the Empress ordered it printed in luxurious style, at government expense, had him presented to her, and made him her reader. He was regarded as a great poet, became a close friend of the imperial family, tutor to the Grand Duchess Alexándra Feódorovna (wife of Nikolái Pávlovitch, afterwards the Emperor Nicholas I.), and his fortune was assured. His career during the last twenty-five years of his life, beginning with 1817, belongs to history rather than to literature. In 1853, wealthy, loaded with imperial favors, richly pensioned, he went abroad, and settled in Baden-Baden, where he married (being at the time sixty years of age, while his bride was nineteen), and never returned to Russia. During the last eleven years of his semi-invalid life, with disordered nerves, he approached very close to mysticism.†

Bátiushkoff, as a poet, was the exact opposite of Zhu-

---

* A translation of this—which is too long to quote here—may be found in Sir John Bowring's "Specimens of the Russian Poets," Vol. II.

† These imperial favors and pensions were continued to his children. His son, an artist, regularly visited Russia as the guest of Alexander III. I met him on two occasions and was enabled to judge of his father's charms of mind and manner.

kóvsky, being the first to grasp the real significance of the mood of the ancient classical poets, and to appropriate not only their views on life and enjoyment, but even their plastic and thoroughly artistic mode of expression. While Zhukóvsky removed poetry from earth and rendered it ethereal, Bátiushkoff fixed it to earth and gave it a body, demonstrating all the entrancing charm of tangible reality. Yet, in language, point of view, and literary affiliations, he belongs, like Zhukóvsky, to the school of Karamzín. But his versification, his subject-matter are entirely independent of all preceding influences. In beauty of versification and plastic worth, Bátiushkoff had no predecessors in Russian literature, and no competitors in the school of Karamzín. He was of ancient, noble family, well educated, and began to publish at the age of eighteen.

We now come, chronologically, to a writer who cannot be assigned either to the old sentimental school of Karamzín, or to the new romantic school of which Púshkin was the first and greatest exponent in Russian literature; to a man who stood apart, in a lofty place, all his own, both during his lifetime and in all Russian literary history; whose name is known to every Russian who can read and write, and whose work enjoys in Russia that popularity which the Odyssey did among the ancient Greeks. Iván Andréevitch Krylóff (1763–1844) began his literary work almost simultaneously with Karamzín, but was not, in the slightest degree, influenced by the style which the latter introduced into Russian literature; and bore himself in no less distant and hostile a manner to the rising romantic school of Púshkin. He was the son of an army officer, who was afterwards in the civil service, a very competent, intel-

ligent man, who left his family in dire poverty at his death.
At the age of fifteen, Krylóff produced his first, and very
creditable, specimen of his future talent, though obliged,
by extreme need, to enter government service at the age
of fourteen, at his father's death. He filled several positions in different places at a very meager salary, until the
death of his mother (1788), when he resigned and determined to devote himself exclusively to literature. He
engaged in journalistic work, became an editor, and soon
published a paper of his own. But his real sphere was
that of fabulist. In 1803 he offered his first three fables,
partly translated, partly worked over from La Fontaine,
and from the moment of their publication, his fame as a
writer of fables began to grow. But he wrote two comedies and a fairy-opera before, in 1808, he finally devoted
himself to fables, to which branch of literature he remained
faithful as long as he lived. By 1811–1812 his fables
were so popular that he was granted a government pension, and became a member of the Empress Márya Feódorovna's circle of court poets and literary men. From
1812–1840, or later, Krylóff had an easy post in the
Imperial Public Library, and in the course of forty years,
wrote about two hundred fables. He is known to have
been extremely indolent and untidy; but all his admirers,
and even his enemies, recognized in him a power which
not one of his predecessors in the literary sphere had possessed—a power which was thoroughly national, bound in
the closest manner to the Russian soil. His fables bear
an almost family likeness to the proverbs, aphorisms,
adages, and tales produced by the wisdom of the masses,
and are quite in their spirit. All the Russian poets had
tried their hand at that favorite form of poetic compo-

sition—the fable—ever since its introduction from western
Europe, in the eighteenth century; and Krylóff's success
called forth innumerable imitators.   But up to that time,
out of all the sorts of poetry existing in Russian literature,
only the fable, thanks to Krylóff, had become, in full
measure, the organ of nationality, both in spirit and in
language; and these two qualities his fables possess in the
most profound, national meaning of the term.   His language is peculiar to himself.   He was the first who dared
to speak to Russian society, enervated by the harmonious,
regular prose of Karamzín, in the rather rough vernacular
of the masses, which was, nevertheless, energetic, powerful, and contained no foreign admixture, or any exclusively
bookish elements.   One of the most popular of his fables,
to which allusion is often made in Russian literature and
conversation, is "Demyán's Fish-Soup."   The manner
in which the lines are rhymed in the original is indicated
by corresponding figures.

DEMYÁN'S FISH-SOUP

"Neighbor, dear, my light! (1)
Eat, I pray thee." (2)
"Neighbor, dear, I'm full to the throat,—" No matter." (1)
Another little plateful; hearken: (2)
This fish soup, I assure you, is gloriously cooked." (3)
"Three platefuls have I eaten."—"O, stop that, why keep
    count, (4)
If only you feel like it, (4)
Why, eat and health be yours: eat to the bottom! (3)
What fish-soup! and how rich in fat (3)
As though with amber covered. (3)
Enjoy yourself, dear friend! (5)
Here's tender bream, pluck, a bit of sterlet here!

Just another little spoonful!
Come, urge him, wife!"
In this wise did neighbor Demyán neighbor Fóka entertain.
And let him neither breathe nor rest;
But sweat from Fóka long had poured in streams.
Yet still another plateful doth he take,
Collects his final strength—and cleans up everything.
"Now, that's the sort of friend I like!"
Demyán did shout: "But I can't bear the stuck-up; come, eat
          another plateful, my dear fellow!"
Thereupon, my poor Fóka,
Much as he loved fish-soup, yet from such a fate,
In his arms seizing his girdle and his cap—
Rushed madly, quickly home,
And since that day, hath never more set foot in Demyán's house.
Writer, thou art lucky if the real gift thou hast,
But if thou dost not know enough to hold thy peace in time,
And dost not spare thy neighbor's ears,
Then must thou know, that both thy prose and verse,
To all will prove more loathsome than Demyán's fish-soup.

Another good specimen is called:

THE SWAN, THE PIKE, AND THE CRAB

When partners cannot agree, their affair will not work
          smoothly,
And torment, not business, will be the outcome.
Once on a time, the Swan, the Crab, and the Pike,
Did undertake to haul a loaded cart,
And all three hitched themselves thereto;
They strained their every nerve, but still the cart budged not.
And yet, the load seemed very light for them;
But towards the clouds the Swan did soar,
Backwards the Crab did march,
While the Pike made for the stream.
Which of them was wrong, which right, 'tis not our place to
          judge.
Only, the cart doth stand there still."

We have seen that Lomonósoff began the task of rendering the modern Russian language adaptable to all the needs of prose and verse; and that the writers who followed him, notably Karamzín, contributed their share to this great undertaking. Púshkin practically completed it and molded the hitherto somewhat harsh and awkward forms into an exquisite medium for every requirement of literature. Alexánder Sergyéevitch Púshkin (1799–1837), still holds the undisputed leadership for simplicity, realism, absolute fidelity to life, and he was the first worthy forerunner of the great men whose names are world-synonyms at the present day for those qualities. Almost every writer who preceded him had been more or less devoted to translations and servile copies of foreign literature. Against these, and the mock-classicism of the French pattern, which then ruled Europe, he waged relentless battle. He vitalized Russian literature by establishing its foundations firmly on Russian soil; by employing her native traditions, life, and sentiment as subjects and inspiration, in place of the worn-out conventionalities of foreign invention. The result is a product of the loftiest truth, as well as of the loftiest art.

His ancestors were nobles who occupied important posts under Peter the Great. His mother was a grand-daughter of Hannibal, the negro of whom Púshkin wrote under the title of "Peter the Great's Arab." This Hannibal was a slave who had been brought from Africa to Constantinople, where the Russian ambassador purchased him, and sent him to Peter the Great. The latter took a great fancy to him, had him baptized, and would not allow his brothers to ransom him, but sent him, at the age of eighteen, abroad to be educated. On his return,

Peter kept his favorite always beside him. Under the reign of the Empress Anna Ioánnovna he was exiled to Siberia, in company with other court favorites of former reigns; and like them, returned to Russia, and was loaded with favors by Peter's daughter, the Empress Elizabeth. His son was a distinguished general of Katherine II.'s day. Púshkin, the poet, had blue eyes, and very fair skin and hair, but the whole cast of his countenance in his portraits is negro. His father was a typical society man, and in accordance with the fashion of the day, Púshkin was educated exclusively by French tutors at home, and his first writings (at the age of ten) were in French, and imitated from writers of that nation. When his father retired from the military service, he settled in Moscow, and the boy knew all the literary men of that day and town before he was twelve years of age, and there can be no doubt that this literary atmosphere had a great influence upon him. When, at the age of twelve, he was placed in the newly founded Lyceum,* at Tzárskoe Seló (sixteen miles from St. Petersburg), whence so many famous men were afterwards graduated, he and the other pupils amused themselves in their play hours by writing a little newspaper, and by other literary pursuits. Here the lad was compelled to learn Russian, and the first use he made of it was to write caustic epigrams. At the school examination in 1815, the aged poet Derzhávin was among the visitors; and when he heard the boy read his "Memories of Tzárskoe Seló," he at once predicted his

* This building still exists, with its garden alluded to in the 'Memories.' But though it still bears its name, it is connected by a glazed gallery with the old palace, famous chiefly as Katherine II.'s residence, across the street; and it is used for suites of apartments, allotted for summer residence to certain courtiers. The exact arrangement of the rooms in Púshkin's day is not now known.

coming greatness. As is natural at his age, there was not much originality of idea in the poem; but it was amazing for its facility and mastery of poetic forms. Karamzín and Zhukóvsky were not long in adding their testimony to the lad's genius, and the latter even acquired the habit of submitting his own poems to the young poet's judgment.

Púshkin was an omnivorous reader, but his parents had never been pleased with his progress in his studies, or regarded him as clever. The praise of competent judges now opened their eyes; but he had a good deal to endure from his father, later on, in spite of this. At this period, Púshkin imitated the most varied poetical forms with wonderful delicacy, and yielded to the most diverse poetical moods. But even then he was entering on a new path, whose influence on later Russian literature was destined to be incalculably great. While still a school-boy, he began to write his famous fantastic-romantic poem, "Rúslan and Liudmíla" (which Glinka afterwards made the subject of a charming opera), and here, for the first time in Russian literary history, a thoroughly national theme was handled with a freedom and naturalness which dealt the death-blow to the prevailing inflated, rhetorical style. The subject of the poem was one of the folk-legends, of which he had been fond as a child; and when it was published, in 1820, the critics were dumb with amazement. The gay, even dissipated, society life which he took up on leaving the Lyceum came to a temporary end in consequence of some biting epigrams which he wrote. The Prefect of St. Petersburg called him to account for his attacks on prominent people, and transferred him from the ministry of foreign affairs to southern Russia—in fact, to polite exile—giving him a corresponding position in another department of the government.

For four years (1820–1824) he lived chiefly in southern Russia, including the Crimea and the Caucasus, and wrote, "The Prisoner of the Caucasus," "The Fountain of Baktchesarái," "The Gypsies," and a part of his famous "Evgény Onyégin," being, at this period, strongly influenced by Byron, as the above-mentioned poems and the short lyrics of the same period show. Again his life and his poetry were changed radically by a caustic but witty and amusing epigram on his uncongenial official superior in Odessa; and on the latter's complaint to headquarters— the complaint being as neat as the epigram, in its way— Púshkin was ordered to reside on one of the paternal estates, in the government of Pskoff. Here, under the influence of his old nurse, Arína Rodiónovna, and her folk-tales, he became thoroughly and definitively Russian, and entered at last on his real career—poetry which was truly national in spirit. His talents were now completely matured. His wonderfully developed harmony of versification has never been approached by any later poet, except, in places, by Lérmontoff. Quite peculiar to himself, at that day—and even much later—are his vivid delineations of character, and his simple but startlingly lifelike and truthful pictures of every-day life. If his claim to immortality rested on no other foundation than these, it would still be incontestable, for all previous Russian writers had scorned such commonplaces.

In 1826 he returned to the capital, having been restored to favor, and resumed his gay life, which on the whole, had a deleterious influence on his talents. In 1831 he married a very beautiful and extravagant woman, after which he was constantly in financial distress, his own social ambitions and lavish expenditure being equally well developed with the same tastes in his wife. His inclination to write poetry was destroyed. He took to historical research, wrote a "History of Pugatchéff's Rebellion," and a celebrated tale, "The Captain's Daughter" (the scene of the latter being laid in the same epoch), and other stories. In these, almost simultaneously with Gógol, he laid the foundations for the vivid, modern school of the Russian novel. He was killed in a duel with Baron George Hekkeren-Dantes, who had been persecuting his wife with unwelcome attentions, in January, 1837. Baron Hekkeren-Dantes died only a year or two ago.

As a school-boy he had instinctively turned into a new path, that of national Russian literature. For this national service, and because he was the first to realize the poetic ideal, his countrymen adored him. To the highest external elegance and the most exquisite beauty, he fitly wedded inward force and wealth of thought, in the most incomparable manner. His finest effort, "Evgény Onyégin" (1822–1829), exhibits the poet in the process of development, from the Byronic stage to the vigorous independence of a purely national writer. The hero, Evgény Onyégin, begins as a society young man of the period; that is to say, he was inevitably a Byronic character. His father's death calls him from the dissipations of the capital to the quiet life of a country estate. He regards his neighbors as his inferiors, both in culture and social standing, and for a long time will have nothing to do with them. At last, rather accidentally, he strikes up a friendship with Lénsky, a congenial spirit, a young poet, who has had the advantage of foreign education, the son of one of the neighbors. Olga Lárin, the young daughter of another neighbor, has long been betrothed to Lénsky, and the latter naturally introduces Onyégin to her family. Olga's elder sister, Tatyána, promptly falls in love with Onyégin, and in a letter, which is always quoted as one of the finest passages in Russian literature, and the most perfect portrait of the noble Russian woman's soul, she declares her love for him. Onyégin politely snubs her, lecturing her in a fatherly way, and no one is informed of the occurrence, except Tatyána's old nurse, who, though stupid, is absolutely devoted to her, and does not betray the knowledge which she has, involuntarily, acquired. Not long afterwards, Tatyána's name-day festival is celebrated by a dinner, at which Onyégin is present, being urged thereto by Lénsky. He goes, chiefly, that no comment may arise from any abrupt change of his ordinary friendly manners. The family, ignorant of what has happened between him and Tatyána, and innocently scheming to bring them together, place him opposite her at dinner. Angered by this, he revenges himself on the wholly innocent Lénsky, by flirting outrageously with Olga (the wedding-day is only a fortnight distant), and Olga, being as vain and weak as she is pretty, does her share. The result is, that Lénsky challenges Onyégin to a duel, and the seconds insist that it must be fought, though Onyégin would gladly apologize. He kills Lénsky, unintentionally, and immediately departs on his travels. Olga speedily consoles herself, and marries a handsome officer. Tatyána, a girl of profound feelings, remains inconsolable, refuses all offers of marriage, and at last, yielding to the entreaties of her anxious relatives, consents to spend a season in Moscow. As a wall-flower, at her first ball, she captivates a wealthy prince, of very high standing in St. Petersburg, and is persuaded by her parents to marry him. When Onyégin returns to the capital he finds the little country girl, whose love he had scorned, one of the greatest ladies at the court and in society; and he falls madly in love with her. Her cold indifference galls him, and increases his love. He writes three letters, to which she does not reply. Then he forces himself into her boudoir and finds her reading one of his letters and weeping over it. She then confesses that she loves him still, but dismisses him with the assurance that she will remain true to her noble and loving husband. Tatyána is regarded as one of the finest, most vividly faithful portraits of the genuine Russian woman in all Russian literature; while Olga is considered fully her equal, as a type, and in popular sympathy; and the other characters are almost equally good in their various lines.

Besides a host of beautiful lyric poems, Púshkin left several dramatic fragments: "The Rusálka" or "Water Nymph," on which Dargomýzhsky founded a beautiful opera, "The Stone Guest," * "The Miserly Knight," and chief of all, and like "Evgény Onyégin," epoch-making in its line, the historical dramatic fragment "Borís Godunóff." This founded a school in Russian dramatic writing. It is impossible to do justice in translation to the exquisite lyrics; but the following soliloquy, from "Borís Godunóff," will serve to show Púshkin's power in blank verse. Borís Godunóff, brother-in-law to the Tzar

---

* "The Stone Guest" is founded on the Don Juan legend, like the familiar opera "Don Giovanni." Músorgsky set it to music, in sonorous, Wagnerian recitative style (though the style was original with him, not copied from Wagner, who came later). It is rarely given in public, but I had the pleasure of hearing it rendered by famous artists, accompanied by the composer Balakíreff, at the house of a noted art and musical critic in St. Petersburg.

Feódor Mikháilovitch, has at last reached the goal of his
ambition, and mounted the throne, at what cost his own
speech shows: Scene: The Imperial Palace.   The Tzar
enters:

> I've reached the height of power;
> 'Tis six years now that I have reigned in peace;
> But there's no happiness within my soul.
> Is it not thus — in youth we thirst and crave
> The joy of love; but once that we have quenched
> Our hungry heart with brief possession,
> We're tired, and cold, and weary on the instant!
> The sorcerers in vain predict long life;
> And promise days of undisturbed power.
> Nor power, nor life, nor aught can cheer my heart;
> My soul forebodeth heaven's wrath and woe.
> I am not happy.   I did think to still
> With plenty and with fame my people here;
> To win for aye their love by bounties free.
> But vain are all my cares and empty toils:
> A living power is hated by the herd;
> They love the dead alone, only the dead.
> What fools we are, when popular applause,
> Or the loud shout of masses thrills our heart!
> God sent down famine on this land of ours;
> The people howled, gave up the ghost in torment;
> I threw the granaries open, and my gold
> I showered upon them; sought out work for them.
> Made mad by suffering, they turned and cursed me!
> By conflagrations were their homes destroyed;
> I built for them their dwellings fair and new;
> And they accused me — said I had set the fires!
> That's the Lord's judgment; — seek its love who will!
> Then dreamed I bliss in mine own home to find;
> I thought to make my daughter blest in wedlock:
> Death, like a whirlwind, snatched her betrothed away,
> And rumor craftily insinuates
> That I am author of my own child's widowhood: —
> I, I, unhappy father that I am!

Let a man die — I am his secret slayer.
I hastened on the death of Feódor;
I gave my sister, the Tzarítza, poison;
I poisoned her, the lovely nun,— still I!
Ah, yes, I know it: naught can give us calm,
Amid the sorrows of this present world;
Conscience alone, mayhap:
Thus, when 'tis pure, it triumphs
O'er bitter malice, o'er dark calumny;
But if there be in it a single stain,
One, only one, by accident contracted,
Why then, all's done; as with foul plague
The soul consumes, the heart is filled with gall,
Reproaches beat, like hammers, in the ears,
The man turns sick, his head whirls dizzily,
And bloody children float before my eyes.*
I'd gladly flee — yet whither? Horrible!
Yea, sad his state, whose conscience is not clean.

QUESTIONS FOR REVIEW

1. How did the reign of Katherine II. mark a distinct advance in the development of Russian literature?

2. Describe the literary activities of Katherine II.

3. Who was Princess Dáshkoff?

4. Describe the early life and character of Von Vízin.

5. What qualities did he show in his play "The Brigadier"?

6. How did the characters in his "The Hobbledehoy" compare with those in the plays of Katherine II.?

7. Give an account of this play.

8. Give the chief events in the life of Derzhávin.

9. Why is he especially worthy to be remembered?

10. What are some of the beautiful thoughts in the ode "God"?

11. How was Kheraskóff regarded in his own day?

---

* The reference is to Godunóff's presumptive share in the murder, at Uglitch, of Iván the Terrible's infant heir, the Tzarévitch Dmítry.

12. What was the character of Bogdanóvitch's poem, " Dushenka "?

13. What influence had the fables of Khémnitzer?

14. Give examples of them.

15. What incidents show the effect of his comedy "Calumny"?

16. Give an account of the life of Karamzín.

17. Give examples of the character of some of his sentimental tales.

18. What real services did he render to Russian literature?

19. What importance had Dmítrieff and Ózeroff?

20. How did the translations of German and French writers, made by Zhukóvsky, affect the literary ideals of his time?

21. Give the chief facts in the life of Krylóff.

22. Give examples of his fables.

23. Describe the ancestry and early life of Púshkin.

24. What is his position in Russian literature?

25. How were his talents shown in Evgény Onyégin?

26. What is the character of the soliloquy from Borís Godunóff?

BIBLIOGRAPHY

The Memoirs of the Empress Katherine II. Written by herself.

The Princess Dáshkoff. Memoirs written by herself, and containing letters of the Empress Katherine II.

Original Fables. Krylóff. (The translation by Mr. Harrison, London, 1884, is regarded as the best of the twelve translations of Krylóff's works.)

Specimens from the Russian Poets. 2 volumes. By Sir John Bowring. Specimens of poetry from Lomonósoff through Zhukóvsky.

Prose Tales. Alexánder Púshkin. Translated by T. Keane.

Translations from Púshkin, in Memory of the Hundredth Anniversary of the Poet's Birthday. C. E. Turner.

CHAPTER VIII

SEVENTH PERIOD, FROM PÚSHKIN TO THE WRITERS OF THE FORTIES.

Even Karamzín's vast influence on his contemporaries cannot be compared with that exercised by Púshkin on the literature of the '20's and '30's of the nineteenth century; and no Russian writer ever effected so mighty a change in literature as Púshkin. Among other things, his influence brought to life many powerful and original talents, which would not have ventured to enter the literary career without Púshkin's friendly support and encouragement. He was remarkably amiable in his relations with all contemporary writers (except certain journalists in St. Petersburg and Moscow), and treated with especial respect three poets of his day, Délvig, Baratýnsky, and Yázykoff. He even exaggerated their merits, exalting the work of the last two above his own, and attributing great significance to Délvig's most insignificant poems and articles. Hence their names have become so closely connected with his, that it is almost impossible to mention him without mentioning them.

Baron Antón Antónovitch Délvig (1798–1831) the descendant of a Baltic Provinces noble, was one of Púshkin's comrades in the Lyceum, and published his first collection of poems in 1829.

Evgény Abrámovitch Baratýnsky (1800–1844) came of a noble family of good standing. His poetry was founded on Byronism, like all European poetry of that day, and was also partly under the influence of the fantastic romanticism introduced by Zhukóvsky. He never developed beyond a point which was reached by Púshkin in his early days in "The Prisoner of the Caucasus," "The Gypsies," "The Fountain of Baktchesarái," and the first chapters of "Evgény Onyégin." He wrote one very fine poem, devoted to Finland.

Nikolái Mikháilovitch Yázykoff (1803–1846) was of noble birth, and published a number of early poems in 1819. One of his best and longest, published about 1836, was a dramatic tale of "The Fire Bird." Between 1837–1842 his "The Lighthouse," "Gastún," "Sea Bathing," "The Ship," "The Sea," and a whole series of elegies, are also very good. Yázykoff's poetry is weaker and paler in coloring than Délvig's or Baratýnsky's, yet richer than all of theirs in really incomparable outward form of the verse, and in poetical expression of thought; in fact, he was "the poet of expression," and rendered great service by his boldness and originality of language, in that it taught men to write not as all others wrote, but as it lay in their individual power to write; in other words, he inculcated individuality in literature.

The only one of the many poets of Púshkin's epoch in Russia who did not repeat and develop, in different keys, the themes of their master's poetry, was Alexánder Sergyéevitch Griboyédoff (1795–1829). He alone was independent, original, and was related to the Púshkin period as Krylóff was to the Karamzín period—merely by the accident of time, not by the contents of his work. Griboyédoff was the first of a series of Russian poets who depicted life in absolutely faithful, but gloomy, colors; and it was quite in keeping with this view, that he did not live to see in print the comedy in which his well-earned fame rested, at the time, and which still keeps it fresh, by performances on the stage at the present day.

There was nothing very cheerful or bright about the social life of the '20's in the nineteenth century to make Russian poets take anything but a gloomy view of matters in general. Griboyédoff, as an unprejudiced man, endowed with great poetical gifts, and remarkable powers of observation, was able to give a faithful and wonderfully complete picture of high life in Moscow of that day, in his famous comedy "Woe from Wit" ("Góre ot Umá"), and introduce to the stage types which had never, hitherto, appeared in Russian comedy, because no one had looked deep enough into Russian hearts, or been capable of limning, impartially and with fidelity to nature, the emptiness and vanity of the characters and aims which preponderated in Russian society.

He was well born and very well educated. After serving in the army in 1812, like most patriotic young Russians of the day, he entered the foreign office, in 1817. There he probably made the acquaintance of Púshkin, but he never became intimate with him, as he belonged to a different literary circle, which included actors and dramatic writers. His first dramatic efforts were not very promising, though his first comedy, "The Young Married Pair," was acted in St. Petersburg in 1816. In 1819 he was offered the post of secretary of legation in Persia, which he accepted; and this took him away from the gay and rather wild society existence which he was leading, with bad results in many ways. In Persia, despite his multifarious occupations, and his necessary study of Oriental languages, Griboyédoff found time to plan his famous comedy in 1821, and in 1822 he wrote it in Georgia, whither he had been transferred. But he remodeled and rewrote portions of it, and it was finished only in 1823, when he spent a year in Moscow, his native city. When it was entirely ready for acting, he went to St. Petersburg, but neither his most strenuous efforts, nor his influence in high quarters, sufficed to secure the censor's permission for its performance on stage, or to get the requisite license for printing it. But it circulated in innumerable manuscript copies, and every one was in raptures over it. Even the glory of Púshkin's "Evgény Onyégin," which appeared at about the same time, did not overshadow Griboyédoff's glory. Strange to say, Púshkin, who had magnified Délvig, Baratýnsky, and Yázykoff far above their merits, and in general, was accustomed to overrate all talent, whether it belonged to his own friends or to strangers, was extremely severe on Griboyédoff's comedy, and detected many grave defects in it.

Griboyédoff was greatly irritated by his failure to obtain proper public recognition of his comedy. He expressed his feelings freely, became more embittered than ever against mankind in general, and went back to Georgia, in 1825, where he added to his previous poems, and took part in the campaign against Persia, in which he rendered great services to the commander-in-chief. As a reward, he was sent to St. Petersburg (1828), to present the treaty of peace to the Emperor. He was promptly appointed minister plenipotentiary to Persia, and on his way thither, in Tiflís, married a Georgian princess. His stern course of action and his disregard of certain rooted Oriental customs aroused the priesthood and the ignorant

masses of Teheran against him, and a riot broke out.
After a heroic defense of the legation, all the Russians,
including Griboyédoff, were torn to pieces. His wife had
been left behind in Tabreez and escaped. She buried his
remains at a monastery near Tiflís, in accordance with a
wish which he had previously expressed.

There is not much plot to "Woe from Wit." Moltchálin, Famúsoff's secretary, a cold, calculating, fickle
young man, has been making love to Famúsoff's only
child, an heiress, Sophia, an extremely sentimental young
person. Famúsoff rails against foreign books and fashions, "destroyers of our pockets and our hearth," and
lauds Colonel Skalozúb, an elderly pretender to Sophia's
hand, explaining the general servile policy of obtaining
rank and position by the Russian equivalent of "pull,"
which is called "connections." He compares his with
Tchátsky, to the disadvantage of the latter, who had been
brought up with Sophia, and had been in love with her
before his departure on his travels three years previously,
though he had never mentioned the fact. Tchátsky gives
rise to this diatribe by returning from his travels at this
juncture, asking for Sophia's hand, and trying to woo
the girl herself with equal unsuccess. Tchátsky's arraign-
ment of the imitation of foreign customs then everywhere
prevalent, does not win favor from any one. Worse yet,
he expresses his opinion of Moltchálin; and Sophia, in
revenge, drops a hint that Tchátsky is crazy. The hint
grows apace, and the cause is surmised to be a bullet-
wound in the head, received during a recent campaign.
Another "authority" contradicts this; it comes from
drinking champagne by the gobletful—no, by the bottle—
no, by the case. But Famúsoff settles the matter by

declaring that it comes from knowing too much. This takes place at an evening party at the Famúsoffs, and Tchátsky returns to the room to meet with an amazing reception. Eventually, he discovers that he is supposed to be mad, and that he is indebted to Sophia for the origin of the lie; also, that she is making rendezvous with the low-minded, flippant Moltchálin. At last Sophia discovers that Moltchálin is making love to her maid through inclination, and to her only through calculation. She casts him off, and orders him out of the house. Tchátsky, cured of all illusions about her, renounces his suit for her hand, and declares that he will leave Moscow forever. Tchátsky, whose woe is due to his persistence in talking sense and truth to people who do not care to hear it, and to his manly independence all the way through, comes to grief through having too much wit; hence the title.

Not one of Púshkin's successors, talented as many of them were, was able to attain to the position of importance which the great poet had rendered obligatory for future aspirants. It is worth noting that Púshkin's best work, in his second, non-Byronic, purely national style, enjoyed less success among his contemporaries than his early, half-imitative efforts, where the characters were weak, lacking in independent creation, and where the whole tone was gloomy. This gloomy tone expressed the sentiments of all Russia of the period, and it was natural that Byronic heroes should be in consonance with the general taste.

At this juncture, a highly talented poet arose, Mikháil Yúrievitch Lérmontoff (1814–1841), who, after first imitating Púshkin, speedily began to imitate Byron—and that with far more success than Púshkin had ever done—with great delicacy and artistic application to the local condi-

tions. Thus, as a vivid, natural echo of this epoch in
Russian life, the poet became dear to the heart of Russians; and in the '40's they regarded him as the equal of
the writers they most loved.

Lérmontoff, the son of a poor but noble family, was
reared by his grandmother, as his mother died when he
was a baby, and his father, an army officer, could not care
for him.   The grandmother did her utmost to give him
the best education possible at that time, and to make him
a brilliant society man.   The early foreign influence over
Púshkin was, as we have seen, French.   That over
Lérmontoff was rather English, which was then becoming
fashionable.   But like many another young Russian of
that day, Lérmontoff wrote his first poems in French,
imitating Púshkin's "The Fountain of Baktchesarái" and
Byron's "The Prisoner of Chillon."   He finished the
preparatory school with the first prize for composition
and history, and entered the University, which he was
soon compelled to leave, in company with a number of
others, because of a foolish prank they had played on a
professor.   In those days, when every one was engrossed
in thoughts of military service and a career, and when the
few remaining paths which were open to a poor young
man had thus been closed to him, but one thing was left
for him to do—enter the army.   Accordingly, in 1832,
Lérmontoff entered the Ensigns' School in St. Petersburg; but during his two years there he did not abandon
verse-making, and here he first began to imitate Byron.
A couple of poems, "Ismail Bey" (1832) and "Hadji
Abrek" (1833) were published by a comrade, without
Lérmontoff's knowledge, at this time.   In general, it may
be said of Lérmontoff at that period that he cared not in

the least for literary fame, and made no haste to publish his writings, as to which he was very severe. Many were not published until five or six years after they were written.

Soon after leaving the military school Lérmontoff wrote a drama, "The Masquerade" (1834), and the fine poem, "Boyárin Órsha," but his fame began only in 1837, with his splendid poem on the death of Púshkin, "The Death of the Poet," beginning, "The poet perished, the slave of honor," in which he expressed his entire sympathy with the poet in his untimely death, and poured out all his bitterness upon the circle which was incapable of appreciating and prizing the genius. This, in a multitude of manuscript copies, created a great sensation in St. Petersburg. Soon afterwards, on hearing contradictory rumors as to the duel and Púshkin's death, he added sixteen verses, beginning, "And you, ye arrogant descendants." One of the prominent persons therein attacked having had his attention called to the matter in public by an officious gossip (he had probably known all about it before, and deliberately ignored the matter), felt obliged to report Lérmontoff. The result was that Lérmontoff was transferred as ensign to a dragoon regiment which was serving in Georgia, and early in 1837 he set out for the Caucasus. Through his grandmother's efforts he was permitted to return from the Caucasus about eight months later, to a hussar regiment. By this time people were beginning to appreciate him; he had written his magnificent "Ballad of Tzar Iván Vasílievitch, the Young Lifeguardsman, and the Bold Merchant Kaláshnikoff," which every one hailed as an entirely new phenomenon in Russian literature, amazing in its highly artistic pictures, full of power and dignity, combined with an exterior like that of the inartistic productions of folk-poetry. This poem was productive of all the more astonishment, because his "The Demon," * written much earlier (1825–1834), was little known. "The Demon" is poor in contents, but surprisingly rich in wealth and luxury of coloring, and in the endless variety of its pictures of Caucasian life and nature.

In 1838, while residing in St. Petersburg, Lérmontoff wrote little at first, but in 1839 he wrote "Mtzyri," and a whole series of fine tales in prose, which eventually appeared under the general title of "A Hero of Our Times." This work, which has lost much of its vivid interest for people of the present day, must remain, nevertheless, one of the most important monuments of that period to which Lérmontoff so completely belonged. In the person of the hero, Petchórin, he endeavored to present "a portrait composed of the vices of the generation of which he was a contemporary," and he "drew the man of the period as he understood him, and as, unfortunately, he was too often met with." Lérmontoff admitted that in Petchórin he had tried to point out the "malady" which had attacked all Russian society of that day. All this he said in a preface to the second edition, after people had begun to declare that in the novel he had represented himself and his own experiences. Naturally Petchórin was drawn on Byronic lines, in keeping with the spirit of the '30's, when individuality loudly protested against the oppressive conditions of life. Naturally, also, all this now appears to be a caricature, true to the life of the highest Russian society as it was when it was written. Before he had quite completed this work, in February,

---

* Rubinstein used this as a foundation for the libretto of his delightful opera, with the same title.

1840, Lérmontoff fought a duel with the son of Baron de Barante, a well-known French historian, and was transferred, in consequence, to an infantry regiment in the Caucasus, whither he betook himself for the third time. A year later, after being permitted to make a brief stay in St. Petersburg, he returned to the Caucasus, and three months afterwards he was killed in a duel (on July 25, O. S., 1841) with a fellow officer, Martýnoff, and was buried on the estate in the government of Pénza, where he had been reared by his grandmother. The latest work of the poet, thus cut off almost before his prime, consisted of lyrics, which were full of power and perfection, and gave plain promise of the approaching maturity of the still young and not fully developed but immense talent.

His famous "Ballad of Tzar Iván Vasílievitch, the Young Lifeguardsman, and the Bold Merchant Kaláshnikoff" must be given in a summary and occasional quotations, as it is too long to reproduce in full. It lends itself better to dignified and adequate reproduction than do his lyrics, because it is not rhymed.* After a brief preface, the poet says: "We have composed a ballad in the ancient style, and have sung it to the sound of the dulcimer."

> The red sun shineth not in the heaven,
> The blue clouds delight not in it;
> But at his banqueting board, in golden crown,
> Sitteth the Terrible Tzar Iván Vasílievitch.
> Behind him stand the table-deckers,
> Opposite him all the boyárs and the princes,
> At his side, all about, the lifeguardsmen;
> And the Tzar feasteth to the glory of God,
> To his own content and merriment.

---

*Rubinstein used this as the libretto foundation for his opera of the same title, which was produced once, prohibited by the censor, produced once again after a lapse of eight or ten years, and again promptly prohibited. After another interval of years it was again permitted.

The ballad goes on to relate how the Tzar then ordered the beakers to be filled with wine from beyond the seas, and how all drank and lauded the Tzar.   One brave warrior, a gallant youth, did not dip his mustache in the golden cup, but dropped his eyes, drooped his head, and meditated.   The Tzar frowned, rapped on the floor with his iron-tipped staff, and finding that the young man still paid no heed, called him to account.   "Hey, there, our faithful servant Kiribyéevitch, art thou concealing some dishonorable thought?   Or art thou envious of our glory?   Or hath our honorable service wearied thee?" and he reproaches the youth.   Then Kiribyéevitch answered him, bowing to his girdle, begging the Tzar not to reproach his unworthy servant, but if he has offended the Tzar, he begs that the latter will order his head to be cut off.   "It oppresseth my heroic shoulders, and itself unto the damp earth doth incline."   The Tzar inquires why the lifeguardsman is sad.   "Has his kaftan of gold brocade grown threadbare?   Has his cap of sables got shabby?   Has he exhausted his treasure?   Has his well-tempered saber got nicked?   Or has some merchant's son from across the Moscow River overcome him in a boxing match?"   The young lifeguardsman shakes his curly head, and says that all these things are as they should be, but that while he was riding his mettlesome steed in the Trans-Moscow River quarter of the town (the merchant's quarter), with his silken girdle drawn taut, his velvet cap rimmed jauntily with black sables, fair young maidens had stood at the board gates, gazing at him, admiring and whispering together; but one there was who gazed not, admired not, but covered her face with her striped veil, "and in all Holy Russia, our Mother, no such beauty is to be found or searched out. She walketh swimmingly, as though she were a young swan. She gazeth sweetly, as though she were a dove. When she uttereth a word, 'tis like a nightingale warbling. Her cheeks are aflame with roses, like unto the dawn in God's heaven. Her tresses of ruddy gold, intertwined with bright ribbons, flow rippling down her shoulders, and kiss her white bosom. She was born in a merchant's family. Her name is Alyóna * Dmítrievna.''

He describes how he has fallen in love with her at first sight, and cares no more for anything in all the world save her, and begs that he may be sent away to the steppes along the Volga, to live a free kazák life, where he may lay his "turbulent head" on a Mussulman's spear (in the fights with the Tatars of Kazán is what is meant), where the vultures may claw out his tearful eyes, and his gray bones be washed by the rain, and his wretched dust, without burial, may be scattered to the four quarters of the compass. Tzar Iván Vasílievitch laughs, advises him to send gifts to his Alyóna, and celebrate the wedding. The lifeguardsman then confesses that he has not told the whole truth; that the beauty is already the wife of a young merchant.

In Part II., the young merchant is represented as seated at his shop-board, a stately, dashing young fellow, Stepán Paramónovitch Kaláshnikoff, spreading out his silken wares, beguiling his patrons (or "guests") with flattering speech, counting out gold and silver. But it is one of his bad days; the wealthy lords pass and do not so much as glance at his shop. "The bells of the holy churches have finished chiming for Vespers. The cloudy

* An unaristocratic form of Eléna—Helen.

glow of evening burneth behind the Kremlin. Little
clouds are flitting athwart the sky. The great Gostíny
Dvor * is empty.'' And Stepán Paramónovitch locks the
oaken door of his shop with a German (that is, a foreign)
spring-lock, fastens the fierce, snarling dog to the iron
chain, and goes thoughtfully home to his young housewife
beyond the Moscow River. On arriving there he is surprised that his wife does not come to meet him, as is her
wont. The oaken table is not set, the taper before the
ikóna (the holy picture) is almost burned out. He sum-
mons the old maid-servant and asks where his wife is at
that late hour, and what has become of his children? The
servant replies that his wife went to Vespers as usual, but
the priest and his wife have already sat down to sup, yet
the young housewife has not returned, and his little children are neither playing nor in bed, but weeping bitterly.
As young Merchant Kaláshnikoff then looks out into the
gloomy street he sees that the night is very dark, snow is
falling, covering up men's tracks, and he hears the outer
door slam, then hasty footsteps approaching, turns round
and beholds his young wife, pale, with hair uncovered
(which is highly improper for a married woman), her
chestnut locks unbraided, sprinkled with snow and hoar-
frost, her eyes dull and wild, her lips muttering unintel-
ligibly. The husband inquires where she has been, the
reason for her condition, and threatens to lock her up
behind an iron-bound oaken door, away from the light of
day. She, weeping bitterly, begs her "lord, her fair little
red sun," to slay her or to listen to her, and she explains,
that as she was coming home from Vespers she heard the
snow crunching behind her, glanced round, and beheld a

* The "Guests' Court," that is, the bazaar.

man running. She covered herself with her veil, but the man seized her hands, bade her have no fear, and said that he was no robber, but the servant of the Terrible * Tzar, Kiribyéevitch, from the famous family of Maliúta, promised her her heart's desire—gold, pearls, bright gems, flowered brocades—if she would but love him, and grant him one embrace. Then he caressed and kissed her, so that her cheeks are still burning, while the neighbors looked on, laughed, and pointed their fingers at her in scorn. Tearing herself from his hands, she fled homewards, leaving in his hands her flowered kerchief (her husband's gift) and her Bokhará veil. She entreats her husband not to give her over to the scorn of their neighbors, she is an orphan, her elder brother is in a foreign land, her younger brother still a mere child.

Stepán Paramónovitch thereupon sends for his two younger brothers, but they send back a demand to know what has happened that he should require their presence on a dark, cold night. He informs them that Kiribyéevitch, the lifeguardsman, has dishonored their family; that such an insult the soul cannot brook, neither a brave man's heart endure. On the morrow there is to be a fight with fists in the presence of the Tzar himself, and it is his intention to go to it, and stand up against that lifeguardsman and fight him to the death until his strength is gone. He asks them, in case he is killed, to step forth for "Holy Mother right," and as they are younger than he, fresher in strength, and with fewer sins on their heads, perchance the Lord will show mercy upon them. And this reply his brethren spake: "Whither the breeze bloweth beneath the

* His Russian name, "Grózny," means, rather, "menacing, threatening," than "terrible," the customary translation, being derived from "grozá," a thunderstorm.

sky, thither hasten the dutiful little clouds. When the dark blue eagle summoneth with his voice to the bloody vale of slaughter, summoneth to celebrate the feast, to clear away the dead, to him do the little eaglets wing their flight. Thou art our elder brother, our second father, do what thou see'st fit, and deemest best, and we will not fail thee, our own blood and bone.''

Part III. picturesquely and vividly describes the scene of the encounter; the challenge to the combatants to stand forth, by command of the Tzar, with a promise in the latter's name that the victors shall receive from him rewards. Then the redoubtable Lifeguardsmen Kiribyée-vitch steps forth. Thrice the challenge is repeated before any one responds. Then young Merchant Kaláshnikoff comes forward, makes his reverence to the Tzar, and when Kiribyéevitch demands his name, he announces it, and adds that he was born of an honorable father and has always lived according to God's law; he has not cast his eyes on another man's wife, nor played the bandit on a dark night, nor hid from the light of heaven, and that he means to fight to the death. On hearing this, Kiribyée-vitch "turned pale as snow in autumn, his bold eyes clouded over, a shiver ran through his mighty shoulders, on his parted lips the words fell dead." With one blow, the young merchant crushes in the lifeguardsman's breast, and the latter falls dead, the death being beautifully described in stately, picturesque language. At sight thereof, the Tzar Iván Vasílievitch waxed wroth, stamped on the earth, scowled with his black brows; ordered that the young merchant be seized and hauled before him. He then demands whether Kaláshnikoff has slain his faithful servant Kiribyéevitch "voluntarily, involuntarily, or

against his will.'' Kaláshnikoff boldly makes answer that
he has done it with deliberate intent, and that the reason
therefor he will not tell to the Tzar, but only to God
alone. He tells the Tzar to order him to be executed,
but not to deprive his little children or his young widow
and his brothers of his favor. The Tzar replies that it
is well Kaláshnikoff has answered truthfully; he will give
the young widow and the children a grant from his treasury, and give command that, from that day forth, his
brothers may traffic throughout the wide Russian realm
free of taxes. But Kaláshnikoff must mount the scaffold,
lay down his turbulent head, and the executioner shall be
ordered to make his axe very sharp, and the great bell
shall be tolled in order that all the men of Moscow may
know that the Tzar has not deprived him of his favor.
The execution and Kaláshnikoff's farewell speeches to his
brothers, with his last messages to his wife not to grieve
so greatly, and his commands that she is not to tell his
children how their father died, together with requests for
prayers for his soul, are described in very touching and
lofty terms, as are also the burial, and the scenes at the
grave.

The influence of Schelling's philosophy on the society of
Moscow (the literary center until half-way through the
'30's of the nineteenth century) was very great. This
philosophy held that every historical nation should express
some idea or other; that a nation could be called historical
only on condition of its being independent in this respect;
and that its importance in the progress of general civilization is determined by its degree of independence. This
set all thoughtful people to considering the place of Russia

among the European nations; and all the problems suggested by this philosophy came up with special force in
the Russian literature of the end of the '30's, and split
society into two great camps—the Slavyanophils (slavo-
phils)* and the Westerners.   These camps had existed
earlier, but had concerned themselves only with the purification of the Russian language, or with sentimental admiration for everything Russian, or for everything foreign,
as the case might be.   But now both parties undertook to
solve the problems connected with the fate of the nation.

Schelling's philosophy also suggested new views as to
the theory of art and the significance of literature in the
life of a nation, and evolved the conclusion, that a nation's
literature, even more than its civilization, should be entirely
independent.   This naturally led the Slavyanophils to
reflect upon the indispensability of establishing Russian
literature on a thoroughly national, independent basis.
Naturally, also, this led to the Slavyanophils contesting
the existence of a Russian literature in the proper sense
of the term; since the whole of it, from Lomonósoff to
Púshkin, had been merely a servile imitation of Western
literature, and did not in the least express the spirit
of the Russian people, and of the Schellingists.   A number of the professors in the Moscow University belonged
to this party.   Naturally the students in their department—the philological faculty—came under their influence, and under this influence was reared the famous
Russian critic, Vissarión Grigórievitch Byelínsky (1811–
1848).   His name is chiefly identified with the journal
"The Annals of the Fatherland" (of St. Petersburg),

---

* Most Russians prefer to have the world "Slavyáne" translated Slavonians, rather than Slavs, as the latter is calculated to mislead.

where he published his brilliant critical articles on Griboyédoff, Gógol's "The Inspector," on Lérmontoff's works, and on those of other writers; on French contemporary literature, and on current topics at home and abroad, among them articles condemning many characteristics of Russian society, both intellectual and moral, such as the absence of intellectual interests, routine, narrowness, and egotism in the middle-class merchants; self-satisfied philistinism; the patriarchal laxity of provincial morals; the lack of humanity and the Asiatic ferocity towards inferiors; the slavery of women and children under the weight of family despotism. His volume of articles on Púshkin constitute a complete critical history of Russian literature, beginning with Lomonósoff and ending with Púshkin. By these Byelínsky's standing as an important factor in literature was thoroughly established, and all the young writers of the succeeding epoch, that of the '50's, gathered around him. Grigoróvitch, Turgéneff, Gontcharóff, Nekrásoff, Apollón Máikoff, Dostoévsky, Tolstóy, and the rest, may be said to have been reared on Byelínsky's criticism, inspired by it to creative activity, and indebted to it for much of their fame. Byelínsky, moreover, educated the minds of that whole generation, and prepared men for the social movement of the '60's, which was characterized by many reforms.

After 1846 Byelínsky was connected with the journal, "The Contemporary," published by the poet Nekrásoff, and I. I. Panáeff, to which the best writers of the day contributed. Here, during the brief period when his health permitted him to work, he expressed even bolder and more practical ideas, and became the advocate of the "natural school," of which he regarded Gógol as the founder, wherein poetry was treated as an integral part of every-day life. Turgéneff has declared, that Byelínsky indisputably possessed all the chief qualities of a great critic, and that no one before him, or better than he, ever expressed a correct judgment and an authoritative verdict, and that he was, emphatically, "the right man in the right place."

One author who deserves to be better known outside of Russia produced the really original and indescribably fascinating works on which his fame rests during the last ten or twelve years of his long life, late in the '40's and '50's, although he was much older than the authors we have recently studied, and began to write much earlier than many of them. His early writing, however, was in the classical style, and does not count in comparison with his original descriptions of nature, and of the life of the (comparatively) distant past. Sergyéi Timoféevitch Aksákoff (1791–1859), the descendant of a very ancient noble family, was born in far-away eastern Russia, in Ufá, and was very well educated by his mother, at schools, and at Kazán University. His talents first revealed themselves in 1847, in his "Notes on Angling," and his "Diary of a Sportsman with a Gun," in the Orenburg Government (1852). Most famous of all, and most delightful, are the companion volumes, "A Family Chronicle and Souvenirs" (1856) and "The Childhood's Years of Bagróff's Grandson" (1858). In these Russian descriptive language made a great stride in advance, even after Púshkin and Gógol; and as a limner of landscape, he has no equal in Russian literature. The most noteworthy point about his work is that there is not a trace of creative fancy or invention; he describes reality, takes everything straight from life, and describes it with amazing faithfulness and artistic harmony. He was the first Russian writer to look on Russian life from a positive instead of from a negative point of view.*

Púshkin's period had been important, not only in rendering Russian literature national, but still more so in bringing literature into close connection with life and its interests.   This had in turn led to a love of reading and of literature all over the country, and had developed latent talents.   This love spread to classes hitherto unaffected by it; and among the talents it thus developed, none was more thoroughly independent than that of Alexéi Vasílievitch Koltzóff (1809–1842), who was so original, so wholly unique in his genius, that he cannot rightly be assigned to any class, and still stands as an isolated phenomenon. He was the son of a merchant of Vorónezh, who was possessed of considerable means, and he spent the greater part of his youth on the steppes, helping his father, a drover, who supplied tallow-factories.   After being taught to read and write by a theological student, young Koltzóff was sent to the district school for four months, after which his education was regarded as finished, because he knew as much as the people about him, and because no more was required for business purposes.   But the lad acquired a strong love of reading, and devoted himself to such literature as he could procure, popular fairy-tales, the "Thousand and One Nights," and so forth.   He was sixteen years of age when Dmítrieff's works fell into his hands, and inspired him with a desire to imitate them, and

* His " Family Chronicle " was the favorite book (during her girlhood) of Maryá Alexandrovna, the daughter of Alexander II., afterwards Duchess of Edinburg, and now Duchess of Saxe-Coburg-Gotha. I made acquaintance with this fascinating work by reading aloud from her copy to a mutual friend, a Russian.

to "make songs" himself. As yet he did not understand the difference between poetry and popular songs, and did not read verses, but sang them. The local book-seller was the first to recognize his poetical tendency, and in a degree, guided him on the right road with a "Russian Prosody," and other suitable books, such as the works of Zhukóvsky, Púshkin, and other contemporary poets. A passion for writing poetry was in the air in the '20's. But although he yielded to this and to the promptings of his genius, it was a long time before he was able to clothe his thoughts in tolerable form. An unhappy love had a powerful influence on the development of his poetical talent, and his versified efforts suddenly became fervent songs of love and hate, of melancholy, soulful cries of grief and woe, full of melodious expressions of the world about him. One of Byelínsky's friends, whose family lived near Vorónezh, made his acquaintance, read his poems and applauded much in them. Three years later, in 1833, at the request and expense of this new friend, Koltzóff published a small collection, containing eighteen poems selected by him, which showed that he possessed an original and really noteworthy poetical gift. In 1835 Koltzóff visited St. Petersburg and made acquaintance with Púshkin, Zhúkovsky, and many other literary men, and between 1836 and 1838 his fame penetrated even to the knowledge of the citizens in his native town. He continued to aid his father in business, but his heart was elsewhere—he longed for the intellectual companionship of his friends in Moscow, and all this rendered him extremely unhappy. In 1840 he spent three months with Byelínsky in St. Petersburg, and after that he remained in Vorónezh, had another unhappy love affair, and dreamed continually of the possibility of quitting the place for good. But his father would not give him a kopék for such a purpose. His health gave way, and he died in 1842, aged thirty-three.

His poems are few in number, and the best of them belong to an entirely peculiar style, which he alone in Russian literature possesses, to which he alone imparted significance — the ballad, the national ballad compact, powerful, rich in expression, and highly artistic. The charm of nationality is so great, as expressed in Koltzóff's songs, that it is almost impossible to read them; one wants to sing them as the author sang the verses of others in his boyhood. Even his peculiar measures, which are not at all adapted to popular songs, do not destroy the harmonious impression made by them, and such pieces as "The Forest," "The Ballads of Cabman Kudryávitch," "The Perfidy of the Affianced Bride," and others, not only belong to the most notable productions of Russian lyric poetry, but are also representatives of an important historical phenomenon, as the first attempt to combine in one organic whole Russian artistic literature and the inexhaustible vast inartistic poetry of the people. "The Perfidy of the Affianced Bride," which is not rhymed in the original, runs as follows:

> Hot in heaven the summer sun doth shine,
> But me, young though I be, it warmeth not!
> My heart is dead with cold
> Through the perfidy of my affianced bride.
>
> Woe-sadness upon me hath fallen,
> Upon my sorrowful head;
> My soul by deadly anguish is tormented,
> And from my body my soul doth long to flee.

Unto men have I resorted for help—
With a laugh have they turned away ;
To the grave of my father, my mother—
But they rise not at my call.

The world grew dark before mine eyes,
Upon the grass I swooned.
At dead of night, in a dreadful storm,
They lifted me from the grave.

At night, in the storm, I saddled my steed;
I set out, caring not whither I went—
To lead a wretched life, to console myself,
With rancor to demand satisfaction from men.

Romanticism established, as its first principles, freedom
of creation and nationality of poetry, and these principles
survived romanticism itself. Now, while romanticism
preached freedom of creation, it circumscribed this freedom by selecting as subjects for poetical compositions
chiefly the extraordinary sides of life, its majestic
moments. Its heroes were always choice, powerful
natures, who suffered profoundly because of the lot of all
mankind, and were capable of gigantic conflicts against
the whole world. Classicism had bequeathed this habit
of regarding as worthy of poetical treatment only heroes
who stood out from the mass, and of depicting these
heroes only at critical crises. All this depended, in a
great degree, upon the political and social conditions
which prevailed at that epoch—the beginning of the nineteenth century. But quieter, more peaceful times dawned,
and with them men's tastes and habits of mind underwent
a change. They grew tired of scorning and hating reality,
because it did not conform to their cherished dreams, and
they began coolly to study it. The titanic heroes, who had

become tiresome and anti-pathetic to the last degree, made way for ordinary mortals in their everyday surroundings. Lyrical exaltation was superseded by calm observation, or disintegrating analysis of the different elements of life; pathetic misery made way for cold irony, or jeeringly melancholy humor; and at last poetry was succeeded by prose, and the ruling poetical forms of the new epoch became the romance and the novel. This change took place almost simultaneously in all the literatures of Europe.

We have seen that Púshkin, towards the end of his career, entered upon this new path, with his prose tales, "The Captain's Daughter," "Dubróvsky," and so forth, and throughout the '30's of the nineteenth century, the romance and novel came, more and more, to occupy the most prominent place in Russian literature. We may pass over the rather long list of second-class writers who adventured in this field (of whom Zagóskin and Márlinsky are most frequently referred to), and devote our attention to the man who has been repeatedly called "the father of modern Russian realism," Nikolái Vasílievitch Gógol (1809–1852). He is credited with having created all the types which we encounter in the works of the great novelists who followed him, and this is almost literally true, at least so far as the male characters are concerned. In particular, this applies to his famous "Dead Souls," which contains if not the condensed characterization in full of these types, at least the readily recognized germs of them. But in this respect, his early Little Russian Stories, "Tales from a Farm-house Near Dikánka," and the companion volume, "Mírgorod," as well as his famous comedy, "The Inspector," must not be forgotten, for they contributed their full quota. Púshkin was one of Gógol's earliest and most ardent admirers, and it was because he recognized the latter's phenomenal talent in seizing the national types that he gave to him the idea for "Dead Souls," which he had intended to use himself. Thanks to his own genius (as well as to the atmosphere of the epoch in which he lived), he solved for himself, quite independently of any foreign influence, the problem of bringing Russian literature down from the clouds to everyday real life. He realized that the world was no longer living in a sort of modern epic, as it had been during the French Revolution and the Napoleonic campaigns, and that literature must conform to the altered conditions. Naturally, in his new quest after truth, Gógol-Yanóvsky (to give him his full name) mingled romanticism and realism at first. But he soon discovered the true path. He was born and reared in Little Russia, at Sorótchinsky, Government of Poltáva, and was separated only by two generations from the famous epoch of the Zaporózhian kazáks, who lived (as their name implies) below the rapids of the Dniepr. He has depicted their life in his magnificent novel "Tarás Búlba." His grandfather had been the regimental scribe—a post of honor—of that kazák army, and the spirit of the Zaporózhian kazáks still lingered over the land which was full of legends, fervent, superstitious piety, and poetry.

Gógol's grandfather, who figures as "Rúdy Pánko, the bee-farmer," in the two volumes of Little Russian stories which established his fame, narrated to him at least one-half of those stories. His father, also, who represented the modern spirit, was an inimitable narrator of comic stories, and the talents of father and grandfather rendered their house the popular center of a very extensive neighborhood.

At school Gógol did not distinguish himself, but he wrote a good deal, all of an imitative character. After leaving school, it was with difficulty that he secured a place as copying-clerk, at a wretched salary, in St. Petersburg. He promptly resigned this when fame came, and secured the appointment as professor of history. But he was a hopelessly incompetent professor of history, despite his soaring ambitions, both on account of his lack of scholarship and the natural bent of his mind. The literary men who had obtained the position for him had discerned his immense talent in a perfectly new style of writing; and after failure had convinced him that heavy, scientific work was not in his line, he recognized the fact himself, and decided to devote himself to the sort of work for which nature had intended him. The first volume of his "Tales from a Farm-house Near Dikánka" appeared at the end of 1831, and had an immense success. The second volume, "Mírgorod," was equally successful, all the more so, as it introduced, together with the pure merriment which had characterized the earlier tales, and the realism which was his specialty, so to speak, a new element—pathos; "laughter piercing through a mist of tears." In this style "Old-fashioned Gentry" * and "How Iván Ivánovitch Quarrelled with Iván Nikifórovitch" are famous examples. Success always turned Gógol's head, and he immediately aspired to some undertaking far beyond his powers. In this case, for instance, despising, as usual, what he could do best, he planned a

* Literally, "Old-fashioned Landed Proprietors," who would, as a matter of course, belong to the gentry, or "nobility," as the Russian term is. This title is often translated, "Old-fashioned Farmers."

huge work, in nine volumes, on the history of the Middle Ages. Fortunately, his preparatory studies in the history of Little Russia led him to write his splendid epic, which is a composition of the highest art, "Tarás Búlba," and diverted him from his ill-digested project.

He began to recognize that literary work was not merely a pastime, but his moral duty; and the first result of this conviction was his great play "The Inspector," finished in April, 1836. The authorities refused to produce it, but the Emperor Nicholas I. heard about it, read it, and gave imperative orders that it should be put on the stage, upholding Gógol with rapturous delight. Everybody—officials, the police, literary people, merchants—attacked the author. They raged at this comedy, refused to recognize their too lifelike portraits, and still endeavored to have the play prohibited. Gógol's health and spirits failed under this persecution, and he fled abroad, whence thereafter he returned to Russia only at long intervals and for brief visits, chiefly to Moscow, where most of his faithful friends resided. He traveled a great deal, but spent most of his time in Rome, where his lavish charities kept him perennially poor despite the eventual and complete success, both artistically and financially, of "The Inspector," and of Part I. of "Dead Souls," which would have enabled him to live in comfort. He was wont to say that he could see Russia plainly only when he was at a distance from her, and in a measure, he proved the truth of his contention in the first volume of "Dead Souls." Thereby he justified Púshkin's expectations in giving him the subject of that work, which he hoped would enable Gógol to depict the classes and localities of the fatherland in the concentrated form of types. But he lived too long in

Rome. The Russian mind in general is much inclined to mysticism, and Little Russia, in Gógol's boyhood, was exceptionally permeated with exaggerated religious sentiment. Mysticism seems to be peculiarly fatal to Russian writers of eminence; we have seen how Von Vízin and Zhukóvsky were affected toward the end of their lives; we have a typical and even more pronounced example of it in a somewhat different form at the present time in Count L. N. Tolstóy. Lérmontoff had inclined in that direction. Hence, it is not surprising that the moral and physical atmosphere of Rome, during a too prolonged residence there, eventually ruined Gógol's mind and health, and extinguished the last sparks of his genius, especially as even in his school-days he had shown a marked tendency (in his letters to his mother) to religious exaltation. Now, under the pressure of his personal tendencies and friendships, and the clerical atmosphere of Rome, he developed into a mystic and an ascetic of the most extreme type. He regarded all his earlier writings as sins which must be atoned for (precisely as Count L. N. Tolstóy regards his masterpieces at the present time); and nevertheless, his overweening self-esteem was so flattered by the tremendous success of "The Inspector" and the first part of "Dead Souls" that he began to regard himself as a sort of divinely commissioned prophet, on whom it was incumbent to preach to his fellow-men. It will be seen that the parallel holds good in this respect also. Extracts from his hortatory letters which he published proved to Russians that his day was over. His failure in his self-imposed mission plunged him into the extremes of self-torment, and his lucid moments grew more and more rare. He destroyed what he had written of the second part of

"Dead Souls," in the attacks of ecstatic remorse at such profane work which followed. (By some authorities it is believed that he did this unintentionally, meaning to destroy an entirely different set of papers.) In 1848 he made a pilgrimage to Jerusalem, and went thence to Moscow, where he resided until his death, becoming more and more extreme in his mysticism and asceticism. He spent sleepless nights in prayer; he tried to carry fasting to the extent of living for a week on one of the tiny double loaves which are used for the Holy Communion in the Eastern Catholic Church, a feat which it is affirmed can be performed with success, and even to more exaggerated extent, by practiced ascetics. Gógol died. His observation was acute; his humor was genuine, natural, infectious; his realism was of the most vivid description; his power of limning types was unsurpassed, and it is these types which have entered, as to their essential ingredients, into the works of his successors, that have rendered the Russian realistic literary school famous. He wrote only one complete play besides "The Inspector," and it is still acted occasionally, but it is not of a sort to appeal to the universal public, as is his famous comedy. The fantastic but amusing plot of this lesser comedy, "Marriage," is founded upon a young girl's meditations on that theme, and the actions which lead up to and follow them. The wealthy heroine of the merchant class, being desirous of marrying, enlists the services of the professional matchmaker, the old-time Russian matrimonial agent, in the merchant and peasant classes. This match-maker offers for her choice several eligible suitors (all strangers), and the girl makes her choice. She is well pleased with it, but suddenly begins to speculate on the future; is moved to tears by the prospect that her daughter may be unhappy in a hypothetical marriage, in the dim future; and at last, driven to despair by this painful picture of her fancy, she evades her betrothed and breaks off the match.

The interest of "The Inspector" is perennial and universal; official negligence, corruption, bribery, masculine vanity and boastfulness, and feminine failings to match, are the exclusive prerogatives of no one nation or epoch. The comedy is not a caricature, but it is a faithful society portrait and satire, with intense condensation of character, and traits which are not only truly and typically Russian, but come within the ken of all fair-minded persons of other lands. The scene opens in a room at the house of the Chief of Police in a provincial town. Those present are: The Chief himself, the Curator of the Board of Benevolent Institutions, the Superintendent of Schools, the Judge, the Commissioner of Police, the Doctor, and two policemen.

CHIEF.—I have summoned you hither, gentlemen, in order to communicate to you an unpleasant piece of news. An Inspector is coming.

JUDGE.—What! An Inspector?

CHIEF.—An Inspector from St. Petersburg, incognito, and with secret orders, to boot.

JUDGE.—I thought so!

CURATOR.—If there's not trouble, I'm mistaken!

CHIEF.—I have warned you, gentlemen. See to it! I have made some arrangements in my own department, and I advise you to do the same. Especially you, Artémy Philípp'itch! Without a doubt, this traveling official will wish, first of all, to inspect your institutions, and therefore, you must arrange things so that they will be decent. The nightcaps should be clean, and the sick people should not look like blacksmiths, as they usually do in private.

CURATOR.—Well, that is a mere trifle. We can put clean nightcaps on them.

CHIEF.—Moreover, you ought to have written up, over the head of each bed, in Latin or some other language—that's your affair—the name of each disease; when each patient was taken sick, the day and the hour. It is not well that your sick people should smoke such strong tobacco that one has to sneeze every time he goes in there. Yes, and it would be better if there were fewer of them; it will be set down at once to bad supervision, or to lack of skill on the doctor's part.

CURATOR.—Oh, so far as the doctoring is concerned, Christián Iván'itch and I have already taken measures; the nearer to nature, the better—we don't use any expensive medicines. Man is a simple creature; if he dies, why then, he dies; if he gets well, why then, he gets well; and moreover, it would have been difficult for Christián Iván'itch to make them understand him; he doesn't know one word of Russian.

CHIEF.—I should also advise you, Ammós Feódor'itch, to turn your attention to court affairs. In the anteroom, where the clients usually assemble, your janitor has got a lot of geese and goslings, which waddle about under foot. Of course it is praiseworthy to be thrifty in domestic affairs, and why should not the janitor be so, too? Only, you know, it is not proper in that place. I intended to mention it to you before, but always forgot it.

JUDGE.—I'll order them to be taken to the kitchen this very day. Will you dine with me?

CHIEF.—And moreover, it is not well that all sorts of stuff should be put to dry in the court-room, and that over the very desk with the documents, there should be a hunting-whip. . . . . Yes, and strange to say, there is no man who has not his faults. God himself has arranged it so, and it is useless for free-thinkers to maintain the contrary.

JUDGE.—What do you mean by 'faults,' Antón Antón'itch? There are various sorts of faults. I tell every one frankly that I take bribes; but what sort of bribes? Greyhound pups. That's quite another thing.

CHIEF.—Well, greyhound pups or anything else, it's all the same.

JUDGE.—Well, no, Antón Antón'itch. But, for example, if some one has a fur coat worth five hundred rubles, and his wife has a shawl—

CHIEF.—Well, and how about your taking greyhound pups as bribes? Why don't you trust in God? You never go to church. I am firm in the faith, at all events, and go to church every Sunday. But you—oh, I know you! If you begin to talk about the creation, one's hair rises straight up on his head.

JUDGE.—It came of itself, of its own accord.

CHIEF.—Well, in some cases, it is worse to have brains than to be entirely without them. As for you, Luká Lúk'itch, as superintendent of schools, you must bestir yourself with regard to the teachers. One of them, for instance, the fat-faced one—I don't recall his name—cannot get along without making grimaces when he takes his seat—like this (*makes a grimace*); and then he begins to smooth his beard out from under his neckerchief with his hand. In short, if he makes such faces at the scholars, there is nothing to be said; it must be necessary; I am no judge as to that. But just consider—if he were to do that to a visitor, it might be very unpleasant; the Inspector, or any-one else, might take it as personal. The Devil knows what might come of it. . . . . And I must also mention the teacher of history. He's a learned man, that's plain; but he expresses himself with so much warmth that he loses control of himself. I heard him once; well, so long as he was talking about the Assyrians and the Babylonians, it was all right; but when he got to Alexander of Macedon, I can't describe to you what came over him. I thought there was a fire, by heavens! He jumped up from his seat, and dashed his chair down against the floor with all his might. Alexander of Macedon was a hero, no doubt; but why smash the chairs?(*) There will be a deficit in the accounts, just as the result of that.

SUPERINTENDENT.—Yes, he is hasty! I have spoken to him about it several times. He says: "What would you have? I would sacrifice my life for science."

CHIEF.—Yes, such is the incomprehensible decree of Fate;

*This expression has become proverbial in Russia, and is used to repress any one who becomes unduly excited.

a learned man is always a drunkard, or else he makes faces that would scare the very saints.

As the play proceeds in this lively vein, two men about town—in a humble way—the public busybodies, happen to discover at the Inn a traveler who has been living on credit for two weeks, and going nowhere. The landlord is on the point of putting the man in prison for debt, when the busybodies jump to the conclusion that he is the Inspector. The Prefect and the other officials accept their suggestion in spite of the traveler's plain statement as to his own identity as an uninfluential citizen. They set about making the town presentable, entertain him, bribe him against his will, and bow down before him. He enters into the spirit of the thing after a brief delay, accepts the hospitality, asks for loans, makes love to the Prefect's silly wife and daughter, betroths himself to the latter, receives the petitions and the bribes of the downtrodden townspeople, and goes off with the best post-horses the town can furnish, ostensibly to ask the blessing of a rich old uncle on his marriage. The Postmaster intercepts a cynically frank letter which the man has written to a friend, and in which he heaps ridicule on his credulous hosts. This opens their eyes at last, and at that moment, a gendarme appears and announces that the Inspector has arrived. Tableau.

Gógol's two volumes of Little Russian Tales, above-mentioned, must remain classics, and the volume of St. Petersburg Tales contains essentially the same ingredients, so that they may be considered as a whole. All the tales in the first two volumes are from his beloved native Little Russia. Some are merely poetical renderings of popular legends, counterparts of which are to be found in the folk-lore of many lands; such are "Vy," and "St. John's

Eve's" and the exquisite "May Night," where the famous
poetical spirit of the Ukráina (borderland) is displayed in
its fullest force and beauty. "Know ye the night of the
Ukráina?" he writes. "O, ye do not know the Ukráina
night! Look upon it; from the midst of the sky gazes the
moon; the illimitable vault of heaven has withdrawn into
the far distance, has spread out still more immeasurably;
it burns and breathes; the earth is all bathed in silvery
light; and the air is wondrous, and cool, and perfumed,
and full of tenderness, and an ocean of sweet odors is
abroad. A night divine! An enchanting night! The
forests stand motionless, inspired, full of darkness, and
cast forth a vast shadow. Calm and quiet are the pools;
the coldness and gloom of their waters is morosely hemmed
in by the dark green walls of gardens. The virgin copses
of wild bird-cherry and black cherry trees stretch forth
their roots towards the coolness of the springs, and from
time to time their leaves whisper as though in anger and
indignation, when a lovely little breeze, and the wind of
the night, creeping up for a moment, kisses them. All
the landscape lies in slumber. But on high, everything
is breathing with life, everything is marvelous, everything
is solemnly triumphant. And in the soul there is something illimitable and wondrous, and throngs of silvery
visions make their way into its depths. Night divine!
Enchanting night! And all of a sudden, everything has
become instinct with life; forests, pools, and steppes.
The magnificent thunder of the Ukráina nightingale
becomes audible, and one fancies that the moon, in the
midst of the sky, has paused to listen to it. . . . . As
though enchanted, the hamlet dreams upon the heights.
The mass of the cottages gleams still whiter, still more

agreeably under the light of the moon; still more dazzlingly do their lowly walls stand out against the darkness. The songs have ceased. Everything is still. Pious people are all asleep. Only here and there are the small windows still a-glow. In front of the threshold of a few cottages only is a belated family eating its late supper.''

Others of the tales are more exclusively national; such as ''The Lost Document,'' ''Sorótchinsky Fair,'' ''The Enchanted Spot,'' and the like. But they display the same fertility of invention, combined with skill in management, and close study of every-day customs, superstitions, and life, all of which render them invaluable, both to Russians and to foreigners. More important are such stories as ''Old-fashioned Gentry,'' ''The Cloak'' (from the volume of ''St. Petersburg Tales''), wherein kindly wit is tempered with the purest, deepest pathos, while characters and customs are depicted with the greatest art and fidelity. ''The Portrait,'' again, is semi-fantastic, although not legendary; and the ''Diary of a Madman'' is unexcelled as an amusing but affecting study of a diseased mind in the ranks of petty officialdom, where the tedious, insignificant routine disperses what few wits the poor man was originally endowed with by nature.

In Gógol's greatest work, ''Dead Souls,'' all his qualities are developed to the highest degree, though there is less pathos than in some of the short stories. This must forever rank as a Russian classic. The types are as vivid, as faithful, for those who know the Russia of to-day, as when they were first introduced to an enthusiastic Russian public, in 1847.

In the pre-emancipation days, a ''soul'' signified a male serf. Women were not taken account of in the periodical revisions; although the working unit, or *tyagló*, consisted of a man, his wife, and his horse—the indispensable trinity in agricultural labors. In the interval between revisions, a landed proprietor continued to pay taxes on all the male serfs accredited to him on the official list, births being considered as an exact offset to deaths, for the sake of convenience. Another provision of the law was, that no one should purchase serfs without the land to which they belonged, except for the purpose of colonization. An ingenious fraud, suggested by a combination of these two laws, forms the basis of plot for "Dead Souls." The hero, Tchítchikoff, is an official who has struggled up, cleverly but not too honestly, through the devious ways of bribe-taking, extortion, and not infrequent detection and disgrace, to a snug berth in the customs service, from which he has been ejected under conditions which render further upward flight quite out of the question. In this dilemma, he hits upon the idea of purchasing from landed proprietors of mediocre probity all their "souls" which are dead, though still nominally alive, and are taxed as such. Land is being given away gratuitously in the southern governments of Khersón and Taúris to any one who will settle on it. This is a matter of public knowledge, and Tchítchikoff's plan consists in buying a thousand non-existent serfs—"dead souls"—at a maximum of one hundred rubles apiece, for colonization on an equally non-existent estate in the south. He will then mortgage them to the loan bank of the nobility, known as the Council of Guardians, and obtain a capital. In pursuance of this clever scheme, the adventurer sets out on his travels, visits provincial towns, and the estates of landed gentry of every shade of character, honesty, and financial standing; and from them he buys for a song (or cajoles from them for nothing, as a gift, when they are a trifle scrupulous over the tempting prospect of illegal gain) huge numbers of "dead souls." Púshkin himself could not have used with such tremendous effect the phenomenal opportunities which this plot of Tchítchikoff's wanderings offered for setting forth Russian manners, characters, customs, all Russian life, in town and country, as Gógol did. The author even contrives, in keen asides and allusions, to throw almost equal light on the life of the capital as well. His portraits of women are not exactly failures; they are more like composite photographs. His portraiture of men is supreme. In fact, there is no such thing in the whole of Gógol's work as a heroine, properly speaking, who plays a first-class part, or who is analyzed in modern fashion. The day was not come for that as yet.

"Tarás Búlba," his great historical novel, offers a vivid picture of the famous kazák republic on the Dniépr, and equally with his other volumes, it stands in the first rank for its poetry, its dramatic force, its truth to life. It alone may be said to have a passionate love story.

QUESTIONS FOR REVIEW

1. What special gift as a writer had Yázykoff?
2. Give the chief events in the career of Griboyédoff.
3. What was the character of Russian social life at this time?
4. What was the plot of "Woe from Wit"?
5. Describe the influence of Lérmontoff.
6. What is the story of his famous "Ballad of the Tzar, the Lifeguardsman, and the Merchant"? Supply full title.
7. What was Schelling's philosophy, and how did it affect Russian thinkers?

8. What important influence had Byelínsky?

9. What marked powers of description had Aksákoff?

10. How does Koltzóff's life illustrate the widening influence of Russian literature?

11. How did the change from poetry to prose writing come about?

12. Give an account of the chief events in the life of Gógol.

13. How was the Russian tendency to mysticism illustrated in his case?

14. Describe his famous play "The Inspector." What qualities does he show in this?

15. What are the characteristics of his "Tales"?

16. Why is "Dead Souls" regarded as his greatest work?

17. What is the character of "Tarás Búlba"?

BIBLIOGRAPHY

A Hero of To-Day. M. Y. Lérmontoff. (Several translations.)

Works of Gógol: *The Inspector*. (Translated by Arthur Sykes.) *Tarás Búlba*. (Translated by I. F. Hapgood.)

Dead Souls, St. John's Eve, and Other Stories. (Selections from the two volumes of *Little Russian and St. Petersburg Tales*. Translated by I. F. Hapgood.)

CHAPTER IX

SEVENTH PERIOD: GONTCHARÓFF. GRIGO-
RÓVITCH. TURGÉNEFF.

Under the direct influence of Byelínsky's criticism, and
of the highly artistic types created by Gógol, a new generation of Russian writers sprang up, as has already been
stated—the writers of the '40's: Grigoróvitch, Gontcharóff, Turgéneff, Ostróvsky, Nekrásoff, Dostoévsky, Count
L. N. Tolstóy, and many others. With several of these
we can deal but briefly, for while they stand high in the
esteem of Russians, they are not accessible in English
translations.

Despite the numerous points which these writers of the
'40's possessed in common, and which bound them together
in one "school," this community of interests did not prevent each one of them having his own definite individuality; his own conception of the world, ideals, character,
and creative processes; his own literary physiognomy, so
to speak, which did not in the least resemble the physiognomy of his fellow-writers, but presented a complete
opposition to them in some respects. Perhaps the one
who stands most conspicuously apart from the rest in this
way is Iván Alexándrovitch Gontcharóff (1812–1890).
He was the son of a wealthy landed proprietor in the
southeastern government of Simbírsk, pictures of which
district are reproduced in his most famous novel, "Oblómoff." This made its appearance in 1858. No one who

did not live in Russia at that time can fully comprehend what an overwhelming sensation it created. It was like a bomb projected into the midst of cultivated society at the moment when every one was profoundly affected by the agitation which preceded the emancipation of the serfs (1861), when the literature of the day was engaged in preaching a crusade against slumberous inactivity, inertia, and stagnation. The special point about Gontcharóff's contribution to this crusade against the order of things, and in favor of progress, was that no one could regard "Oblómoff" from the objective point of view. Every one was compelled to treat it subjectively, apply the type of the hero to his own case, and admit that in greater or less degree he possessed some of Oblómoff's characteristics. In this romance the gift of generalization reached its highest point. Oblómoff not only represented the type of the landed proprietor, as developed by the institution of serfdom, but the racial type, which comprised the traits common to Russians in general, without regard to their social rank, class, or vocation. In fact, so typical was this character that it furnished a new word to the language, "oblómovshtchina,"—the state of being like Oblómoff. Oblómoff carried the national indolence— "khaládtnost," or dressing-gown laziness, the Russians call it in general—to such a degree that he not only was unable to do anything, but he was not able even to enjoy himself. Added to this, he was afflicted with aristocratic enervation of his faculties, unhealthy timidity, incapacity to take the smallest energetic effort, dove-like gentleness, and tenderness of soul, rendering him utterly incapable of defending his own interests or happiness in the slightest degree. And these characteristics were recognized as appertaining to Russians in general, even to those who had never owned serfs, and thus the type presented by Oblómoff may be said to be not only racial, but to a certain extent universal—one of the immortal types, like Don Quixote, Don Juan, Hamlet, and the like. The chief female character in the book, Olga, can hardly be called the heroine; she appears too briefly for that. But she is admitted to be a fine portrait of the Russian woman as she was about to become, not as she then existed. Gontcharóff's "An Every-day Story" is also celebrated; equally so is his "The Ravine," a very distressing picture of the unprincipled character of an anarchist. As the author changed his mind about the hero in part while writing the book, it is not convincing.

Another of the men who made his mark at this time was Dmítry Vasílievitch Grigoróvitch (born in 1812), who wrote a number of brilliant books between 1847–1855. His chief merit is that he was the first to begin the difficult study of the common people; the first who talked in literature about the peasants, their needs, their virtues, their helplessness, their misfortunes, and their sufferings. Of his early short stories, "Antón Goremýka" (wretched fellow) is the best. In it he is free from the reproach which was leveled at his later and more ambitious long stories, "The Emigrants" and "The Fishermen." In the latter, for the sake of lengthening the tale, and of enlisting interest by making it conform to the general taste of readers, he made the interest center on a love-story, in which the emotions and procedure were described as being like those in the higher walks of life; and this did not agree with the facts of the case. But the remainder of the stories are founded on a genuine study of peasant ways and feelings. Grigoróvitch had originally devoted himself to painting, and after 1855 he returned to that profession, but between 1884–1898 he again began to publish stories.

Among the writers who followed Grigoróvitch in his studies of peasant life, was Iván Sergyévitch Turgéneff (1818–1883), who may be said not only to have produced the most artistic pictures of that sphere ever written by a Russian, but to have summed up in his longer novels devoted to the higher classes, in a manner not to be surpassed, and in a language and style as polished and brilliant as a collection of precious stones—a whole obscure period of changes and unrest. He was descended from an ancient noble family, and his father served in a cuirassier regiment. On the family estate in the government of Orel * (where, later in life, he laid the scene of his famous "Notes of a Sportsman"), he was well provided with teachers of various nationalities—Russian excepted. One of his mother's serfs, a man passionately fond of reading, and a great admirer of Kheraskóff, was the first to initiate the boy into Russian literature, with "The Rossiad." In 1834 Turgéneff entered the Moscow University, but soon went to St. Petersburg, and there completed his course in the philological department. Before he graduated, however, he had begun to write, and even to publish his literary efforts. After spending two years in Berlin, to finish his studies, he returned to Moscow, in 1841, and there made acquaintance with the Slavyanophils—the Aksákoffs, Khomyakóff (a military man, chiefly known by his theological writings), and others, the leaders of the new cult. But Turgéneff, thoroughly imbued with western ideas, did

* Pronounced Aryól.

not embrace it. He entered the government service, although there was no necessity for his so doing, but soon left it to devote himself entirely to literature, Byelínsky having written an enthusiastic article about a poem which Turgéneff had published under another name. But poetry was not Turgéneff's strong point, any more than was the drama, though he wrote a number of plays later on, some of which have much merit, and are still acted occasionally. He found his true path in 1846, when the success of his first sketch from peasant life, "Khor and Kalínitch," encouraged him to follow it up with more of the same sort; the result being the famous collection "The Notes (or Diary) of a Sportsman." These, together with numerous other short stories, written between 1844–1850, won for him great and permanent literary fame.

The special strength of the "school of the '40's" consisted in its combining in one organic and harmonious whole several currents of literature which had hitherto flowed separately and suffered from one-sidedness. The two chief currents were, on the one hand, the objectivity of the Púshkin school, artistic contemplation of everything poetical in Russian life; and on the other hand, the negatively satirical current of naturalism, of the Gógol school, whose principal attention was directed to the imperfections of Russian life. To these were added, by the writers of the '40's, a social-moral movement, the fermentation of ideas, which is visible in the educated classes of Russian society in the '40's and '50's. As this movement was effected under the influence of the French literature of the '30's and '40's, of which Victor Hugo and Georges Sand were the leading exponents (whose ideas were expressed under the form of romanticism), these writers exercised the most influence on the Russian writers of the immediately succeeding period. But it must be stated that their influence was purely intellectual and moral, and not in the least artistic in character. The influence of the French romanticists on the Russian writers of the '40's consisted in the fact that the latter, imbued with the ideas of the former, engaged in the analysis of Russian life, which constitutes the strength and the merit of the Russian literature of that epoch.

Of all the Russian writers of that period, Turgéneff was indisputably the greatest. No one could have been more advantageously situated for the study of the mutual relations between landed proprietors and serfs. The Turgéneff family offered a very sharp type of old-fashioned landed-proprietor manners. Not one gentle or heartfelt trait softened the harshness of those manners, which were based wholly upon merciless despotism, and weighed oppressively not only upon the peasants, but upon the younger members of the family. Every one in the household was kept in a perennial tremor of alarm, and lived in hourly, momentary expectation of some savage punishment. Moreover, the author's father (who is depicted in the novel "First Love"), was much younger than his wife, whom he did not love, having married her for her money. His mother's portrait is to be found in "Púnin and Babúrin." Extremely unhappy in her childhood and youth, when she got the chance at last she became a pitiless despot, greedy of power, and indulged the caprices and fantastic freaks suggested by her shattered nerves upon her family, the house-servants, and the serfs. It is but natural that from such an experience as this Turgéneff should have cherished, from the time of his miserable childhood (his disagreements with his mother later in life are matters of record also), impressions which made of him the irreconcilable foe of serfdom. In depicting, in his "Notes of a Sportsman," the tyranny of the landed gentry over their serfs, he could have drawn upon his personal experience and the touching tale "Mumú;" actually is the reproduction of an episode which occurred in his home. His "Notes of a Sportsman" constitutes a noteworthy historical monument of the period, not only as a work of the highest art, but also as a protest against serfdom. In a way these stories form a worthy continuation of Gógol's "Dead Souls." In them, as in all his other stories, at every step the reader encounters not only clear-cut portraits of persons, but those enchanting pictures of nature for which he is famous.

The publication of his short sketches from peasant life in book form—"Notes of a Sportsman"—aroused great displeasure in official circles; officialdom looked askance upon Turgéneff because also of his long residence abroad. Consequently, when, in 1852, he published in a Moscow newspaper a eulogistic article on Gógol (when the latter died), which had been prohibited by the censor in St. Petersburg, the authorities seized the opportunity to punish him. He was arrested and condemned to a month in jail, which the daughter of the police-officer who had charge of him, contrived to convert into residence in their quarters, where Turgéneff wrote "Mumú"; and to residence on his estate, which he was not allowed to leave for about two years. In 1855 he went abroad, and thereafter he spent most of his time in Paris, Baden-Baden (later in Bougival), returning from time to time to his Russian estate. During this period his talent attained its zenith, and he wrote all the most noteworthy works which assured him fame: "Rúdin," "Faust," "A Nest of Nobles," "On the Eve," and "First Love," which alone would have sufficed to immortalize him. In 1860 he published an article entitled "Hamlet and Don Quixote," which throws a brilliant light upon the characters of all his types, and upon their inward springs of action. And at last, in 1862, came his famous "Fathers and Children." The key to the comprehension of his works is contained in his "Hamlet and Don Quixote." His idea is that in these two types are incarnated all the fundamental, contrasting peculiarities of the human race—both poles of the axis upon which it revolves—and that all people belong, more or less, to one of these two types; that every one of us inclines to be either a Hamlet or a Don Quixote. "It is true," he adds, "that in our day the Hamlets have become far more numerous than the Don Quixotes, but the Don Quixotes have not died out, nevertheless." Such is his hero "Rúdin," that central type of the men of the '40's—a man whose whole vocation consists in the dissemination of enlightening ideas, but who, at the same time, exhibits the most complete incapacity in all his attempts to realize those ideas in practice, and scandalous pusillanimity when there is a question of any step which is, in the slightest degree, decisive—a man of the head alone, incapable of doing anything himself, because he has no nature, no blood. Such, again, is Lavrétzky ("A Nest of Nobles"), that concentrated type, not only of the man from the best class of the landed gentry, but in general, of the educated Slavonic man—a man who is sympathetic in the highest degree, full of tenderness, of gentle humanity and kindliness, but who, at the same time, does not contribute to life the smallest active principle, who passively yields to circumstances, like a chip borne on the stormy torrent. Such are the majority of Turgéneff's heroes, beginning with the hero of "Ásya," and ending with Sánin, in "Spring Floods," and Litvínoff, in "Smoke." Several Don Quixotes are to be found in his works, but not many, and they are of two sorts. One typically Russian category includes Andréi Kólosoff, and Yákoff Pásinkoff, Púnin, and a few others; the second are Volýntzeff and Uvár Ivánovitch, in "On the Eve." A third type, invented by Turgéneff as an offset to the Hamlets, is represented by Insároff in "On the Eve."

With the publication, in 1862, of "Fathers and Children," a fateful crisis occurred in Turgéneff's career. In his memoirs and in his letters he insists that in the character of Bazároff he had no intention of writing a caricature on the young generation, and of bearing himself in a negative manner towards it. "My entire novel," he writes, "is directed against the nobility as the leading class." Nevertheless, the book raised a tremendous storm. His mistake lay in not recognizing in the new type of men depicted under the character of Bazároff enthusiasts endowed with all the merits and defects of people of that sort; but on the contrary, they impressed him as skeptics, rejecters of all conventions, and he christened them with the name of "nihilists," which was the cause of the whole uproar, as he himself admitted. But he declares that he employed the word not as a reproach, or with the aim of insulting, but merely as an accurate and rational expression of an historical fact, which had made its appearance.

Turgéneff always regarded himself as a pupil of Púshkin, and a worthy pupil he was, but he worked out his

own independent style, and in turn called forth a horde of
imitators. It may be said of Turgéneff, that he created
the artistic Russian novel, carrying it to the pitch of perfection in the matter of elegance, and finely proportioned
exposition and arrangement of its parts—its architecture,
so to speak—combined with artless simplicity and realism.
The peculiarity of Turgéneff's style consists in the remarkable softness and tenderness of its tones, combined with
a certain mistiness of coloring, which recalls the air and
sky of central Russia. Not a single harsh or coarse line
is to be found in Turgéneff's work; not a single glaring
hue. The objects depicted do not immediately start forth
before you, in full proportions, but are gradually depicted
in a mass of small details with all the most delicate shades.
Turgéneff is most renowned artistically for the landscapes
which are scattered through his works, and principally
portray the nature of his native locality, central Russia.
Equally famous, and executed with no less mastery and
art, are his portrayal and analysis of the various vicissi-
tudes of the tender passion, and in this respect, he was
regarded as a connoisseur of the feminine heart. A
special epithet, "the bard of love," was often applied to
him. Along with a series of masculine types, Turgéneff's
works present a whole gallery of Russian women of the
'50's and '60's, portrayed in a matchless manner with the
touch of absolute genius. And it is a fact worth noting
that in his works, as in those of all the "authors of the
'40's," the women stand immeasurably higher than the
men. The heroines are frequently set forth in all their
moral grandeur, as though with the express intention of
overshadowing the insignificance of the heroes who are
placed beside them.

Towards the beginning of the '60's, the germs of pessimism began to make their appearance in Turgéneff's work, and its final expression came in "Poems in Prose." The source of this pessimism must be sought in his whole past, beginning with the impressions of his childhood, and the disintegrating influence of the reaction of the '50's, when the nation's hopes of various reforms seemed to have been blighted, and ending with a whole mass of experiences of life and the literary failures and annoyances which he underwent during the second half of his life. And in this connection it must not be forgotten that the very spirit of analysis and skepticism wherewith the school of writers of the '40's is imbued, leads straight to pessimism, like any other sort of skepticism.

The following specimen, from "The Notes of a Sportsman," is selected chiefly for its comparative brevity:

"THE WOLF."

I was driving from the chase one evening alone in a racing gig.* I was about eight versts from my house; my good mare was stepping briskly along the dusty road, snorting and twitching her ears from time to time; my weary dog never quitted the hind wheels, as though he were tied there. A thunderstorm was coming on. In front of me a huge, purplish cloud was slowly rising from behind the forest; overhead, and advancing to meet me, floated long, gray clouds; the willows were rustling and whispering with apprehension. The stifling heat suddenly gave way to a damp chill; the shadows swiftly thickened. I slapped the reins on the horse's back, descended into a ravine, crossed a dry brook, all overgrown with scrub-willows, ascended the hill, and drove into the forest. The road in front of me wound along among thick clumps of hazel-bushes, and was already inundated with gloom; I advanced with difficulty. My

* This vehicle, which is also the best adapted as a convenient runabout for rough driving in the country, consists merely of a board, attached, without a trace of springs, to two pairs of wheels, identical in size.

gig jolted over the firm roots of the centenarian oaks and lindens, which incessantly intersected the long, deep ruts—the traces of cart-wheels; my horse began to stumble. A strong wind suddenly began to drone up above, the trees grew turbulent, big drops of rain clattered sharply, and splashed on the leaves, the lightning and thunder burst forth, the rain poured in torrents. I drove at a foot-pace, and was speedily compelled to halt; my horse stuck fast. I could not see a single object. I sheltered myself after a fashion under a wide-spreading bush. Bent double, with my face wrapped up, I was patiently awaiting the end of the storm, when, suddenly, by the gleam of a lightning-flash, it seemed to me that I descried a tall figure on the road. I began to gaze attentively in that direction—the same figure sprang out of the earth as it were beside my gig.

"Who is this?" asked a sonorous voice.

"Who are you yourself?"

"I 'm the forester here."

I mentioned my name.

"Ah, I know; you are on your way home?"

"Yes. But you see what a storm—"

"Yes, it is a thunderstorm," replied the voice. A white flash of lightning illuminated the forester from head to foot; a short, crashing peal of thunder resounded immediately afterwards. The rain poured down with redoubled force.

"It will not pass over very soon," continued the forester.

"What is to be done?"

"I'll conduct you to my cottage if you like," he said, abruptly.

"Pray do."

"Please take your seat."

He stepped to the mare's head, took her by the bit, and turned her from the spot. We set out. I clung to the cushion of the drózhky, which rocked like a skiff at sea, and called the dog. My poor mare splashed her feet heavily through the mire, slipped, stumbled; the forester swayed from right to left in front of the shafts like a specter. Thus we proceeded for rather a long time. At last my guide came to a halt. "Here we are at home, master," he said, in a calm voice.

A wicket gate squeaked, several puppies began to bark all together. I raised my head, and by the glare of the lightning, I descried a tiny hut, in the center of a spacious yard, surrounded with wattled hedge. From one tiny window a small light cast a dull gleam. The forester led the horse up to the porch, and knocked at the door. " Right away! right away!" resounded a shrill little voice, and the patter of bare feet became audible, the bolt screeched, and a little girl, about twelve years of age, clad in a miserable little chemise, girt about with a bit of list, and holding a lantern in her hand, made her appearance on the threshold.

" Light the gentleman," he said to her:—"and I will put your carriage under the shed."

The little lass glanced at me, and entered the cottage. I followed her. The forester's cottage consisted of one room, smoke-begrimed, low-ceiled and bare, without any sleeping-shelf over the oven, and without any partitions; a tattered sheepskin coat hung against the wall. On the wall-bench hung a single-barreled gun; in the corner lay scattered a heap of rags; two large pots stood beside the oven. A pine-knot was burning on the table, sputtering mournfully, and on the point of dying out. Exactly in the middle of the room hung a cra-dle, suspended from the end of a long pole. The little maid extinguished the lantern, seated herself on a tiny bench, and began to rock the cradle with her left hand, while with her right she put the pine-knot to rights. I looked about me, and my heart grew sad within me; it is not cheerful to enter a peasant's hut by night. The baby in the cradle was breathing heavily and rapidly.

" Is it possible that thou art alone here?" I asked the little girl.

"Yes," she uttered, almost inaudibly.

" Art thou the forester's daughter? "

"Yes," she whispered.

The door creaked, and the forester stepped across the threshold, bending his head as he did so. He picked up the lantern from the floor, went to the table, and ignited the wick.

"Probably you are not accustomed to a pine-knot," he said, as he shook his curls.

I looked at him. Rarely has it been my fortune to behold such a fine, dashing fellow. He was tall of stature, broad-shouldered, and splendidly built. From beneath his dripping shirt, which was open on the breast, his mighty muscles stood prominently forth. A curly black beard covered half of his surly and manly face; from beneath his broad eyebrows, which met over his nose, small, brown eyes gazed bravely forth. He set his hands lightly on his hips, and stood before me.

I thanked him, and asked his name.

"My name is Fomá," he replied—"but my nickname is "The Wolf."*

"Ah, are you The Wolf?"

I gazed at him with redoubled curiosity. From my Ermolái and from others I had often heard about the forester, The Wolf, whom all the peasants round about feared like fire. According to their statements, never before had there existed in the world such a master of his business. "He gives no one a chance to carry off trusses of brushwood, no matter what the hour may be; even at midnight, he drops down like snow on one's head, and you need not think of offering resistance—he's as strong and as crafty as the Devil. . . . . And it's impossible to catch him by any means; neither with liquor nor with money; he won't yield to any allurement. More than once good men have made preparations to put him out of the world, but no, he doesn't give them a chance."

That was the way the neighboring peasants expressed themselves about The Wolf.

"So thou art The Wolf," I repeated. "I've heard of you, brother. They say that thou givest no quarter to any one."

"I perform my duty," he replied, surlily; "it is not right to eat the master's bread for nothing."

He pulled his axe from his girdle, sat down on the floor, and began to chop a pine-knot.

"Hast thou no housewife?" I asked him.

* In the government of Orel (pronounced Aryól) a solitary, surly man is called a wolf-*biriúk*.

"No," he replied, and brandished his axe fiercely.

"She is dead, apparently."

"No—yes—she is dead," he added, and turned away.

I said nothing; he raised his eyes and looked at me.

"She ran away with a petty burgher who came along," he remarked, with a harsh smile. The little girl dropped her eyes; the baby waked up and began to cry; the girl went to the cradle. "There, give it to him," said The Wolf, thrusting into her hand a soiled horn.* "And she abandoned him," he went on, in a low tone, pointing at the baby. He went to the door, paused, and turned round.

"Probably, master," he began, "you cannot eat our bread; and I have nothing but bread."

"I am not hungry."

"Well, suit yourself. I would boil the samovár for you. only I have no tea. . . . . I'll go and see how your horse is."

He went out and slammed the door. I surveyed my surroundings. The hut seemed to me more doleful than before, The bitter odor of chilled smoke oppressed my breathing. The little girl did not stir from her place, and did not raise her eyes, from time to time she gave the cradle a gentle shove, or timidly hitched up on her shoulder her chemise which had slipped down; her bare legs hung motionless.

"What is thy name?" I asked.

"Ulíta," she said, drooping her sad little face still lower.

The forester entered, and seated himself on the wall-bench.

"The thunderstorm is passing over," he remarked, after a brief pause; "if you command, I will guide you out of the forest."

I rose. The Wolf picked up the gun, and inspected the priming.

"What is that for?" I inquired.

"They are stealing in the forest. They're felling a tree at the Hare's Ravine," he added, in reply to my inquiring glance.

"Can it be heard from here?"

"It can from the yard."

---

* For a nursing-bottle, the Russian peasants use a cow's horn, with a cow's teat tied over the tip.

We went out together. The rain had ceased. Heavy masses of cloud were piled up in the distance, long streaks of lightning flashed forth, from time to time; but over our heads, the dark blue sky was visible; here and there, little stars twinkled through the thin, swiftly flying clouds. The outlines of the trees, besprinkled with rain and fluttered by the wind, were beginning to stand out from the gloom. We began to listen. The forester took off his cap and dropped his eyes. "The—there," he said suddenly, and stretched out his arm; "you see what a night they have chosen."

I heard nothing except the rustling of the leaves. The Wolf led my horse out from under the shed. "But I shall probably let them slip this way," he added aloud—"I'll go with you, shall I?"—"All right," he replied, and backed the horse. "We'll catch him in a trice, and then I'll guide you out. Come on."

We set out, The Wolf in advance, I behind him. God knows how he found the road, but he rarely halted, and then only to listen to the sound of the axe. "You see," he muttered between his teeth. "You hear? do you hear?" "But where?" The Wolf shrugged his shoulders. We decended into a ravine, the wind died down for an instant, measured blows clearly reached my ear. The Wolf glanced at me and shook his head. We went on, over the wet ferns and nettles. A dull, prolonged roar rang out. . . . .

"He has felled it," muttered The Wolf.

In the mean time the sky had continued to clear; it was almost light in the forest. We made our way out of the ravine at last. "Wait here," the forester whispered to me, bent over, and raising his gun aloft, vanished among the bushes. I began to listen with strained intentness. Athwart the constant noise of the wind, I thought I discerned faint sounds not far away: an axe was cautiously chopping on branches, a horse was snorting.

"Where art thou going? Halt!" the iron voice of The Wolf suddenly thundered out. Another voice cried out plaintively, like a hare. . . . . A struggle began. "Thou li-iest. Thou li-iest," repeated The Wolf, panting; "thou shalt not escape." . . . . I dashed forward in the direction of the noise, and ran to the scene of battle, stumbling at every step. Beside the felled tree on the earth the forester was moving about: he held the thief beneath him, and was engaged in tying the man's hands behind his back with his girdle. I stepped up. The Wolf rose, and set him on his feet. I beheld a peasant, soaked, in rags, with a long, disheveled beard. A miserable little nag, half-covered with a small, stiff mat, stood hard by, with the running-gear of a cart. The forester uttered not a word; the peasant also maintained silence, and merely shook his head.

"Let him go," I whispered in The Wolf's ear. "I will pay for the tree."

The Wolf, without replying, grasped the horse's foretop with his left hand; with his right he held the thief by the belt. "Come, move on, simpleton!" he ejaculated surlily.

"Take my axe yonder," muttered the peasant. "Why should it be wasted," said the forester, and picked up the axe. We started. I walked in the rear. . . . . The rain began to drizzle again, and soon was pouring in torrents. With difficulty we made our way to the cottage. The Wolf turned the captured nag loose in the yard, led the peasant into the house, loosened the knot of the girdle, and seated him in the corner. The little girl, who had almost fallen asleep by the oven, sprang up, and with dumb alarm began to stare at us. I seated myself on the wall-bench.

"Ekh, what a downpour," remarked the forester. "We must wait until it stops. Wouldn't you like to lie down?"

"Thanks."

"I would lock him up in the lumber-room, on account of your grace," he went on, pointing to the peasant, "but, you see, the bolt. . . . ."

"Leave him there, don't touch him," I interrupted The Wolf.

The peasant cast a sidelong glance at me. I inwardly registered a vow that I would save the poor fellow at any cost. He sat motionless on the wall-bench. By the light of the lantern I was able to scrutinize his dissipated, wrinkled face, his pendant, yellow eyebrows, his thin limbs. . . . . The little girl lay down on the floor, at his very feet, and fell asleep again.

The Wolf sat by the table with his head propped on his hands. A grasshopper chirped in one corner. . . . . The rain beat down upon the roof and dripped down the windows; we all maintained silence.

"Fomá Kúzmitch," began the peasant suddenly, in a dull, cracked voice: "hey there, Fomá Kúzmitch!"

"What do you want?"

"Let me go."

The Wolf made no reply.

"Let me go . . . . hunger drove me to it . . . . let me go."

"I know you," retorted the forester, grimly. "You're all alike in your village, a pack of thieves."

"Let me go," repeated the peasant. "The head clerk . . . . we're ruined, that's what it is . . . . let me go!"

"Ruined! . . . . No one ought to steal!"

"Let me go, Fomá Kúzmitch . . . . don't destroy me. Thy master, as thou knowest, will devour me, so he will."

The Wolf turned aside. The peasant was twitching all over as though racked with fever. He kept shaking his head, and he breathed irregularly.

"Let me go," he repeated with melancholy despair. "Let me go, for God's sake, let me go! I will pay, that I will, by God. By God, hunger drove me to it . . . . the children are squalling, thou knowest thyself how it is. It's hard on a man, that it is."

"All the same, don't go a-thieving."

"My horse," continued the peasant, "there's my horse, take it if you choose . . . . it's my only beast . . . . let me go!"

"Impossible, I tell thee. I also am a subordinate, I shall be held responsible. And it isn't right, either, to connive at thy deed."

"Let me go! Poverty, Fomá Kúzmitch, poverty, that's what it is . . . . let me go!"

"I know thee!"

"But let me go!"

"Eh, what's the use of arguing with you; sit still or I'll give it to you, don't you know? Don't you see the gentleman?"

The poor fellow dropped his eyes. . . . . The Wolf yawned,

and laid his head on the table. The rain had not stopped. I
waited to see what would happen.

The peasant suddenly straightened himself up. His eyes
began to blaze, and the color flew to his face. " Well, go ahead,
devour! Go ahead, oppress! Go ahead," he began, screwing up
his eyes, and dropping the corners of his lips, " go ahead,
accursed murderer of the soul, drink Christian blood, drink!"

The forester turned round.

" I'm talking to thee, to thee, Asiatic blood-drinker, to
thee!"

" Art thou drunk, that thou hast taken it into thy head to
curse!" said the forester with amazement. " Hast thou gone
crazy?"

" Drunk! . . . . It wasn't on thy money, accursed soul-
murderer, wild beast, beast, beast!"

" Akh, thou . . . . I'll give it to thee!"

" What do I care? It's all one to me—I shall perish any-
way; where can I go without a horse? Kill me—it comes to
the same thing; whether with hunger or thus, it makes no
difference. Deuce take them all: wife, children—let them all
perish. . . . . But just wait, thou shalt hear from us!"

The Wolf half-rose to his feet.

" Kill, kill—" the peasant began again in a savage voice;
" Kill, go ahead, kill . . . . ." (The little girl sprang up from
the floor, and riveted her eyes on him.) " Kill, kill!"

" Hold thy tongue!" thundered the forester, and advanced
a couple of strides.

" Enough, that will do, Fomá," I shouted—" let him alone.
. . . . Don't bother with him . . . . ."

"I won't hold my tongue," went on the unfortunate man.
" It makes no difference how he murders me. Thou soul-mur-
derer, thou wild beast, hanging is too good for thee. . . . . But
just wait. Thou hast not long to vaunt thyself! They'll
strangle thy throat for thee. Just wait a bit!"

The Wolf seized him by the shoulder. . . . . I rushed to
the rescue of the peasant.

" Don't touch us, master!" the forester shouted at me.

I did not fear his threats, and was on the point of stretching out my arm, but to my extreme amazement, with one twist, he tore the girdle from the peasant's elbow, seized him by the collar, banged his cap down over his eyes, flung open the door, and thrust him out.

"Take thyself and thy horse off to the devil!" he shouted after him; "and see here, another time I 'll . . . . "

He came back into the cottage, and began to rake over the ashes.

"Well, Wolf," I said at last, "you have astonished me. I see that you are a splendid young fellow."

"Ekh, stop that, master," he interrupted me, with vexation. "Only please don't tell about it. Now I 'd better show you your way," he added, "because you can't wait for the rain to stop."

The wheels of the peasant's cart rumbled through the yard.

"You see, he has dragged himself off," he muttered; "but I 'll give it to him! "

Half an hour later he bade me farewell on the edge of the forest.

QUESTIONS FOR REVIEW

1. At what critical period of Russian history was Gontcharóff's famous novel "Oblómoff" written?

2. Why did it furnish a new word to the Russian language?

3. What traits did this word represent?

4. What was the peculiar merit of the short stories of Grigoróvitch?

5. What was the special strength of the "School of the Forties"?

6. Give an account of the life of Turgéneff.

7. What did he try to show in "Hamlet and Don Quixote"?

8. What opposition arose to his "Fathers and Children"?

9. What are the striking features of his style?

10. What characteristics of this style are shown in "The Wolf"?

BIBLIOGRAPHY

The works of Turgéneff are easily accessible in several English translations.

CHAPTER X

The new impulse imparted to all branches of literature in Russia during the '50's and the '60's could not fail to find a reflection in the fortunes of the drama also. Nowhere is the spirit of the period more clearly set forth than in the history of the Russian theater, by the creation of an independent Russian stage.

Russian comedy had existed from the days of Sumarókoff, as we have seen, and had included such great names as Von Vízin, Griboyédoff, and Gógol. But great as were the works of these authors, they cannot be called its creators, in the true sense of the word, because their plays were like oases far apart, separated by great intervals of time, and left behind them no established school. Although Von Vízin's comedies contain much that is independent and original, they are fashioned after the models of the French stage, as is apparent at every step. "Woe from Wit" counts rather as a specimen of talented social satire than as a model comedy, and in its type, this comedy of Griboyédoff also bears the imprint of the French stage. Gógol's comedies, despite their great talent, left behind them no followers, and had no imitators. In the '30's and the '40's the repertory of the Russian theater consisted of plays which had nothing in common with "Woe from Wit," "The Inspector," or "Marriage," and the latter was rarely played. As a whole, the stage was given over to translations of sensational French melodramas and to patriotic tragedies.

The man who changed all this and created Russian drama, Alexánder Nikoláevitch Ostróvsky (1823–1886), was born in Moscow, the son of a poor lawyer, whose business lay with the merchant class of the Trans-Moscow River quarter, of the type which we meet with in Alexánder Nikoláevitch's celebrated comedies. The future dramatist, who spent most of his life in Moscow, was most favorably placed to observe the varied characteristics of Russian life, and also Russian historical types; for Moscow, in the '30's and '40's of the nineteenth century, was the focus of all Russia, and contained within its walls all the historical and contemporary peculiarities of the nation. On leaving the University (where he did not finish the course), in 1843, Ostróvsky entered the civil service in the commercial court, where he enjoyed further opportunities of enlarging his observations on the life of the Trans-Moscow quarter. In 1847 he made his first appearance in literature, with "Scenes of Family Happiness in Moscow," which was printed in a Moscow newspaper. Soon afterwards he printed, in the same paper, several scenes from his comedy "Svoí liúdi-sotchtyémsya," which may be freely translated, "It's All in the Family: We'll Settle It Among Ourselves." This gained him more reputation, and he resigned from the service to devote himself entirely to literature, as proof-reader, writer of short articles, and so forth, earning a miserably small salary. When the comedy just mentioned was printed, in 1847, it bore the title of "The Bankrupt," and was renamed in deference to the objections of the censor.

It made a tremendous commotion in Russian society, where it was read aloud almost daily, and one noted man remarked of it, "It was not written; it was born." But the Moscow merchants took umbrage at the play, made complaints in the proper quarter, and the author was placed under police supervision, while the newspapers were forbidden to mention the comedy. Naturally it was not acted. The following summary will not only indicate the reason therefor, and for the wrath of the merchants, but will also afford an idea of his style in the first comedy which was acted, his famous "Don't Seat Yourself in a Sledge Which is not Yours" ("Shoemaker, Stick to Your Last," is the English equivalent), produced in 1853, and in others:

It's All in the Family: We'll Settle It Among Ourselves.

Samsón Sílitch Bolshóff (Samson, son of Strong Big), a Moscow merchant, has a daughter, Olympiáda, otherwise known as Lípotchka.

Lípotchka has been "highly educated," according to the ideas of the merchant class, considers herself a lady, and despises her parents and their "coarse" ways. This remarkable education consists in a smattering of the customary feminine accomplishments, especial value being attached to a knowledge of French, which is one mark of the gentry in Russia.

Like all merchants' daughters who have been educated above their sphere, Lípotchka aspires to marry a noble, preferably a military man. The play opens with a soliloquy by Lípotchka, who meditates upon the pleasures of the dance.

"What an agreeable occupation these dances are! Just think how fine! What can be more entrancing? You enter an assembly, or some one's wedding, you sit down; naturally, you are all decked with flowers, you are dressed up like a doll, or like a picture in a paper; suddenly a cavalier flies up, 'Will you grant me the happiness, madam?' Well, you see if he is a man with understanding, or an army officer, you half-close your eyes, and reply, 'With pleasure!' Ah! Cha-a-arming! It is simply beyond comprehension! I no longer like to dance with students or shop-clerks. 'Tis quite another thing to distinguish yourself with military men! Ah, how delightful! How enchanting! And their mustaches, and their epaulets, and their uniforms, and some even have spurs with bells. . . . I am amazed that so many women should sit with their feet tucked up under them. Really, it is not at all difficult to learn. Here am I, who was ashamed to take a teacher. I have learned everything, positively everything, in twenty lessons. Why should not one learn to dance? It is pure superstition! Here is mama, who used to get angry because the teacher was always clutching at my knees. That was because she is not cultured. Of what importance is it? He's only the dancing-master."

Lípotchka proceeds to picture to herself that she receives a proposal from an officer, and that he thinks she is uneducated because she gets confused. She has not danced for a year and a half, and decides to practice a little. As she is dancing, her mother enters, and bids her to stop—dancing is a sin. Lípotchka refuses, and an acrimonious wrangle ensues between mother and daughter, about things in general. The mother reproaches Lípotchka for her ways, reminds her that her parents have educated her, and so forth. To this Lípotchka retorts that other people have taught her all she knows—and why have her parents refused that gentleman of good birth who has asked for her hand? Is he not a Cupid? (she pronounces it "Capid.") There is no living with them, and so forth. The female match-maker comes to inform them how she is progressing in her search for a proper match for Lípotchka, and the latter declares stoutly, that she will never marry a merchant. The match-maker, a famous figure in old Russia life, and irresistibly comic on the stage, habitually addresses her clients as, "my silver ones," "my golden ones," "my emerald ones," "my brilliant (or diamond) ones," which she pronounces "brilliant." Matters are nearly arranged for Lípotchka's marriage with a man of good birth.

Old Bolshóff, however, is represented as being in a financial position where he can take his choice between paying all his debts and being thus left penniless but honest; and paying his creditors nothing, or, at most, a quarter of their dues, and remaining rich enough to indulge in the luxury of a noble son-in-law, the only motive on whose part for such a marriage being, naturally, the bride's dowry.

Old Bolshóff decides to defraud his creditors, with the aid of a pettifogging lawyer, and he makes over all his property to his clerk, Podkhaliúzin. The latter has long sighed for Lípotchka, but his personal repulsiveness, added to his merchant rank, has prevented his ever daring to hint at such a thing. Now, however, he sees his chance. He promises the legal shyster a round sum if he will arrange matters securely in his favor. He bribes the match-maker to get rid of the noble suitor, and to bring about his marriage with Lípotchka, promising her, in case of success, two thousand rubles and a sable-lined cloak.

Matters have gone so far that Lípotchka is gorgeously arrayed to receive her nobly born suitor, and accept him. Her mother is feasting her eyes on her adored child, in one of the intervals of her grumbling and bickering with her "ungrateful offspring," and warning the dear idol not to come in contact with the door, and crush her finery. But the match-maker announces that the man has beaten a retreat; Lípotchka falls in a swoon. Her father declares that there is no occasion for that, as he has a suitable match at hand. He calls in Podkhaliúzin, whom Lípotchka despises, and presents him, commanding his daughter to wed. Lípotchka flatly refuses. But after a private interview with the ambitious clerk, in which the latter informs her that she no longer possesses a dowry wherewith to attract a noble suitor, and in which he promises that she shall have the greatest liberty and be indulged in any degree of extravagance, she consents.

The marriage takes place. But old Bolshóff has been put in prison by his enraged creditors, while the young couple have been fitting up a new house in gorgeous style on the old merchant's money. The pettifogging lawyer comes for his promised reward. Podkhaliúzin cheats him out of it. The match-maker comes for her two thousand rubles and sable-lined cloak and gets one hundred rubles and a cheap gown. As these people depart cursing, old Bolshóff is brought in by his guard. He has come to entreat his wealthy son-in-law to pay the creditors twenty-five per cent and so release him from prison. Podkhaliúzin declares that this is impossible ; the old man has given him his instructions to pay only ten per cent, and really, he cannot afford to pay more. The old man's darling Lípotchka joins in and supports her husband's plea that they positively cannot afford more. The old man is taken back to prison, preliminary to being sent to Siberia as a fraudulent bankrupt. The young couple take the matter quite coolly until the policeman comes to carry off Podkhaliúzin to prison, for collusion. Even then the rascally ex-clerk does not lose his coolness, and when informed by the policeman—in answer to his question as to what is to become of him—that he will probably be sent to Siberia, " Well, if it is to be Siberia, Siberia let it be! What of that! People live in Siberia also. Evidently there is no escape. I am ready."

Although "Shoemaker, Stick to Your Last," the central idea of which is that girls of the merchant class will be much happier if they marry in their own class than if they wed nobles, who take them solely for their money (the usual reason for such alliances, even at the present day), had an immense success, both in Moscow and in St. Petersburg, Ostróvsky received not a penny from it. In the latter city, also, the censor took a hand, because "the nobility was put to shame for the benefit of the merchant class," and the theater management was greatly agitated when the Emperor and all the imperial family came to the first performance. But the Emperor remarked, "There are very few plays which have given me so much pleasure; it is not a play, it is a lesson."

"The Poor Bride" (written in 1852) was then put on the stage, and the author received a small payment on the spot. In 1854 "Poverty is not a Vice" appeared, and confirmed the author's standing as a writer of the first class. This play, a great favorite still, contains many presentations of old Russian customs. It was the first from which the author received a regular royalty, ranging from one-twentieth to two-thirds of the profits.

After many more comedies, all more or less noted, all more or less objected to by the censor, for various reasons, and hostility and bad treatment on the part of the theatrical authorities, Ostróvsky attained the zenith of his literary fame with his masterpiece, "Grozá" ("The Thunderstorm"). It was not until 1856, in his comedy "A Drunken Headache from Another Man's Banquet" (meaning, "to bear another's trouble"), that Ostróvsky invented the words which have passed into the language, *samodúr* and *samodúrstvo* (which mean, literally, "self-fool" and "the state of being a self-fool"). The original "self-fool" is "Tit Tititch Bruskóff (provincially pronounced "Kit Kititch" in the play), but no better example of the pig-headed, obstinate, self-complacent, vociferous, intolerable tyrant which constitutes the "self-fool" can be desired than that offered in "The Thunderstorm" by Márfa Ignátievna Kabánoff, the rich merchant's widow. She rules her son, Tíkhon, and his wife, Katerína, with a rod of iron. Her daughter, Varvára, gets along with her by consistent deceitfulness, and meets her lover, Kudryásh, whenever she pleases. Tíkhon goes off for a short time on business, and anxious to enjoy a little freedom, he persistently refuses to take his wife with him, despite her urgent entreaties. She makes the request because she feels that she is falling in love with Borís.

After his departure, Varvára takes charge of her fate

and persuades her to indulge her affection and to see Borís. Katerína eventually yields to Varvára's representations. A half-mad old lady, who wanders about attended by a couple of lackeys, has previously frightened the sensitive Katerína (who was reared amid family affection, and cannot understand or endure the tyranny of her mother-in-law) by vague predictions and threats of hell; and when a thunderstorm suddenly breaks over the assembled family, after her husband's return, and the weird old lady again makes her appearance, Katerína is fairly crazed. She thinks the terrible punishment for her wayward affections has arrived; she confesses to her husband and mother-in-law that she loves Borís. Spurned by the latter—though the husband is not inclined to attach overmuch importance to what she says, in her startled condition—she rushes off and drowns herself. The savage mother-in-law, who is to blame for the entire tragedy, sternly commands her son not to mourn for his dead wife, whom he has loved in the feeble way which such a tyrant has permitted. This outline gives hardly an idea of the force of the play, and its value as a picture of Russian manners of the old school in general, and of the merchant class (who retained them long after they were much ameliorated in other classes of society) in particular.

But Ostróvsky did not confine his dramas within narrow limits. On the contrary, they present a wonderfully broad panorama of Russian life, and attain to a universality which has been reached by no other Russian writer save Púshkin and Count L. N. Tolstóy. There are plays from prehistoric, mythical times, and historical plays, which deal with prominent epochs in the life of the nation. A great favorite, partly because of its pictures of old

Russian customs, is "The Voevóda" or "The Dream on the Volga" (1865). "Vasilísa Meléntieff" is popular for the same reasons (1868). Ostróvsky's nervous organization was broken down by the incessant toil necessary to support his family, and these historical plays were written, with others, to relieve the pressure. His dramas were given all over Russia, and he received more money from private than from the government theaters. But towards the end of his life comfort came, and during the last year of his life he was in charge of the Moscow (government) Theater. At last he was master of the Russian stage, and established a school of dramatic art on the lines laid down by himself. But the toil was too great for his shattered health, and he died in 1886. His plays are wonderfully rich as a portrait-gallery of contemporary types, as well as of historical types, and the language of his characters is one of the most surprising features of his work. It is far too little to say of it that it is natural, and fits the characters presented: in nationality, in figurativeness, in keen, unfeigned humor and wit it represents the richest treasure of the Russian speech. Only three writers are worthy of being ranked together in this respect: Púshkin, Krylóff, and Ostróvsky.

While, like all the writers of the '40's, Ostróvsky is the pupil of Gógol, he created his own school, and attained an independent position from his very first piece. His plays have only one thing in common with Gógol's—he draws his scenes from commonplace, every-day life in Russia, his characters are unimportant, every-day people. Gógol's comedies were such in the strict meaning of the word, and their object was to cast ridicule on the acting personages, to bring into prominence the absurd sides of their characters; and this aim accomplished, the heroes leave the stage without having undergone any change in their fates. With Ostróvsky's comedies it is entirely different. The author is not felt in them. The persons of the drama talk and act in defiance of him, so to speak, as they would talk and act in real life, and decided changes in their fate take place. But Ostróvsky accomplished far more than the creation of a Russian theater: he brought the stage to the highest pitch of ideal realism, and discarded all ancient traditions. The subjects of his plays are distinguished for their classic simplicity; life itself flows slowly across the stage, as though the author had demolished a wall and were exhibiting the actual life within the house. His plays, like life, break off short, after the climax, with some insignificant scene, generally between personages of secondary rank, and he tries to convince the audience that in life there are no beginnings, no endings; that there is no moment after which one would venture to place a full period. Moreover, they are "plays of life" rather than either "comedies" or "tragedies," as he chanced to label them; they are purely presentations of life. In their scope they include almost every phase of Russian life, except peasant and country life, which he had no chance to study.

For the sake of convenience we may group the other dramatic writers here. The conditions under which the Russian stage labored were so difficult that the best literary talent was turned into other channels, and the very few plays which were fitted to vie with Ostróvsky's came from the pens of men whose chief work belonged to other branches of literature. Thus Iván Sergyéevitch Turgéneff, who wrote more for the stage than other contemporary writers, and whose plays fill one volume of his collected works, distinguished himself far more in other lines. Yet several of these plays hold the first place after Ostróvsky's. "The Boarder" (1848), "Breakfast at the Marshal of Nobility's" (1849), "The Bachelor" (1849), "A Month in the Country" (1850), "The Woman from the Rural Districts" (1851) are still acted and enjoyed by the public.

Alexéi Feofiláktovitch Písemsky (best known for his "Thousand Souls" and his "Troubled Sea," romances of a depressing sort) contributed to the stage a play called "A Bitter Fate" (among others), wherein the Russian peasant appeared for the first time in natural guise without idealization or any decoration whatever.

Count Alexéi Konstantínovitch Tolstóy (1817–1875) wrote a famous trilogy of historical plays: "The Death of Iván the Terrible" (1866), "Tzar Feódor Ivánovitch" (1868), and "Tzar Borís" (1870). The above are the dates of their publication. They appeared on the stage, the first in 1876, the other two in 1899, though they had been privately acted at the Hermitage Theater, in the Winter Palace, long before that date. They are fine reading plays, offering a profound study of history, but the epic element preponderates over the dramatic element, and the characters set forth their sentiments in extremely long monologues and conversations. There have been many other dramatic writers, but none of great distinction.

Count A. K. Tolstóy stood at the head of the school of purely artistic poets who claimed that they alone were the faithful preservers of the Púshkin tradition. But in this they were mistaken. Púshkin drew his subjects from life; they shut themselves up in æsthetic contemplation of the beautiful forms of classical art of ancient and modern times, and isolated themselves from life in general. The result was, that they composed poetry of an abstract, artistically dainty, elegantly rhetorical sort, whose chief defect lay in its lack of individuality, and the utter absence of all colors, sounds, and motives by which Russian nationality and life are conveyed. The poetry of this school contains no sharply cut features of spiritual physiognomy. All of them flow together into a featureless mass of elegantly stereotyped forms and sounds.

Count A. K. Tolstóy, who enjoyed all the advantages of education and travel abroad (where he made acquaintance with Goethe), began to scribble verses at the age of six, he says in his autobiography. Born in 1817, he became Master of the Hounds at the imperial court in 1857, and died in 1875. He made his literary debut in 1842 with prose tales, and only in 1855 did he publish his lyric and epic verses in various newspapers. His best poetical efforts, beautiful as they are in external form, are characterless, and remind one of Zhúkovsky's, in that they were influenced by foreign or Russian poets—Lérmontoff, for instance. But they have not a trace of genuine, unaffected feeling, of vivid, burning passion, of inspiration. His best work is his prose historical romance, "Prince Serébryany," which gives a lively and faithful picture of Iván the Terrible, his court, and life in his day. The dramas already mentioned are almost if not equally famous in Russia, though less known abroad. "Prince Serébryany," and "War and Peace" by the former author's more illustrious cousin, Count L. N. Tolstóy, are the best historical novels in the Russian language.

Another poet of this period was Apollón Nikoláevitch Máikoff, born in 1821, the son of a well-known painter. During his first period he gave himself up to classical, bloodless poems, of which one of the most noted is "Two Worlds," which depicts the clash of heathendom and Christianity at the epoch of the fall of Rome. This poem he continued to write all his life; the prologue, "Three Deaths," begun in 1841, was not finished until 1872. To this period, also, belong "Two Judgments," "Sketches of Rome," "Anacreon," "Alcibiades," and so forth. His second and best period began in 1855, when he abandoned his cold classicism and wrote his best works: "Clermont Cathedral," "Savonarola," "Foolish Dúnya," "The Last Heathens," "Pólya," "The Little Picture," and a number of beautiful translations from Heine.

Still another poet was Afanásy Afanásievitch Shénshin, who wrote under the name of Fet. Born in 1820, he began to write at the age of nineteen. About that time, on entering the Moscow University, he experienced some difficulty in furnishing the requisite documents, whereupon he assumed the name of his mother during her first marriage—Fet. He reacquired his own name, Shénshin, in 1875, by presenting the proper documents, whereupon an imperial order restored it to him. From 1844 to 1855 he served in the army, continuing to write poetry the while. Before his death, in 1892, he published numerous volumes of poems, translations from the classics, and so forth. Less talented than Count Alexéi K. Tolstóy, Apollón Máikoff, and other poets of that school, his name, in Russian criticism, has become a general appellation to designate a poet of pure art, for he was the most typical exponent of his school. Most of his poems are short, and present a pic-

ture of nature, or of some delicate, fleeting psychical emotion, but they are all filled with enchanting, artistic charm.
His poetry is the quintessence of æsthetic voluptuousness,
such as was evolved on the soil of the sybaritism of the
landed gentry in the circles of the '40's of the nineteenth
century.

The oldest of all these worshipers of pure art was
Feódor Ivánovitch Tiútcheff (1803–1873). At the age of
seventeen he made a remarkably fine translation of some
of Horace's works. He rose to very fine positions in the
diplomatic service and at court. Although his first poems
were printed in 1826, he was not widely known until
1850–1854. His scope is not large, and he is rather weari-
some in his faultless poems. The majority of them are
rather difficult reading.

A poet who did not wholly belong to this school, but
wrote in many styles, was Yákoff Petróvitch Polónsky
(1820–1898).* Under different conditions he might have
developed fire and originality, both in his poems and his
prose romances. His best known poem is "The Grass-
hopper-Musician" (1863). He derived his inspiration
from various foreign poets, and also from many of his
fellow-countrymen. Among others, those in the spirit of
Koltzóff's national ballads are not only full of poetry and
inspiration, art and artless simplicity, but some of them
have been set to music, have made their way to the populace, and are sung all over Russia. Others, like "The
Sun and the Moon" and "The Baby's Death" are to be
found in every Russian literary compendium, and every
child knows them by heart.

*I had the pleasure of knowing Polónsky and his wife, a gifted sculptress.
He was a great favorite in society, for his charming personality, as well as
for his poetry. He served on the Committee of Foreign Censure.

But while the poetry of this period could not boast of any such great figures as the preceding period, it had, nevertheless, another camp besides that of the "pure art" advocates whom we have just noticed. At the head of the second group, which clung to the æsthetic doctrine that regarded every-day life as the best source of inspiration and contained several very talented expositors, stood Nikolái Alexyéevitch Nekrásoff (1821–1877). Nekrásoff belonged to an impoverished noble family, which had once been very wealthy, and was still sufficiently well off to have educated him in comfort. But when his father sent him to St. Petersburg to enter a military school he was persuaded to abandon that career and take a course at the University. His father was so enraged at this step that he cast him off, and the lad of sixteen found himself thrown upon his own resources. He nearly starved to death and underwent such hardships that his health was injured for life, but he did not manage to complete the University course. These very hardships contributed greatly, no doubt, to the power of his poetry later on, even though they exerted a hardening effect upon his character, and aroused in him the firm resolve to acquire wealth at any cost. Successful as his journalistic enterprises were in later life, it is known that he could not have assured himself the comfortable fortune he enjoyed from that source alone, and he is said to have won most of it at the gambling-table. This fact and various other circumstances may have exercised some influence upon the judgment of a section of the public as to his literary work. There is hardly any other Russian writer over whose merits such heated discussions take place as over Nekrásoff, one party maintaining that he was a true poet, with genuine inspiration; the other, that he was as clever with his poetry in a business sense, as he was with financial operations, and that he possessed no feeling, inspiration, or poetry.* The truth would seem to lie between these two extremes. Like all the other writers of his day—like writers in general—he was unconsciously impressed by the spirit of the time, and changed his subjects and treatment as it changed; and like every other writer, some of his works are superior in feeling and truth to others.

The most important period of his life was that from 1841 to 1845, when his talent was forming and ripening. Little is known with definiteness regarding this period, but it is certain that while pursuing his literary labors, he moved in widely differing circles of society—fashionable, official, literary, theatrical, that of the students, and others —which contributed to the truth of his pictures from these different spheres in his poems. In 1847 he was able (in company with Panáeff) to buy "The Contemporary," of which, eventually, he became the sole proprietor and editor, and with which his name is indelibly connected. When this journal was dropped, in 1866, he became the head, in 1868, of "The Annals of the Fatherland," where he remained until his death. It was during these last ten years of his life that he wrote his famous poems, "Russian Women" and "Who in Russia Finds Life Good,"

---

*I permit myself to quote from my "Russian Rambles" Count L. N. Tolstóy's opinion, in which he succinctly expressed to me the view of this second party: "There are three requisites which go to make a perfect writer. First, he must have something worth saying. Second, he must have a proper way of saying it. Third, he must have sincerity. Dickens had all three of these qualities. Thackeray had not much to say ; he had a great deal of art in saying it, but he had not enough sincerity. Dostoévsky possessed all three requisites. Nekrásoff knew well how to express himself, but he did not possess the first quality; he forced himself to say something— whatever would catch the public at the moment, of which he was a very keen judge, as he wrote to suit the popular taste, believing not at all in what he said. He had none of the third requisite."

with others of his best poems. He never lost his adoration of the critic Byelínsky, to whom he attributed his own success, as the result of judicious development of his powers.

One of the many conflicting opinions concerning him is, that he is merely a satirist, "The Russian Juvenal," which opinion is founded on his contributions to "The Whistle," a publication added, as a supplement, to "The Contemporary," about 1857. Yet his satirical verses form but an insignificant part of his writings. And although there does exist a certain monotony of gloomy depression in the tone of all his writings, yet they are so varied in form and contents that it is impossible to classify them under any one heading without resorting to undue violence. He is not the poet of any one class of society, of any one party or circle, but expresses in his poetry the thoughts of a whole cycle of his native land, the tears of all his contemporaries and fellow-countrymen. This apparently would be set down to the credit of any other man, and regarded as a proof that he kept in intimate touch with the spirit and deepest sentiments of his time, instead of being reckoned a reproach, and a proof of commercialism. Moreover, he wrote things which were entirely peculiar to himself, unknown hitherto, and which had nothing in common with the purely reflective lyricism of the '40's of the nineteenth century. These serve to complete his significance as the universal bard of his people and his age, to which he is already entitled by his celebration of all ranks and elements of society, whose fermentation constitutes the actual essence of that period.

There is one point to be noted about Nekrásoff which was somewhat neglected by the critics during his lifetime.

No other Russian poet of that day was so fond of calling attention to the bright sides of the national life, or depicted so many positive, ideal, brilliant types with such fervent, purely Schilleresque, enthusiasm as Nekrásoff. And most significant of all, his positive types are not of an abstract, fantastic character, clothed in flesh and blood of the period and environment, filled with conflicting, concrete characteristics—not one of them resembles any other. He sought and found them in all classes of society; in "Russian Women" he depicts the devoted princesses in the highest circle of the social hierarchy, with absolute truth, as faithful representatives of Russian life and Russian aristocrats, capable of abandoning their life of ease and pleasure, and with heroism worthy of the ancient classic heroines, accompanying their exiled husbands to Siberia, and there cheerfully sharing their hardships. His pictures of peasant life are equally fine; that in "Red-Nosed Frost" (the Russian equivalent of Jack Frost) is particularly famous, and the peasant heroine, in her lowly sphere, yields nothing in grandeur to the ladies of the court.

The theme of "Red-Nosed Frost" may be briefly stated in a couple of its verses, in the original meter:

> There are women in Russian hamlets
>   With a dignified calmness of face;
> With a beautiful strength in their movements,
>   With mien and glance of an empress in grace.
>
> A blind man alone could ignore them;
>   And he who can see them must say:
> "She passes—'tis as though the sun shineth!
>   She looks—'tis giving rubles away!"

A noble-minded, splendid peasant woman, who has worthily fulfilled all the duties of her hard lot, at last

becomes a widow. The manner of it; the quaint folk-
remedies employed to heal the sick man; the making of
the shroud by the bereaved wife; the digging of his grave
by his father; the funeral; all are described. The widow
drives the sledge with the coffin to the grave. On her
return home she finds that the fire is out and that there is
no wood on hand. Intrusting her two children to the
care of a neighbor, she drives off with the sledge to the
forest to cut some. As she collects the fuel, her thoughts
wander back over the past, and she sees a vision of her
life, its joys and sorrows. Just as she is about to set out
for home, she pauses, approaches a tall pine-tree with her
axe, and there Jack Frost woos and wins her, and she
remains, frozen stiff. The beauty and interest of the
poem quite escape in this (necessarily) bald summary.
The same is the case with "Russian Women." The first
poem of this is entitled "Princess Trubetzkóy." It
begins by narrating how the "Count-father" prepares the
covered traveling sledge for the Princess, who is bent
upon the long journey to Siberia, to join her husband, one
of the "Decembrists," exiled for participation in the
tumults of 1825, on the accession to the throne of Nicholas I. He spreads a thick bear-skin rug, puts in down-
pillows, hangs up a holy image (*ikóna*) in the corner,
grieving the while. After this prologue, the journey of
the devoted wife is described; the monotonous way being
spent in great part by the noble woman in vision-like
memories of her happy childhood, girlhood, and married
life. On arriving at Irkútsk she receives a visit from the
governor, an old subordinate of her father, who endeavors
by every possible means to deter her from pursuing her journey. She persists in demanding that fresh horses be put

to her sledge, and that she be allowed to proceed to the Nertchínsk mines, where her husband is. Failing to frighten her by the description of the hardships she will be compelled to endure, by telling her that she will have to live in the common ward of the prison with hundreds of prisoners, never see her husband alone, and the like, he at last informs her that she can proceed only on condition that she renounces all her rights, title, property. She demands the document on the instant and signs it, and again demands her horses. The governor (who, by pleading illness, has already detained the impatient woman a whole week) then tells her that, having renounced her rights, she must traverse the remaining eight hundred versts * on foot, like a common prisoner, and that the majority fall by the way in so doing. Her only thought is the extra time which this will require. The governor, having done his duty, tells her that she shall have her horses and sledge as before; he will assume the responsibility. She proceeds. Here the poem ends. But the second poem, entitled "Princess Volkónsky," and dated 1826–1827 carries the story further for both women. It takes the form of a tale told to her grandchildren, to whom says the Princess Volkónsky, she will bequeath flowers from her sister Muraviéff's grave (in Siberia), a collection of butterflies, the flora of Tchitá, views of that savage country, and an iron bracelet forged by their grandfather from his chains. She narrates how, at the age of seventeen, she married the Prince, a friend of her father, and the hero of many campaigns, much older than herself, who even after the wedding, is absent the greater part of the time on his military duties. Once,

* A verst is about two-thirds of a mile.

when they meet again after one of these prolonged separations, he is suddenly seized with panic, burns many documents in her presence, and takes her home to her father without, however, explaining anything. After that she hears nothing about him for many months; no letters reach her, every one professes ignorance as to his whereabouts, but assures her he is engaged in his duties. Even when her son is born he makes no sign, and all further efforts to pacify her prove useless. She goes to St. Petersburg, finds out the truth, and insists on joining her husband who, with Prince Trubetzkóy and the other noble Decembrists, is in Siberia. Every effort on the part of friends and relatives to prevent her leaving her baby and taking this step prove of no avail. She obtains the Emperor's permission, and sets out. The description of her journey is even more graphic and touching than that of Princess Trubetzkóy's. She hears on the way about the efforts which have been made to turn the latter from her purpose, and that probably the same measures will be used with her. At one point she meets the caravan which is bringing the silver from the Nertchínsk mines to the capital, and she asks the young officer in charge if the exiles are alive and well. He replies insultingly that he knows nothing about such people. But one of the peasant-soldiers of the caravan quietly gives her the desired information, and she adds, that invariably throughout her long and trying experience the peasant men have been truly sympathetic, helpful, and kind to the last degree, when their superiors were not. Efforts to turn her aside fail. She overtakes Princess Trubetzkóy, and the two friends pursue their sad journey together. On arriving in Nertchínsk, the commandant questions their right to see their husbands, refuses to recognize the Emperor's own signature, says he will send to Irkútsk for information (they had offered to go back themselves for it), and until it is received, they will not be permitted to hold communication with those whom they have come so far to see. The women resign themselves, and pass the night in a peasant hut, so small that their heads touch the wall, their feet the door. Princess Volkónsky, waking early, sets out on a stroll through the village, and comes to the mouth of the mine-shaft, guarded by a sentry. She prevails upon this sentry to let her descend, contrary to orders, and after a long and arduous passage through the rough, dripping corridors, and after running the risk of discovery by an official, and even of death (when she extinguishes her torch to escape the official, and proceeds in the dark), she reaches her husband and the other Decembrist exiles, and delivers to them the letters from their friends, which she has with her. The poem is most beautiful and affecting.

A third very famous poem is "Who in Russia Finds Life Good?" Seven peasants meet by chance on the highway, and fall into a dispute on that theme. One says, "the landed proprietor"; another, "the official"; a third, "the priest." Others say, respectively, "the fat-bellied merchant," "the minister of the empire," "the Tzar." All of the peasants had started out at midday upon important errands, but they argue hotly until sundown, walking all the while, and do not notice even that until an old woman happens along and asks them, "Where are they bound by night?" On glancing about them, the peasants perceive that they are thirty versts from home, and they are too fatigued to undertake the return journey at once. They throw the blame on the Forest-Fiend, seat themselves in the woods, and light a fire. One man goes off to procure liquor, another for food, and as they consume these, they begin the discussion all over again in such vehement wise that all the beasts and birds of the forest are affrighted. At last Pakhóm, one of the peasants, catches a young bird in his hand and says that, frail and tiny as it is, it is more mighty than a peasant man, because its wings permit it to fly whithersoever it wishes; and he beseeches the birdling to give them its wings, so that they may fly all over the empire and observe and inquire, "Who dwelleth happily and at ease in Russia?" Surely, Iván remarks, wings are not needed; if only they could be sure of half a pud (eighteen pounds) of bread a day (meaning the sour, black rye bread), they could "measure off Mother Russia" with their own legs. Another of the peasants stipulates for a vedró (two and three-quarters gallons) of vódka; another for cucumbers every morning; another for a wooden can of kvas (small beer, brewed from the rye bread, or meal) every noon; another for a teapot of boiling tea every evening. A peewit circles above them in the air, listening, then alights beside their bonfire, chirps, and addresses them in human speech. She promises that if they will release her offspring she will give them all they desire. The compact is made; she tells them where to go in the forest and dig up a coffer containing a "self-setting table-cloth," which will carry them all over the country at their behest. They demand, in addition, that they shall be fed and clothed; granted. They get the carpet; their daily supply of food appears from its folds, on demand (they may double, but not treble the allowance), and they vow not to return to their families until they shall have succeeded in their quest of a happy man in Russia. Their first encounter is with a priest, who in response to their questions, asks if happiness does not consist in "peace, wealth, and honor?" He then describes his life, and demonstrates that a priest gets none of these things. As they proceed on their way, they meet and interrogate people from all ranks and classes. This affords the poet an opportunity for a series of pictures from Russian life, replete with national characteristics, stories, arguments, songs, described in varying meters. The whole forms a splendid and profoundly interesting national picture-gallery.

The movements of the '40's and the '60's brought to the front several poets who sprang directly from the people. On the borderland of the two epochs stands the most renowned of Little Russian poets, Tarás Grigórievitch Shevtchénko (1814–1861). He was the contemporary of Koltzóff and Byelínsky, rather than of Nekrásoff; nevertheless, he may be regarded as a representative of the latter's epoch, in virtue of the contents and the spirit of his poetry.

His history is both interesting and remarkable. He was the son of a serf, in the government of Kíeff. When he was eight years old his mother died, and his father married again. His stepmother favored her own children, and to constant quarrels between the two broods, incessant altercation between the parents was added. At the age of eleven, when his father died, he began a roving life. He ran away from a couple of ecclesiastics who had undertaken to teach him to read and write (after having acquired the rudiments of those arts), and made numerous ineffectual attempts to obtain instruction in painting from

various wretched daubers of holy pictures, having been
addicted, from his earliest childhood, to scrawling over
the walls of the house and the fences with charcoal draw-
ings. He was obliged to turn shepherd. In 1827 he was
taken on as one of his master's household servants, and
sent to Vílna, where at first he served as scullion.
Later on, it was decided that he "was fitted to become
the household painter."

But he served at first as personal attendant on his
master and handed him a light for his pipe, until his master caught him one night drawing a likeness of Kazák
Plátoff, whereupon he pulled Shevtchénko's ears, cuffed
him, ordered him to be flogged, but simultaneously acquired
the conviction that the lad might be converted into a
painter to the establishment. So Shevtchénko began to
study under a Vílna artist, and a year and a half later, by
the advice of his teacher, who recognized his talent, the
master sent the lad to a portrait-painter in Warsaw. In
1831 he was sent to his master in St. Petersburg on foot
by the regular police "stages" (*étape*), arriving almost
shoeless, and acted as lackey in the establishment. At
last his master granted his urgent request, and apprenticed
him for four years to an instructor in painting. Here
Shevtchénko made acquaintance with the artist I. M.
Sóshenko, and through him with an author of some little
note, who took pity on the young fellow's sorry plight, and
began to invite him to his house, give him books to read,
furnish him with various useful suggestions, and with
money. Thus did Shevtchénko come to know the Russian and western classical authors, history, and so forth.
Through Sóshenko's agency, the aid of the secretary of
the Academy of Arts was invoked to rescue the young

man from his artist master's intolerable oppression, and his literary friend introduced Shevtchénko to Zhukóvsky, who took an ardent interest in the fate of the talented young fellow. They speedily began operations to free Shevtchénko from serfdom; and the manner in which it was finally affected is curious. A certain general ordered a portrait of himself from Shevtchénko for which he was to pay fifty rubles. The general was not pleased with the portrait, and refused to accept it. The offended artist painted the general's beard over with a froth of shaving-soap, and sold the picture for a song to the barber who was in the habit of shaving the general, and he used it as a sign. The general flew into a rage, immediately purchased the portrait, and with a view to revenging himself on the artist, he offered the latter's master a huge sum for him. Shevtchénko was so panic-stricken at the prospect of what awaited him, that he fled for aid to the artist Briulóff, entreating the latter to save him. Briulóff told Zhukóvsky, and Zhukóvsky repeated the story to the Empress Alexándra Feódorovna, wife of Nicholas I. Shevtchénko's master was ordered to stop the sale. The Empress then commanded Briulóff to complete a portrait of her which he had begun, and she put it up as the prize in a lottery among the members of the imperial family for the sum of ten thousand rubles—the price offered for Shevtchénko by the enraged general. Shevtchénko thus received his freedom in May, 1838, and immediately began to attend the classes in the Academy of Arts, and speedily became one of Briulóff's favorite pupils and comrades.

In 1840 he published his "Kobzár" * which made an

* The player on the Little Russian twelve-stringed guitar, the Kóbza, literally translated.

impression in Little Russia.   In 1842 he began the publication of his famous poem, "The Haïdamák" (A Warrior of Ancient Ukráina).   In 1843 he was arrested and sent back to Little Russia, where he lived until 1847, and during this period his talent bore its fairest blossoms, and his best works appeared: "The Banquet of the Dead," "The Hired Woman," "The Dream," "The Prisoner," "Iván Gus" (the goose), "The Cold Hillside," and so forth.   His literary fame reached its zenith, and brought with it the friendship of the best intellectual forces of southern Russia, and with the aid of Princess Ryépnin (cousin to the minister of public education) and Count Uvároff, he obtained the post of drawing-master in Kíeff University.   But in 1847 some one overheard and distorted a conversation in which Shevtchénko and several friends had taken part, the result being that all were arrested, while Shevtchénko, after being taken to St. Petersburg, was sent to the Orenburg government in the far southeast, to serve as a common soldier in the ranks, and was forbidden to paint or to write.   There he remained for ten years, when he returned to the capital, and settled down at the Academy of Arts, where he was granted a studio, in accordance with his right as an academician.   He never produced anything of note in the literary line thereafter, and the last three years of his life were chiefly devoted to releasing his relatives from serfdom, and furnishing them with land for cottages, which object he accomplished a few months before the general emancipation of the serfs.

In the work of Shevtchénko it is possible to follow the curious transformation from what may be called the collective-folk creative power, to the purely individual.   His figures, subjects, and the quiet, heart-rending sadness of his poems are precisely the same as those to be met with in any Little Russian folk-ballad. The majority of his poems are not inventions, but are taken directly from popular legends and traditions, and the personality of the poet vanishes in a flood of purely popular poetry. Nevertheless, he is not a slavish copyist of this folk-poetry. The language of his compositions is strikingly simple, and comprehensible not only to native-born Little Russians, but also to those who are not acquainted with the dialect of that region. Most writers who have employed the Little Russian dialect are difficult of comprehension not only to educated Great Russians, but also to ordinary Little Russians, because their language is artificial, intermingled with a mass of new words and expressions invented in educated circles of Little Russia. But Shevtchénko wrote in the living tongue of the Ukráina, in which its people talk and sing. His best work, after he came under the influence of Zhukóvsky, is "The Hired Woman." This is the story of a girl who is betrayed, then forced by outsiders to abandon her child, after which she hires herself out as servant to the people at whose door she has left the child, and so is enabled to rear it, only revealing the secret to her child on her deathbed.

The sufferings of the people in serfdom form the subject of another series of his poems, and in this category, "Katerina" is the best worked out and most dramatic of his productions. A third category comprises the historical ballads, in which he celebrates the days of kazák freedom. This class comprises two long poems, "The Haïdamák" (The Kazák Warrior of Ancient Ukráina) and "Gamáliya," besides a number of short rhapsodies. In these poems

the writer has expressed his political and social views, and
they are particularly prized by his fellow-landsmen of the
Ukráina. The fourth (or, in the order of their appearance,
the first) class of Shevtchénko's poems consists of ballads
in the folk-style, and sentimental, romantic pieces, which
have no political or social tendencies. Such are the ballads, "The Cause," "The Drowned Woman," "The
Water Nymph," "The Poplar Tree," which he wrote in
St. Petersburg on scraps of paper in the summer garden.

Of less talent and importance was a fellow-citizen of
Koltzóff, Ivan Sávitch Nikítin (1824–1861). Perhaps the
most interesting thing about him is that Count L. N.
Tolstóy took a lively interest in this gifted plebeian, and
offered to bear the cost of publishing his poems, regarding
him as a new Koltzóff. Count Tolstóy has since arrived
at the conclusion that all poetry is futile and an unnecessary waste of time, as the same ideas can be much better
expressed in prose, and with less labor to both writer and
reader.

The poet from the educated classes of society who
deserves the most attention as a member of Nekrásoff's
camp, is Alexyéi Nikoláevitch Pleshtchéeff (1825–1893),
the descendant of an ancient family of the nobility. In
1849 he was arrested for suspected implication in what is
known as "The Petrashévsky Affair" (from the name of
the leader), and imprisoned in the Peter-Paul Fortress.
Together with Dostoévsky and nineteen others he was
condemned to be shot, but all the prisoners were pardoned
by the Emperor (the charge was high treason) at the last
moment, and after spending nine months in the fortress,
Pleshtchéeff was sent to serve as a common soldier in the
troops of the line, in the Orenburg government, with the

loss of all his civil rights.   There he remained nine years,
taking part in several border campaigns, and rising to the
rank of ensign, after which he entered the civil service.
In 1859 he was allowed to return to Moscow, whence he
removed to St. Petersburg in 1872.*

The principal writers of satirical verse during this
period were: Alexyéi Mikháilovitch Zhemtchúzhnikoff
(1822), V. S. Kúrotchkin (1831-1875), who founded the
extremely popular journal "The Spark," in 1859, and
D. D. Mináeff (1835-1889).

* I saw him, a majestic old man, surrounded by an adoring throng of
students and young men, at one of the requiem services for M. E. Saltykóff
(Shtchedrín), in the Kazán Cathedral, St. Petersburg, in April, 1889.

QUESTIONS FOR REVIEW

1. What had been the progress of the drama in Russia up
to the time of Ostróvsky?

2. How did " It Is All in the Family " make its appearance,
and with what result?

3. What especial value has the play " The Thunderstorm " ?

4. What variety of subjects are treated in Ostróvsky's
plays?

5. Why does his work rank so high?

6. What plays by Turgéneff hold the next place to Ostróvsky's?

7. What are the best historical novels in the Russian
language?

8. What was the character of the poetry of this period?

9. What ballads by Polónsky have a national reputation?

10. Give the chief events in the life of Nekrásoff.

11. What hostile criticism have his works received?

12. What may be said in his favor?

13. What is the story of " Red-Nosed Frost"?

14. What pictures of Russian society are given in " Russian
Women "?

15. How is the poet's wide knowledge shown in his poem "Who in Russia Finds Life Good"?

16. Give an account of the eventful career of Shevtchénko.

17. What are the noteworthy features of his poetry?

BIBLIOGRAPHY

The Thunderstorm. Ostróvsky.

Prince Serébryany; The Death of Ivan the Terrible. Count Alexéi K. Tolstóy.

Red-Nosed Frost. N. A. Nekrásoff.

CHAPTER XI

DOSTOÉVSKY

All the writers of the '40's of the nineteenth century had their individual peculiarities. But in this respect, Feódor Mikháilovitch Dostoévsky (1821–1886) was even more sharply separated from all the rest by his characteristics, which almost removed him from the ranks of the writers of the epoch, and gave him a special place in literature.

The chief cause of this distinction lies in the fact that while most of the other writers sprang from the country regions, being members of the landed gentry class, Dostoévsky represents the plebeian, toiling class of society, a nervously choleric son of the town; and in the second place, while the majority of them were well-to-do, Dostoévsky alone in the company belonged to the class of educated strugglers with poverty, which had recently made its reappearance.

His father was staff physician in the Márya Hospital in Moscow, and he was the second son in a family of seven children. The whole family lived in two rooms, an ante-room and kitchen, which comprised the quarters allotted to the post by the government. Here strictly religious and patriarchal customs reigned, mitigated by the high cultivation of the head of the family.

In 1837 Feódor Mikháilovitch and his elder brother were taken to St. Petersburg by their father to be placed

in the School for Engineers, but the elder did not succeed
in entering, on account of feeble health. Dostoévsky had
already evinced an inclination for literature, and naturally
he was not very diligent in his studies of the dry, applied
sciences taught in the school. But he found time to make
acquaintance with the best works of Russian, English,
French, and German classical authors. In 1843 he completed his course, and was appointed to actual service in
the draughting department of the St. Petersburg engineer
corps.

With his salary and the money sent to him by his
guardian (his father being dead), he had about five thousand rubles a year, but as he was extremely improvident,
bohemian, and luxurious in his tastes, he could never make
both ends meet. He was still more straitened in
his finances when, in 1844, he resigned from the service,
which was repugnant to him, and utterly at variance with
his literary proclivities, and was obliged to resort to
making translations. In May, 1844, he completed his
first romance, "Poor People," and sent it to Nekrásoff
by his school-friend Grigoróvitch. In his "Diary" Dostoévsky has narrated the manner of its reception by Nekrásoff (who was preparing to publish a collection), and by
Byelínsky, to whom the latter gave it. Grigoróvitch and
Nekrásoff sat up all night to read it, so fascinated were
they, and then hastened straight to communicate their
rapture to the author. Nekrásoff then gave the manuscript to Byelínsky with the exclamation, "A new Gógol
has made his appearance!" to which Byelínsky sternly
replied, "Gógols spring up like mushrooms with you."
But when he had read the romance, he cried out, with
emotion, "Bring him, bring him to me!"

Even before the romance made its appearance in print (early in 1846), Dostoévsky had won a flattering literary reputation. The young author's head was fairly turned with his swift success, and he grew arrogant, the result of which was that he soon quarreled with Byelínsky, Nekrá-soff, and their whole circle, and published his later writings (with one exception) elsewhere than in "The Contemporary." His coolness towards the circle of "The Contemporary" was not a little aided by the difference in opinions which began to make themselves felt. Dostoévsky was carried away by the political and social ideas which reigned in that circle, but at the same time he obstinately upheld his own religious views. The result of this was, that the members of the circle began to regard him as behind the times. He became more and more interested in socialism, and soon went to live with his new friends in quarters where the principles of association ruled. He then entered the Dúroff circle of Fourierists, the most moderate of all the Petrashévsky circles, which a good authority declares to have entertained no purely revolutionary ideas whatever. They rebelled against the maintenance of the strict censorship then in force, serfdom, and administrative abuses, but paid little attention to the question of a change in the form of government, and attributed no importance to political upheavals. Dostoévsky himself was, in general, very far from cherishing any revolutionary designs; he enthusiastically declaimed Púshkin's verses about slavery falling "at the wave of the Tzar's hand," and insisted that no socialistic theories had the slightest importance for Russians, since in the commune, and the working unions (*artél*), and mutual guarantee system there had long existed in their land more solid and normal foundations than all the dreams of Saint Simon and his school, and that life in a community and phalanstery seemed to him more terrible and repulsive than that of any galley-slave.

Notwithstanding this, in May, 1849, Dostoévsky was arrested, along with the other followers of Petrashévsky, confined in the fortress, and condemned by court-martial on the charge of having "taken part in discussions concerning the severity of the censorship, and in one assembly, in March, 1849, had read a letter from Byelínsky to Gógol, received from Pleshtchéeff in Moscow, and had then read it aloud in the assemblies at Dúroff's, and had given copies of it to Mombelli to copy. In the assemblies at Dúroff's he had listened to the reading of articles, knew of the intention to set up a printing-press, and at Spyéshneff's had listened to the reading of 'A Soldier's Conversation.'"

All the Petrashévskyians were condemned to be shot, and the sentence was read to them on January 3, 1850, on the scaffold, where they stood stripped, in the freezing cold, for twenty minutes, in momentary expectation of their execution. But the death sentence was mitigated in different degrees by the Emperor, Dostoévsky's sentence being commuted to exile with hard labor for four years, and then service as a common soldier in the ranks. He was dispatched to Siberia two days later, which was on Christmas Eve, according to the Russian reckoning.

The wives of the Decembrists (the men exiled for revolutionary plots in 1825, at the accession to the throne of the Emperor Nicholas I.), visited the Petrashévskyians in prison at Tobólsk and gave Dostoévsky a copy of the Gospels. No other book made its way within the prison walls, and after reading nothing else for the next three years, Dostoévsky, according to his own words, "forced by necessity to read the Bible only, was enabled more clearly and profoundly to grasp the meaning of Christianity." In his "Notes from a Dead House" he has described in detail his life in the prison at Omsk, and all his impressions. Prison life produced an extremely crushing and unfavorable impression on him. He was brought into close contact with the common people, was enabled to study them, but he also became thoroughly imbued with that spirit of mysticism which is peculiar to ignorant and illiterate people. His own view of the universe was that of childlike faith, and prison life strengthened this view by leading him to see in it the foundation of the national spirit and the national life. During the last year of his prison life, under a milder commandant, he was able to renew his relations with former schoolmates and friends in the town, and through them obtain more money, write home, and even come into possession of books.

But his health was much affected, his nerves having been weak from childhood, and already so shattered that, in 1846, he was on the verge of insanity. Even at that time he had begun to have attacks by night of that "mystical terror," which he has described in detail in "Humiliated and Insulted," and he also had occasional epileptic fits. In Siberia epilepsy developed to such a point that it was no longer possible to entertain any doubt as to the character of his malady.

On leaving prison, in 1854, and becoming a soldier, Dostoévsky was much better off. He was soon promoted to the rank of ensign, wrote a little, planned "Notes from a Dead House," and in 1856 married. At last, after prolonged efforts, he received permission to return to

European Russia, in July, 1859, and settled in Tver. In the winter of that year, his rights, among them that of living in the capital, were restored to him, and in 1861 he and his elder brother began to publish a journal called "The Times." The first number contained the first installment of "Humiliated and Insulted," and simultaneously, during 1861–1862, "Notes from a Dead House" appeared there also, in addition to critical literary articles from his pen. This and other editorial and journalistic ventures met with varying success, and he suffered many reverses of fortune. In 1865–1866 he wrote his masterpiece, "Crime and Punishment." His first wife having died, he married his stenographer, in 1867, and traveled in western Europe for the next four years, in the course of which he wrote his romances: "The Idiot" (1868), "The Eternal Husband" (1870), and "Devils" (1871–72). After his return to Russia he wrote (1875) "The Stripling," and (1876) began the publication of "The Diary of a Writer," which was in the nature of a monthly journal, made up of his own articles, chiefly of a political character, and bearing on the Serbo-Turkish War. But it also contained literary and autobiographical articles, and had an enormous success, despite the irregularity of its appearance.

In June, 1880, he delivered a speech before the Society of Lovers of Russian Literature, which won him such popularity as he had never before enjoyed, and resulted in a tremendous ovation, on the part of the public, at the unveiling of the monument to Púshkin. He was besieged with letters and visits; people came to him incessantly from all parts of St. Petersburg and of Russia, with expressions of admiration, requests for aid, questions, complaints against others, and expressions of opinions hostile to him personally. In the last half of 1880 he finished "The Karamázoff Brothers." His funeral, on February 15, 1881, was very remarkable; the occasion of an unprecedented "manifestation," which those who took part in it are still proud of recalling. Forty-two deputations bearing wreaths and an innumerable mass of people walked miles after his coffin to the cemetery of the Alexander Névsky Monastery.

Under the various influences to which Dostoévsky was subjected, he eventually became what is known in Russia as "a native-soiler," in literature—the leader, in fact, of that semi-Slavyánophil, semi-Western school—and towards the end of his life was converted into a genuine Slavophil and mystic. In this conversion, as well as in the mystical theories which he preached in his "Diary," and afterwards in his romances, beginning with "Crime and Punishment," Dostoévsky has something in common with Count L. N. Tolstóy. Both writers were disenchanted as to European progress, admitted the mental and moral insolvency of educated Russian society, and fell into despair, from which the only escape, so it seemed to them, was becoming imbued with the lively faith of the common people, and both authors regarded this faith as the sole means of getting into real communion with the people. Then, becoming more and more imbued with the spirit of the Christian doctrine, both arrived at utter rejection of material improvement of the general welfare; Count Tolstóy came out with a theory of non-resistance to evil by force, and Dostoévsky with a theory of moral elevation and purification by means of suffering, which in essence are identical; for in what manner does non-resistance to evil manifest itself, if not in unmurmuring endurance of the sufferings caused by evil?

Nevertheless, a profound difference exists between Count Tolstóy and Dostoévsky. In the former we see an absence of conservatism and devotion to tradition. His attitude towards all doctrines is that of unconditional freedom of thought, and subjecting them to daring criticism, he chooses from among them only that which is in harmony with the inspirations of his own reason. He is a genuine individualist, to his very marrow. By the masses of the common people, he does not mean the Russian nation only, but all the toilers and producers of the earth, without regard to nationality; while by the faith which he seeks among those toilers, he does not mean any fixed religious belief, but faith in the reasonableness and advantageousness of life, and of everything which exists, placing this faith in dependence upon brisk, healthy toil.

Dostoévsky, on the contrary, is a communist, or socialist. He cares nothing for freedom and the self-perfection of the individual. The individual, according to his teaching, should merely submit, and resignedly offer itself up as a sacrifice to society, for the sake of fulfilling that mission which Russia is foreordained, as God's chosen nation, to accomplish. This mission consists in the realization upon earth of true Christianity in orthodoxy,* to which the Russian people remain faithful and devoted; union with the common people is to be accomplished in that manner alone; like the common people, with the same boundless faith and devotion, orthodoxy must be professed, for in it

---

* Meaning the faith of the Holy Catholic Apostolic Church of the East. A great many Russians believe this. and that Russia's mission on earth is a moral and spiritual one, founded upon precisely this basis.

alone lies all salvation, not only for the world as a whole, but for every individual.

The character of Dostoévsky's works is determined by the fact that he was a child of the town. In their form they possess none of that elegant regularity, of that classical finish and clear-cut outline, which impress us in the works of Turgéneff and Gontcharóff. On the contrary, they surprise us by their awkwardness, their prolixity, their lack of severe finish, which requires abundant leisure. It is evident that they were written in haste, by a man who was eternally in want, embarrassed with debts, and incapable of making the two ends meet financially. At the same time one is struck by the entire absence in Dostoévsky's works of those artistic elements in which the works of the other authors of the '40's are rich. They contain no enchanting pictures of nature, no soul-stirring love scenes, meetings, kisses, the bewitching feminine types which turn the reader's head, for which Turgéneff and Tolstóy are famous. Dostoévsky even ridicules Turgéneff for his feminine portraits, in "Devils," under the character of the writer Karmazínoff, with his passion for depicting kisses not as they take place with all mankind, but with gorse or some such weed growing round about, which one must look up in a botany, while the sky must not fail to be of a purplish hue, which, of course, no mortal ever beheld, and the tree under which the interesting pair is seated must infallibly be orange-colored, and so forth.

Dostoévsky's subjects also present a sharp difference from those of his contemporaries, whose subjects are characterized by extreme simplicity and absence of complication, only a few actors being brought on the stage—not more than two, three, or four—and the entire plot being, as a rule, confined to the rivalry of two lovers, and to the question upon which of them the heroine will bestow her love. It is quite the contrary with Dostoévsky. His plots are complicated and entangled, he introduces a throng of acting personages. In reading his romances, one seems to hear the roar of the crowd, and the life of a town is unrolled before one, with all its bustle, its incessantly complicated and unexpected encounters, and relations of people one to another. Like a true child of the town, Dostoévsky does not confine himself to fashionable drawing-rooms, or to the educated classes; he is fond of introducing the reader to the dens of poverty and vice, which he invests, also, with their own peculiar, gloomy poetry. In his pictures of low life, he more resembles Dickens than the followers of Georges Sand of his day.

But the most essential quality of Dostoévsky's creative art is the psychical analysis, which occupies the foreground in the majority of his romances, and constitutes their chief power and value. A well-known alienist doctor, who has examined these romances from a scientific point of view, declares himself amazed by the scientific accuracy wherewith Dostoévsky has depicted the mentally afflicted. In his opinion, about one-fourth of this author's characters are more or less afflicted in this manner, some romances containing as many as three who are not normal, in one way or another. This doctor demonstrates that Dostoévsky was a great psycopathologist, and that, with his artistic insight, he anticipated even exact science. And much that he has written will certainly be incorporated in psychological text-books. It is superfluous, after such competent testimony, to insist upon the life-likeness and the truth to nature of his portraits. The effect of his books on a reader is overwhelming, even stunning and nerve-shattering.

One further point is to be noted: that notwithstanding the immense number of characters presented to the reader by Dostoévsky, they all belong to a very limited number of types, which are repeated, with slight variations, in all his romances. Thus, in conformity with the doctrine of the "native-soilers," he places at the foundation of the majority of his works one of the two following types: (1) The gentle type of the man overflowing with tender affection of utter self-sacrifice, ready to forgive everything, to justify everything, to bear himself compassionately towards the treachery of the girl he loves, and to go on loving her, even to the point of removing the obstacles to her marriage with another man, and so forth. Such is the hero of "Crime and Punishment"; such is Prince Mýshkinh in "The Idiot," and so on; (2) The rapacious type, the type of the egoist, brimming over with passion, knowing no bounds to his desires, and restrained by no laws, either human or divine. Such are: Stavrógin in "Devils," Dmítry Karamázoff ("The Karamázoff Brothers"), and so forth. His women also can be divided into two similar, contrasting types; on the one hand, the gentle—the type of the woman who possesses a heart which is tender and loving to self-abnegation, like Nelly and Natásha, in "Humiliated and Insulted"; Raskólnikoff's mother and Sónya, in "Crime and Punishment"; Nétotchka Nezvánoff, in "The Stripling." On the other hand, there are the rapacious types of capricious, charming women who are tyrannical to the point of cruelty, like Polína, in "The Gambler," Nástasya Filíppovna in "The Idiot,"

Grúshenka and Katerina Ivánovna in "The Karamázoff Brothers," and Várvara Petróvna, in "Devils."

The reactionary tendency made its appearance in Dostoévsky almost contemporaneously with its appearance in Turgéneff and Gontcharóff, unhappily. The first romance in which it presented itself was "Crime and Punishment," the masterpiece in which his talent attained its zenith. This work, in virtue of its psychical and psychological analyses, deserves to rank among the greatest and best monuments of European literary art in the nineteenth century. Unfortunately, it produced a strange impression on all reasonable people, because of the fact that the author suddenly makes the crime of his hero, Raskólnikoff, dependent upon the influence of new ideas, as though they justified crimes, committed with good objects. No less surprising is the manner in which the romance winds up with the moral regeneration of Raskólnikoff under the influence of exile with hard labor.

Dostoévsky, to be fully appreciated, requires—perhaps more than most writers—to be read at length. But the following brief extract will afford a glimpse of his manner. The extract is from the "Notes from a Dead House." Sushíloff was a prisoner who had been sent to Siberia merely for colonization, for some trifling breach of the laws. During a fit of intoxication he had been persuaded by a prisoner named Mikháiloff to exchange names and punishments, in consideration of a new red shirt and one ruble in cash. Such exchanges were by no means rare, but the prisoner to whose disadvantage the bargain redounded, generally demanded scores of rubles; hence, every one ridiculed Sushíloff for the cheap rate at which he had sold his light sentence. Had he been able to return the ruble (which he had immediately spent for liquor), he might have bought back his name, but the prisoners' artél, or guild, always insisted upon the strict fulfilment of such bargains in default of the money being refunded; and if the authorities suspected such exchanges, they did not pry into them, it being immaterial to the officials (in Siberia at least) what man served out the sentence, so long as they could make their accounts tally. Thus much in explanation abbreviated from Dostoévsky's statement.

"Sushíloff and I lived a long time together, several years in all. He gradually became greatly attached to me; I could not help perceiving this, as I had, also, become thoroughly used to him. But one day—I shall never forgive myself for it—he did not comply with some request of mine, although he had just received money from me, and I had the cruelty to say to him, 'Here you are taking my money, Sushíloff, but you don't do your duty." Sushíloff made no reply, but seemed suddenly to grow melancholy. Two days elapsed. I said to myself, it cannot be the result of my words. I knew that a certain prisoner, Anton Vasílieff, was urgently dunning him for a petty debt. He certainly had no money, and was afraid to ask me for any. So on the third day, I said to him: 'Sushíloff, I think you have wanted to ask me for money to pay Anton Vasílieff. Here it is.' I was sitting on the sleeping-shelf at the time; Sushíloff was standing in front of me. He seemed very much surprised that I should offer him the money of my own accord; that I should voluntarily remember his difficult situation, the more so as, in his opinion, he had already, and that recently, taken altogether too much from me in advance, so that he dared not hope that I would give him any more. He looked at the money, then at me, abruptly turned away and left the room. All this greatly amazed me. I followed him and found him behind the barracks. He was standing by the prison stockade with his face to the fence, his head leaning against it, and propping himself against it with his arm. 'Sushíloff, what's the matter with you?' I asked him. He did not look at me, and to my extreme surprise, I observed that he was on the verge of weeping. 'You think—Alexánder Petróvitch—'* he began, in a broken voice, as he endeavored to look another way, 'that I serve you—for money—but I—I—e-e-ekh !' Here he turned again to the fence, so that he even banged his brow against it—and how he did begin to sob ! It was the first time I had beheld a man weep in the prison. With difficulty I comforted him, and although from that day forth, he began to serve me more zealously than ever, if that were possible, and to watch over me, yet I perceived, from almost imperceptible signs, that his heart could never pardon me for my reproach ; and yet the others laughed at us, persecuted him at every convenient opportunity, sometimes cursed him violently—but he lived in concord and friendship with them and never took offense. Yes, it is sometimes very difficult to know a man thoroughly, even after long years of acquaintance!''

Dostoévsky, in all his important novels, has much to say about religion, and his personages all illustrate some phase of religious life.   This is nowhere more apparent than in his last novel, "The Karamázoff Brothers," wherein the religious note is more powerfully struck than in any of the others.   The ideal of the Orthodox Church of the East is embodied in Father Zosím, and in his gentle disciple, Alexyéi (Alyósha) Karamázoff; the reconciling power of redemption is again set forth over the guilty soul of the principal hero, Dmítry Karamázoff, when he is overtaken by chastisement for a suspected crime.   The doubting element is represented by Iván Karamázoff, who is tortured by a constant conflict with anxious questions.   In "The Legend of the Grand Inquisitor," which the author puts into Iván's mouth, Dostoévsky's famous and characteristic power of analysis reached its greatest height.

*The narrator, in "Notes from a Dead House," is assumed to be a prisoner named Alexánder Petróvitch Goryántchikoff.

Belonging to no class, and famous for but one book, which does not even count as literature, yet chronologically a member of this period, was Nikolai Gavrílovitch Tchernyshévsky (1828–1889). After 1863 he exerted an immense influence on the minds of young people of both sexes; and of all the writers of the "storm and stress" period, he is the most interesting, because, in his renowned book, "What Is to Be Done?" he applied his theories to practical life. His success was due, not to the practicability of his theories, to his literary qualities, to his art, but to the fact that he contrived to unite two things, each one of which, as a rule, is found in a writer; he simultaneously touched the two most responsive chords in the human heart—the thirst for easy happiness, and the imperative necessity for ascetic self-sacrifice. Hence, he won a response from the most diametrically conflicting natures.

"What Is to Be Done" is the story of a young girl who, with the greatest improbability, is represented as being of the purest, most lofty character and sentiments, yet the daughter of two phenomenally (almost impossibly) degraded people. Instead of marrying the rich and not otherwise undesirable man whom her parents urge on her, and who is deeply in love with her, she runs away with her teacher, and stipulates in advance for life in three rooms. She is only seventeen, yet she promptly establishes a fashion-shop which thrives apace, and puts forth numerous branches all over the capital. Her workinggirls are treated ideally and as equals, she working with them, in which lies the answer to "What Is to Be Done?" After a while she falls in love with her husband's dearest friend, who is described as so exactly like him that the reader is puzzled to know wherein she descried favorable difference, and the husband, perceiving this, makes things easy by pretending to drown himself, but in reality going off to America. Several years later he returns—as an American—and his ex-wife's present husband, having become a medical celebrity, helps him to a bride by informing her panic-stricken parents (who oppose the match, although they are ignorant at first of any legal impediment to the union), that she will certainly die if they do not yield. The two newly assorted couples live in peace, happiness, and prosperity ever after. Work and community life are the chief themes of the preachment. ⁕He was exiled to Siberia in 1864, and on his return to Russia (when he settled in Ástrakhan, and was permitted to resume his literary labors), he busied himself with translations, critical articles, and the like, but was unable to regain his former place in literature.

QUESTIONS FOR REVIEW

1. Describe the early life of Dostoévsky.
2. How were his first writings received?
3. What relation had he to the social agitations of the times?
4. Upon what charge was he exiled to Siberia?
5. How were his views affected by his prison life?
6. Give some account of his literary activities.
7. How did his views resemble those of Tolstóy?
8. How did they differ?
9. What are the characteristics of Dostoévsky's style?
10. What are the chief types portrayed in his novels?
11. What two periods of his life are represented by his "Notes From a Dead House" and his later works?
12. Why has "What Is to Be Done?" achieved such popularity?

BIBLIOGRAPHY

Buried Alive; or, Ten Years' Penal Servitude in Siberia. ("Notes From a Dead House.") There are also other translations bearing various titles.

Poor Folk. Crime and Punishment. Humbled and Insulted. (The last two abbreviated are translated by F. Wishaw.) F. M. Dostoévsky.

What is to be Done? A Vital Question. (Two translations of the same work.) N. G. Tchernyshevsky.

CHAPTER XII

SEVENTH PERIOD: DANILÉVSKY, SALTYKOFF, L.
N. TOLSTÓY, GÓRKY, AND OTHERS.

Under the influence of the romantic movement in western Europe, in the '30's of the nineteenth century, and in
particular under the deep impression made by Sir Walter
Scott's novels, historical novels and historical studies
began to make their appearance in Russia, and in the
'50's underwent two periods of existence, which totally
differed from each other.

During the first period the romance-writers, including
even Púshkin, treated things from a governmental point
of view, and dealt only with such epochs, all more or less
remote, as the censorship permitted. For example, Zagóskin, the best known of the historical novelists, wrote
"Áskold's Grave," from the epoch of the baptism of the
Russians, in the tenth century, and "Yúry Miloslávsky,"
from the epoch of the Pretender, early in the seventeenth
century; while Lazhétchnikoff wrote "The Mussulman,"
from the reign of Iván III., sixteenth century, and "The
Last Court Page," from the epoch of Peter the Great's
wars with Sweden. The historical facts were alluded to
in a slight, passing way, or narrated after the fashion of
Karamzín, in lofty terms, with artificial patriotic inspiration. As the authors lacked archæological learning, the
manners and accessories of the past were merely sketched
in a general, indefinite way, and often inaccurately, while

the pages were chiefly filled with the sentimental love-passages of two or three virtuous heroes of stereotyped patterns, who were subjected to frightful adventures, perished several times, and were resuscitated for the purpose of marrying in ordinary fashion at the end.

In the '50's people became far too much interested in the present to pay much heed to the past. Yet precisely at that time the two finest historians came to the front, Sergyei M. Soloviéff and N. I. Kostomároff, and effected a complete revolution in historiography. Soloviéff's great history brings the narrative down to the reign of Katherine II. Kostomároff dealt with periods, giving a complete picture of each one; hence each study, while complete in itself, does not of necessity always contain the whole career of the personages who figure in it. But both writers are essentially (despite Kostomároff's not very successful attempts at historical novels) serious historians.

As we have already seen, the novels of the two Counts Tolstóy, "War and Peace" and "Prince Serébryani," stand quite apart, and far above all others.

But among the favorites of lesser rank are Grigóry Petróvitch Danilévsky (born in 1829), whose best historical novel is "Miróvitch," though it takes unwarrantable liberties with the personages of the epoch depicted (that of Katherine II.) and those in the adjacent periods. Less good, though popular, is his "Princess Tarakánoff," the history of a supposed daughter of the Empress Elizabeth.

Half-way between the historians and the portrayers of popular life, and in a measure belonging to both ranks, are several talented men. The most famous of them was Pável Ivánovitch Mélnikoff (1819–1883), whose official duties enabled him to make an exhaustive study of the "Old Ritualists" * along the middle Volga.

His two novels, "In the Forests" and "On the Hills" (of the eastern and western banks of the Volga, respectively), are utterly unlike anything else in the language, and are immensely popular with Russians. They are history in that they faithfully reproduce the manners and beliefs of a whole class of the population; they are *genre* studies of a very valuable ethnographical character in their fidelity to nature. Long as they are, the interest never flags for a moment, but it is not likely that they will ever appear in an English translation. Too extensive and intimate a knowledge of national ways and beliefs (both of the State Church and the schismatics) are required to allow of their being popular with the majority of foreigners who read Russian; for the non-Russian reading foreigner an excessive amount of explanatory notes would be required, and they would resemble treatises. But they are two of the most delightful books of the epoch, and classics in their way. Mélnikoff wrote, for a long time, under the pseudonym of "Andréi Petchérsky."

Nikolái Seménovitch Lyeskóff (1837-1895), who long wrote under the pseudonym of "M. Stebnítzky," is another author famous for his portraits of a whole class of the population, his specialty being the priestly class. He was of noble birth, and was reared in luxury, but was orphaned and ruined at a very early age, so that he was obliged to earn a hard living, first in government service, then as traveler for a private firm. This extensive traveling afforded him the opportunity of making acquaintance

* The "Old Ritualists" or *raskólniki*, are those who do not accept the corrections to the Church books, and so forth, made in seventeenth century, by the Patriarch Nikon.

with the life of all classes of the population. He began to write in 1860, but a few incautious words, in 1862, raised a storm against him in the liberal press, which accused him of instigating the police to their attacks upon young people. As Count Tolstóy remarked to me, this incident prevented Lyeskóff ever receiving the full meed of recognition which his talent merited; a large and influential section of the press was permanently in league against him. This, eventually, so exasperated and embittered Lyeskóff that he really did go over to the conservative camp, and the first result of his wrath was the romance "No Thoroughfare," published in 1865. Its chief characters are two ideal socialists, a man and a woman, recognized by contemporaries as the portraits of living persons. Both are represented as finding so-called socialists to be merely crafty nihilists. This raised another storm, and still further embittered Lyeskóff, who expressed himself in "To the Knife" (in the middle of the '70's), a mad production, wherein revolutionists (or "nihilists," as they were then generally called) were represented as condensed incarnations of the seven deadly sins. These works had much to do with preventing Lyeskóff from taking that high place in the public estimation which his other works (a mass of novels and tales devoid of political tendency) and his great talent would have otherwise assured to him. Of his large works, "The Cathedral Staff," with its sympathetic and life-like portraits of Archpriest Savély Tuberósoff and his athletic Deacon Achilles, and his "Episcopal Trifles" rank first. The latter volume, which consists of a series of pictures setting forth the dark sides of life in the highest ecclesiastical hierarchy, created a great sensation in the early '80's, and raised a third

storm, and the author fell into disfavor in official circles.
Perhaps the most perfect of his works is one of the
shorter novels, "The Sealed Angel," which deals with
the ways and beliefs of the Old Ritualists (though in the
vicinity of Kíeff, not in Mélnikoff's province), and is
regarded as a classic, besides being a pure delight to the
initiated reader.   Count L. N. Tolstóy greatly admired
(he told me) Lyeskóff's "At the End of the World," a
tale of missionary effort in Siberia, which is equally
delightful in its way, though less great.   Towards the
end of his career, Lyeskóff was inclined to mysticism, and
began to work over ancient religious legends, or to invent
new ones in the same style.*

The direct and immediate result of the democratic
tendency on Russian thought and attraction to the common people during this era was the creation of a school
of writers who devoted themselves almost exclusively to
that sphere, in addition to the contributions from Turgéneff, Tolstóy, Dostoévsky.   Among these was a well-
known woman writer, Márya Alexándrevna Markóvitch,
who published her first Little Russian Tales, in 1859,
under the name of "Márko Vovtchék."   She immediately
translated them into Russian, and they were printed in
the best journals of the day.   I. S. Turgéneff translated
one volume into Russian (for her Little Russian language
was not of the supreme quality that characterized
Shevtchénko's, which needed no translating), and Dobro-
liúboff, an authoritative critic of that period, expressed
himself in the most flattering manner about them.   But

---

* Count L. N. Tolstóy presented me with a copy of one of these legends
—a most distressing and improbable affair—with the remark, "Lyeskóff has
spoiled himself by imitating me."   He meant that Lyeskóff was imitating his
little moral tales and legends, to which he had been devoting himself for
some time past.   I agreed with Tolstóy, as to the effect.

her fame withered away as quickly as it had sprung up. The weak points of her tales had been pardoned because of their political contents; in ten years they had lost their charm, and their defects—a too superficial knowledge of the people's life, the absence of living, authentic coloring in portraiture, its restriction to general, stereotyped types, such as might have been borrowed from popular tales and ballads, and excess of sentimentality—became too apparent to be overlooked by a more enlightened public.

The only other woman writer of this period who acquired much reputation may be mentioned here, although she cannot be classed strictly with portrayers of the people: Nadézhda Dmítrievna Khvóshtchinsky, whose married name was Zaióntchkovsky, and who wrote under the pseudonym of "V. Krestóvsky" (1825–1889). She published a great many short stories of provincial town life, rather narrow as to their sphere of observation. Her best work was "The Great Bear" (referring to the constellation), which appeared in 1870–1871.*

When literature entered upon a fresh phase of development in the '70's of the last century, the careful study of the people, two men headed the movement, Glyeb Ivánovitch Uspénsky and Nilkolái Nikoláevitch Zlatovrátsky. Uspénsky (1840) took the negative and pessimistic view. Zlatovrátsky (1845) took the positive, optimistic view.†

Like many authors of that period, adverse conditions hindered Uspénsky's march to fame. Shortly after his first work, "The Manners of Rasteryáeff Street," began to appear in "The Contemporary," that journal was

* Although she was very ill and weak, she was good enough to ask me to visit her, a few months before she died, in 1889.

† Count L. N. Tolstóy told me that Uspénsky had never been sufficiently appreciated. He also praised Zlatovrátsky highly.

stopped. He continued it in another journal, which also was stopped before his work was finished, and that after he had been forced to cut out everything which gave a hint at its being a "continuation," so that it might appear to be an independent whole. He was obliged to publish the mangled remains in "The Woman's News," because there was hardly any other journal then left running. After the Servian War (generally called abroad "the Russo-Turkish War") of 1877–1878, Uspénsky abandoned the plebeian classes to descend to "the original source" of everything—the peasant. When he published the disenchanting result of his observations, showing to what lengths a peasant will go for money, there was a sensation. This was augmented by his sketch, "Hard Labor"; and a still greater sensation ensued on the publication of his " 'Tis Not a Matter of Habit" (known in book form as "The Eccentric Master"). In "Hard Labor" he set forth, contrary to all theoretical beliefs, that the peasants of villages which had belonged to private landed proprietors prior to the emancipation, were incomparably and incontestably more industrious and moral than the peasants on the crown estates, who had always been practically free men.†

Readers were still more alarmed by the deductions set forth in his "An Eccentric Master." The hero is an educated man, Mikháil Mikháilovitch, who betakes himself to the rural wilds with the express object of "toiling there exactly like the rest, as an equal in morals and duties, to sleep with the rest on the straw, to eat from one pot with them" (the Tolstóyan theory, but in advance of him), "while the money acquired thus by general toil was to be

† Former crown serfs repeatedly told me how free they had been—how much better off than those of private persons.

the property of a group of people to be formed from peasants and from actually ruined former members of the upper classes." But the peasants, not comprehending the master's lofty aims, treated him as an eccentric fool, and began to rob him in all directions, meanwhile humoring him to the top of his bent in all his instincts of master. It ends in Mikháil Mikháilovitch becoming thoroughly disillusioned, dejected, and taking to drink after having expended the whole of his capital on the ungrateful peasants. This will serve to illustrate Uspénsky's pessimistic point of view, for which he certainly had solid grounds.

While Uspénsky never sought artistic effects in his work, and his chief strength lay in humor, in ridicule which pitilessly destroyed all illusions, Zlatovrátsky never indulges in a smile, and is always, whether grieving or rejoicing, in a somewhat exalted frame of mind, which often attains the pitch of epic pathos, so that even his style assumes a rather poetical turn, something in the manner of hexameters. Moreover, he is far from despising the artistic element. He established his fame in 1874 by his first large work, "Peasant Jurors."

As Zlatovrátsky (whose father belonged to the priestly class) regards as ideal the commune and the peasant guild (*artél*), with their individualistic, moral ideals of union in a spirit of brotherly love and solidarity, both in work and in the enjoyment of its products, his pessimism is directed against the Russian educated classes, not excepting even their very best representatives. This view he expresses in all his works which depict the educated classes: "The Golden Heart," "The Wanderer," "The Kremléff Family," "The Karaváeffs," "The Hetman," and so forth. In these he represents educated people—

the better classes, called "intelligent" people by Russians—under the guise of sheep who have strayed from the true fold, and the only thing about them which he regards as a sign of life (in a few of the best of them) is their vain efforts to identify themselves with the common people, and thus, as it were, restore the lost paradise.*

There are many others who have written sketches and more ambitious works founded on a more or less intimate study and knowledge of the peasants. On one of these we must turn our attention, briefly, as the author of one famous and heartrending book, "The Inhabitants of Podlípovo." Feódor Mikháilovitch Ryeshétnikoff (1841–1871) was one of three middle-class ("plebeian" is the Russian word) writers who made a name, the others being Alexánder Ivánovitch Levítoff and Nikolái Ivánovitch Naúmoff. For in proportion as culture spread among the masses of society, and the center of the intellectual movement was transferred from the noble class to the plebeian, in the literary circles towards the end of the '50's there appeared a great flood of new forces from the lower classes. The three writers above mentioned, as well as Uspénsky and Zlatovrátsky, belonged to the priestly plebeian class. Ryeshétnikoff's famous romance —rather a short story—was the outcome of his own hardships, sufferings, and experiences. He was scantily educated, had no æsthetic taste, wrote roughly, not always grammatically, and always in excessively gloomy colors, yet he had the reputation of being a passionate lover of the people, despite the fact that his picture of the peasants in his best known work is generally regarded as almost a

* Naturally, it is this feature of his writings which made Count Tolstóy laud him so highly to me.

caricature in its exaggerated gloom, and he enjoys wide popularity even at the present time.

The spirits of people rose during the epoch of Reform (after the Emancipation of the serfs in 1861) and the general impulse to take an interest in political and social questions was speedily reflected in literature by the formation of a special branch of that art, which was known as "tendency literature," although its more accurate title would have been "publicist literature." The peculiarity of most writers of this class was their pessimistic skepticism. This publicist literature was divided into three classes: democratic, moderately liberal, and conservative.

At the head of the democratic branch stood the great writer who constituted the pride and honor of the epoch, as the one who most profoundly and fully reflected it, Mikháil Evgráfovitch Saltykóff (1826–1889). He was the son of landed proprietors, of an ancient family, with a famous name of Tatár descent. He finished his education in the Tzárskoe Seló Lyceum, which, from the time of Púshkin on, graduated so many notable statesmen and distinguished men. The authorities of the Lyceum were endeavoring to exterminate the spirit of Púshkin, who had died only the year before, and severely repressed all scribbling of poetry, which did not in the least prevent almost every boy in the school from trying his hand at it and dreaming of future fame. Thus incited, Saltykóff, from the moment of his entrance, earned the ill-will of the authorities by his passionate love of verse writing and reading, and when he graduated, in 1844, it was in the lower half of his class, and with one rank lower in the civil service than the upper half of the class.

In 1847 he published (under the name of "M. Nepá-noff") his first story, "Contradictions," and in 1848 his second, "A Tangled Affair," both in "The Annals of the Fatherland." When the strictness of the censorship was augmented during that same year, after "the Petrashévsky affair," all literary men fell under suspicion. When Salty-kóff asked for leave of absence from the service to go home during the holidays, he was commanded to produce his writings. Although these early writings contained hardly a hint of the satirical talents which he afterwards developed, the person to whom was intrusted the task of making a report of them (and who was a sworn enemy to the natural school and "The Annals of the Fatherland") gave such an alarming account of them that the Count Tchérnysheff was frightened at having so dangerous a man in his ministerial department. The result was, that in May, 1848, a posting-tróïka halted in front of Salty-kóff's lodgings, and the accompanying gendarme was under orders to escort the offender off to Vyátka on the instant.

In Saltykóff's case, as in the case of many another Russian writer, exile not only removed him from the distracting pleasures of life at the capital, but also laid the foundation for his future greatness. In Vyátka, Saltykóff first served as one of the officials in the government office, but by the autumn he was appointed the official for special commissions immediately attached to the governor's service. He was a valued friend in the family of the vice-governor, for whose young daughters he wrote a "Short History of Russia," and after winning further laurels in the service, he was allowed to return to St. Petersburg in 1856, when he married one of the young girls, and published his "Governmental Sketches," with the materials for which his exile had furnished him. Two years later he was appointed vice-governor of Ryazán, then transferred to Tver, where he acted as governor on several occasions. In 1862 he retired from the service and devoted himself to literature, but he returned to it a couple of years later, and only retired definitively in 1868. These items are of interest as showing the status of political exiles in a different light from that usually accepted as the unvarying rule.

As we have said, Saltykóff's exile was of incalculable service to him, in that it made him acquainted with the inward life of Russia and of the people. This knowledge he put to unsparing use in his famous satires. In order fully to understand his works, one must be thoroughly familiar with the general spirit and the special ideas of the different periods to which they refer, as well as with Russia and its life and literature in general. Saltykóff (who wrote under the name of "Shtchedrín") was very keen to catch the spirit of the moment, and very caustic in portraying it, with the result that very often the names he invented for his characters clove to whole classes of society, and have become by-words, the mere mention of which reproduces the whole type. For example, after the Emancipation, when the majority of landed proprietors were compelled to give up their parasitic life on the serfs, there arose a class of educated people who were seeking fresh fields for their easy, parasitic existence. One of the commonest expedients, in the '70's, for restoring shattered finances was to go to Tashként, where the cultured classes imagined that regular gold mines awaited them. Saltykóff instantly detected this movement, and not only branded the pioneers in the colonization of Central Asia with the name of "Tashkéntzians" (in "Gospodá Tashkéntzy" Messrs. Tashkéntzians), but according to his wont, he rendered this nickname general by applying it to all cultured classes who had nothing in their souls but an insatiable appetite. In other works he branded other movements and classes with equal ineffaceableness.

His masterpiece (in his third and most developed period), the work which foreigners can comprehend almost equally well with Russians, is "Gospodá Golovlévy" ("The Messrs. Golovléff" *). It contains that element of the universal in humanity which his national satires lack, and it alone would suffice to render him immortal. The type of Iúdiushka (little Judas) has no superior in all European literature, for its cold, calculating, cynical hypocrisy, its miserly ferocity. The book is a presentment of old ante-reform manners among the landed gentry at their worst.

The following favorite little story furnishes an excellent example of Saltykóff's (Shtchedrín's) caustic wit and satire:

THE STORY OF HOW ONE PEASANT MAINTAINED TWO GENERALS.

Once upon a time there lived and flourished two Generals; and as both were giddy-pated, by jesting command, at my desire, they were speedily transported to an uninhabited island.

The Generals had served all their lives in some registry office or other; they had been born there, reared there, had grown old there, and consequently they understood nothing whatever.

* Or, "The Golovléffs," the above being the more formal translation. Saltykóff was too ill to receive strangers when I was in Russia. But I attended a requiem service over his body, at his home; another at the Kazán Cathedral, where all the literary lights assembled; and went to his funeral in the outlying cemetery, thereby having the good fortune to behold one of the famous "demonstrations" in which the Russian public indulges on such occasions.

They did not even know any words except, "accept the assurance of my complete respect and devotion."

The registry was abolished as superfluous, and the Generals were set at liberty. Being thus on the retired list, they settled in Petersburg, in Podyátchesky (Pettifoggers) Street, in separate quarters; each had his own cook, and received a pension. But all of a sudden, they found themselves on an uninhabited island, and when they awoke, they saw that they were lying under one coverlet. Of course, at first they could not understand it at all, and they began to talk as though nothing whatever had happened to them.

"'Tis strange, your Excellency, I had a dream to-day," said one General; "I seemed to be living on a desert island."

No sooner had he said this than he sprang to his feet. The other General did the same.

"Heavens! What's the meaning of this? Where are we?" cried both, with one voice.

Then they began to feel each other, to discover whether this extraordinary thing had happened to them not in a dream, but in their waking hours. But try as they might to convince themselves that all this was nothing but a vision of their sleep, they were forced to the conviction of its sad reality.

On one side of them stretched the sea, on the other side lay a small plot of land, and beyond it again stretched the same boundless sea. The Generals began to weep, for the first time since the registry office had been closed.

They began to gaze at each other, and they then perceived that they were clad only in their night-shirts, and on the neck of each hung an order.

"How good a little coffee would taste now!" ejaculated one General, but then he remembered what unprecedented adventure had happened to him, and he began to cry again.

"But what are we to do?" he continued, through his tears; "if we were to write a report, of what use would it be?"

"This is what we must do," replied the other General. "Do you go to the east, your Excellency, and I will go to the west, and in the evening we will meet again at this place; perhaps we shall find something."

So they began their search to find which was the east and which the west. They recalled to mind that their superior official had once said, " If you wish to find the east, stand with your eyes towards the north, and you will find what you want on your right hand." They began to seek the north, and placed themselves first in one position, then in another, and tried all quarters of the compass in turn, but as they had spent their whole lives in the registry office, they could decide on nothing.

"This is what we must do, your Excellency; do you go to the right, and I will go to the left; that will be better," said the General, who besides serving in the registry office had also served as instructor of calligraphy in the school for soldiers' sons, and consequently had more sense.

So said, so done. One General went to the right, and saw trees growing, and on the trees all sorts of fruits. The General tried to get an apple, but all the apples grew so high that it was necessary to climb for them. He tried to climb, but with no result, except that he tore his shirt to rags. The General came to a stream, the fish were swimming there in swarms, as though in a fish-shop on the Fontánka canal. "If we only had such fish in Pettifoggers Street!" said the General to himself, and he even changed countenance with hunger.

The General entered the forest, and there hazel-hens were whistling, blackcocks were holding their bragging matches, and hares were running.

"Heavens! What victuals! What victuals!" said the General, and he felt that he was becoming fairly sick at his stomach with hunger.

There was nothing to be done; he was obliged to return to the appointed place with empty hands. He reached it but the other General was already waiting for him.

"Well, your Excellency, have you accomplished anything?"

"Yes, I have found an old copy of the 'Moscow News'; that is all."

The Generals lay down to sleep again, but gnawing hunger kept them awake. They were disturbed by speculations as to who would receive their pension for them; then they recalled the fruits, fish, hazel-hens, blackcock, and hares which they had seen that day.

"Who would have thought, your Excellency, that human food, in its original shape, flies, swims, and grows on trees?" said one General.

"Yes," replied the other General; "I must confess that until this day I thought that wheaten rolls came into existence in just the form in which they are served to us in the morning with our coffee."

"It must be that, for instance, if one desires to eat a partridge, he must first catch it, kill it, pluck it, roast it. . . . . But how is all that done?"

"How is all that done?" repeated the other General, like an echo. They fell into silence, and tried to get to sleep; but hunger effectually banished sleep. Hazel-hens, turkeys, sucking-pigs flitted before their eyes, rosy, veiled in a slight blush of roasting, surrounded with cucumbers, pickles, and other salads.

"It seems to me that I could eat my own boots now!" said one General.

"Gloves are good also, when they have been worn a long time!" sighed the other General.

All at once the Generals glanced at each other; an ominous fire glowed in their eyes, their teeth gnashed, a dull roar forced its way from their breasts. They began slowly to crawl toward each other, and in the twinkling of an eye they were exasperated to fury. Tufts of hair flew about, whines and groans resounded; the General who had been a teacher of calligraphy bit off his adversary's Order, and immediately swallowed it. But the sight of flowing blood seemed to restore them to their senses.

"The power of the cross defend us!" they exclaimed simultaneously; "if we go on like this we shall eat each other!"

"And how did we get here? What malefactor has played us this trick?"

"We must divert our minds with some sort of conversation, your Excellency, or there will be murder!" said the other General.

"Begin!" replied the other General.

"Well, for instance, what do you think about this, Why does the sun rise first and then set, instead of acting the other way about?"

"You are a queer man, your Excellency; don't you rise first, then go to the office, write there, and afterward go to bed?"

"But why not admit this reversal of the order; first I go to bed, have divers dreams, and then rise?"

"Hm, yes. . . . . But I must confess that when I served in the department I always reasoned in this fashion: now it is morning, then it will be day, then supper will be served, and it will be time to go to bed."

But the mention of supper plunged them both into grief, and broke the conversation off short at the very beginning.

"I have heard a doctor say that a man can live for a long time on his own juices," began one of the Generals.

"Is that so?"

"Yes, sir, it is; it appears that the juices proper produce other juices; these in their turn, engender still other juices, and so on, until at last the juices cease altogether. . . . "

"What then?"

"Then it is necessary to take some sort of nourishment "

"Tfu!"

In short, no matter what topic of conversation the Generals started, it led inevitably to a mention of food, and this excited their appetites still more. They decided to cease their conversation, and calling to mind the copy of the " Moscow News " which they had found, they began to read it with avidity.

"Yesterday," read one General, with a quivering voice, " the respected governor of our ancient capital gave a grand dinner. The table was set for one hundred persons, with wonderful luxury. The gifts of all lands seemed to have appointed a rendezvous at this magical feast. There was the golden sterlet of the Sheksna, the pheasant, nursling of the Caucasian forests, and strawberries, that great rarity in our north in the month of February. . . . ."

"Tfu, heavens! Cannot your Excellency find some other subject?" cried the other General in desperation, and taking the newspaper from his companion's hand, he read the following: "A correspondent writes to us from Tula: 'There was a festival here yesterday at the club, on the occasion of a sturgeon being caught in the river Upá (an occurrence which not even old residents can recall, the more so as private Warden B. was recognized in the sturgeon). The author of the festival was brought in on a huge wooden platter, surrounded with cucumbers, and holding a bit of green in his mouth. Doctor P., who was on duty that day as presiding officer, saw to it carefully that each of the guests received a piece. The sauce was extremely varied, and even capricious. . . . . "

"Permit me, your Excellency, you also seem to be not sufficiently cautious in your choice of reading matter!" interrupted the first General, and taking the paper in his turn, he read: "A correspondent writes to us from Viátka: 'One of the old residents here has invented the following original method of preparing fish soup: Take a live turbot, and whip him as a preliminary; when his liver has become swollen with rage.' . . . . "

The Generals dropped their heads. Everything on which they turned their eyes—everything bore witness to food. Their own thoughts conspired against them, for try as they would to banish the vision of beefsteak, this vision forced itself upon them.

And all at once an idea struck the General who had been a teacher of calligraphy. . . . .

"How would it do, your Excellency," he said joyfully, "if we were to find a peasant?"

"That is to say . . . . a muzhík?"

"Yes, exactly, a common muzhík . . . . such as muzhíks generally are. He would immediately give us rolls, and he would catch hazel-hens and fish!"

"Hm . . . . a peasant . . . . but where shall we find him, when he is not here?"

"What do you mean by saying that he is not to be found? There are peasants everywhere, and all we have to do is to look him up! He is certainly hiding somewhere, about because he is too lazy to work!" This idea cheered the Generals to such a degree that they sprang to their feet like men who had received a shock, and set out to find a peasant.

They roamed for a long time about the island without any success whatever, but at last the penetrating smell of bread-crust and sour sheepskin put them on the track. Under a tree, flat on his back, with his fists under his head, lay a huge peasant fast asleep, and shirking work in the most impudent manner. There were no bounds to the wrath of the Generals.

"Asleep, lazybones!" and they flung themselves upon him; "and you don't move so much as an ear, when here are two Generals who have been dying of hunger these two days! March off, this moment, to work!"

The man rose; he saw that the Generals were stern. He would have liked to give them the slip, but they had become fairly rigid when they grasped him.

And he began to work under their supervision.

First of all he climbed a tree and picked half a score of the ripest apples for the Generals, and took one, a sour one, for himself. Then he dug in the earth and got some potatoes; then he took two pieces of wood, rubbed them together, and produced fire. Then he made a snare from his own hair and caught a hazel-hen. Last of all, he arranged the fire, and cooked such a quantity of different provisions that the idea even occurred to the Generals, "would it not be well to give the lazy fellow a little morsel?"

The Generals watched the peasant's efforts, and their hearts played merrily. They had already forgotten that they had nearly died of hunger on the preceding day, and they thought, "What a good thing it is to be a general—then you never go to destruction anywhere."

"Are you satisfied, Generals?" asked the big, lazy peasant.

"We are satisfied, my dear friend, we perceive your zeal," replied the Generals.

"Will you not permit me to rest now?"

"Rest, my good friend, only first make us a rope."

The peasant immediately collected wild hemp, soaked it in water, beat it, worked it—and by evening the rope was done.

With this rope the Generals bound the peasant to a tree so that he should not run away, and then they lay down to sleep.

One day passed, then another; the big, coarse peasant became so skilful that he even began to cook soup in the hollow of his hand. Our Generals became jovial, light-hearted, fat, and white. They began to say to each other that, here they were living with everything ready to hand while their pensions were accumulating and accumulating in Petersburg.

"What do you think, your Excellency, was there really a tower of Babel, or is that merely a fable?" one General would say to the other, as they ate their breakfast.

"I think, your Excellency, that it really was built; because, otherwise, how can we explain the fact that many different languages exist in the world?"

"Then the flood must have occurred also?"

"The flood did happen, otherwise, how could the existence of antediluvian animals be explained? The more so as it is announced in the 'Moscow News' . . . ."

"Shall we not read the 'Moscow News'?

Then they would hunt up that copy, seat themselves in the shade, and read it through from end to end; what people had been eating in Moscow, eating in Túla, eating in Pénza, eating in Ryazán—and it had no effect on them; it did not turn their stomachs.

In the long run, the Generals got bored. They began to refer more and more frequently to the cooks whom they had left behind them in Petersburg, and they even wept, on the sly.

"What is going on now in Pettifoggers Street, your Excellency?" one General asked the other.

"Don't allude to it, your Excellency! My whole heart is sore!" replied the other General.

"It is pleasant here, very pleasant—there are no words to describe it; but still, it is awkward for us to be all alone, isn't it? And I regret my uniform also."

"Of course you do! Especially as it is of the fourth class,* so that it makes you dizzy to gaze at the embroidery alone!"

* This refers to the Table of Ranks, established by Peter the Great. The fourth class of officials from the top of the ladder, have attained a very respectable amount of embroidery, dignity, and social position.

Then they began to urge the peasant: Take them, take them to Pettifoggers Street! And behold! The peasant, it appeared, even knew all about Pettifoggers Street; had been there; his mouth had watered at it, but he had not had a taste of it!

"And we are Generals from Pettifoggers Street, you know!" cried the Generals joyfully.

"And I, also, if you had only observed; a man hangs outside a house, in a box, from a rope, and washes the wall with color, or walks on the roof like a fly. I am that man," replied the peasant.

And the peasant began to cut capers, as though to amuse his Generals, because they had been kind to him, an idle sluggard, and had not scorned his peasant toil. And he built a ship—not a ship exactly, but a boat—so that they could sail across the ocean-sea, up to Pettifoggers Street.

"But look to it, you rascal, that you don't drown us!" said the Generals, when they saw the craft pitching on the waves.

"Be easy, Generals, this is not my first experience," replied the peasant, and began to make preparations for departure.

The peasant collected soft swansdown, and lined the bottom of the boat with it; having done this, he placed the Generals on the bottom, made the sign of the cross over them, and set sail. The pen cannot describe, neither can the tongue relate, what terror the Generals suffered during their journey, from storms and divers winds. But the peasant kept on rowing and rowing, and fed the Generals on herrings.

At last, behold Mother Nevá, and the splendid Katherine Canal, and great Pettifoggers Street! The cook-maids clasped their hands in amazement at the sight of their Generals, so fat, white, and merry! The Generals drank their coffee, ate rolls made with milk, eggs, and butter, and put on their uniforms. Then they went to the treasury, and the pen cannot describe, neither can the tongue relate, how much money they received there.

But they did not forget the peasant; they sent him a wine-glass of vódka and a silver five-kopék piece.* "Make merry, big, coarse peasant!"

* About two cents and a half.

While Turgéneff represented the "western" and liberal element (with a tinge of the "red") in the school of the '40's, and Gontcharóff stood for the bourgeois and opportunist ideals of the St. Petersburg bureaucrats, Count Lyéff Nikoláevitch Tolstóy penetrated more profoundly into the depths of the spirit of the times than any other writer of the period in the matter of analysis and skepticism which characterized that school, and carried them to the extremes of pitiless logic and radicalness, approaching more closely than any other to democratic and national ideals. But notwithstanding all his genius, Count Tolstóy was not able to free himself to any great extent from his epoch, his environment, his contemporaries. His special talents merely caused him to find it impossible to reconcile himself to the state of affairs existing around him; and so, instead of progressing, he turned back and sought peace of mind and a firm doctrine in the distant past of primitive Christianity. Sincere as he undoubtedly is in his propaganda of self-simplification and self-perfection—one might almost call it "self-annihilation"—his new attitude has wrought great and most regrettable havoc with his later literary work, with some few exceptions.

And yet, in pursuing this course, he did not strike out an entirely new path for himself; his youth was passed in an epoch when the ideal of personal perfection and self-surrender stood in the foreground, and constituted the very essence of Russian progress.

Count L. N. Tolstóy was born on August 28, O. S., 1828 (September 9th, N. S.), in the village of Yásnaya Polyána, in the government of Túla. His mother, born Princess Volkónsky (Márya Nikoláevna), died before he was two years old, and his father's sister, Countess A. T.

Osten-Saken, and a distant relative, Madame T. A. Ergól-sky, took charge of him. When he was nine years old the family removed to Moscow, and his father died soon afterwards. Lyéff Nikoláevitch, his brother Dmítry, and his sister Márya then returned to the country estate, while his elder brother Nikolái remained in Moscow with Countess Osten-Saken and studied at the University of Moscow. Three years later, the Countess Osten-Saken died, and another aunt on the father's side, Madame P. I. Yúshkoff, who resided in Kazán, became their guardian. Lyéff Nikoláevitch went there to live, and in 1843 he entered the University of Kazán in the philological course, but remained in it only one year, because the professor of history (who had quarreled with Tolstóy's relatives) gave him impossibly bad marks, in addition to which he received bad marks from the professor of German, although he was better acquainted with that language than any other member of his course. He was com-pelled to change to the law course, where he remained for two years. In 1848 he took the examination for "candi-date" in the University of St. Petersburg. "I knew liter-ally nothing," he says of himself, "and I literally began to prepare myself for the examination only one week in advance." He obtained his degree of candidate, or bachelor of arts, and returned to Yásnaya Polyána, where he lived until 1851, when he entered the Forty-fourth Battery of the Twentieth Brigade of Artillery as "yúnker" or supernumerary officer, with no official rank, but eligible to receive a commission as ensign, and thence advance in the service. This battery was stationed on the Térek River, in the Caucasus, and there Tolstóy remained with it until the Crimean War broke out.

Thus during the first twenty-six years of his life he spent less than five years in towns, the rest in the country; and this no doubt laid the foundation for his deep love for country life, which has had so profound an effect upon his writings and his views of existence in general.

The dawning of his talent came during the four years he spent in the Caucasus, and he wrote "Childhood," "The Incursion, " "Boyhood," "The Morning of a Landed Proprietor," and "The Cossacks." During the Turkish campaign he was ordered to the staff of Prince M. D. Gortchakóff, on the Danube, and in 1855 received the command of a mountain battery, and took part in the fight at Tchérnaya, and the siege of Sevastópol. The literary fruits of this experience were "Sevastópol," in December, May, and August, three sketches.

It is convenient to finish his statistical history at this point with the statement that in 1862 he married, having firmly resolved, two years previously, that he never would do so, and clinched the bargain with himself by selling the big manor-house at Yásnaya Polyána for transportation and re-erection elsewhere. Between that date and 1888 he had a family of fifteen* children, of whom seven are still alive.

In his very first efforts in literature we detect certain characteristics which continue to distinguish him throughout his career, and some of which, on attaining their legitimate and logical development seem, to the ordinary reader, to be of extremely recent origin. In "Childhood" and "Boyhood" ("Youth," the third section, was written late

---

*I have seen the number variously stated at from eleven to thirteen; but Countess Sophía Andréevna, his wife, told me there had been fifteen, and I regard her as the final authority on this point, a very interesting one, in view of some of his latter-day theories and exhortations. Countess Tolstóy was the daughter of Dr. Behrs, of Moscow.

in the '50's) we meet the same keen analysis which is a leading feature in his later works, and in them is applied with such effect to women and to the tender passion, neither of which elements enters into his early works in any appreciable degree. He displays the most astounding genius in detecting and understanding the most secret and trivial movements of the human soul. In this respect his methods are those of a miniature painter. Another point must be borne in mind in studying Tolstóy's characters, that, unlike Turgéneff, who is almost exclusively objective, Tolstóy is in the highest degree subjective, and has presented a study of his own life and soul in almost every one of his works, in varying degrees, and combined with widely varying elements. In the same way he has made use of the spiritual and mental state of his relatives. For example, who can fail to recognize a self-portrait from the life in Levín ("Anna Karénin"), and in Prince Andréi Bolkónsky ("War and Peace")? And the feminine characters in these great novels are either simple or composite portraits of his nearest relations, while many of the incidents in both novels are taken straight from their experience or his own, or the two combined.

It is useless to catalogue his many works with their dates in this place. Unquestionably the finest of them (despite the author's present erroneous view, that they constitute a sin and a reproach to him) are his magnificent "War and Peace" and "Anna Karénin." Curiously enough, neither met with prompt or enthusiastic welcome in Russia when they first made their appearance.* The public had grown used to the very different methods of

---

* Turgéneff, who afterwards called Tolstóy "The Great Writer of the Russian Land," pronounced emphatically against him at this time; and so did many others, who became his enthusiastic admirers.

the other celebrated romance-writers of the '40's, with whom we have already dealt. Gontcharóff had accustomed them to the delineation of character by broad, sweeping strokes; Dostoévsky to lancet-like thrusts, penetrating the very soul; Turgéneff to tender touches, which produced soft, melting outlines. It was long before they could reconcile themselves to Tolstóy's original mode of painting a vast series of miniature portraits on an immense canvas. But the effect of this procedure was at last recognized to be the very acme of throbbing, breathing life itself. Moreover, it became apparent that Tolstóy's theory of life was, that great generals, statesmen, and as a whole, all active persons who seem or try to control events, do nothing of the kind. Somewhere above, in the unknown, there is a power which guides affairs at its own will, and (here is the special point) deliberately thwarts all the efforts of the active people. According to his philosophy, the self-contained, thoroughly egotistical natures, who are wedded solely to the cult of success, generally pass through this earthly life without any notable disasters; they attend strictly to their own selfish ends, and do not attempt to sway the destinies of others from motives of humanity, patriotism, or anything else in the lofty, self-sacrificing line. On the contrary, the fate of the people who are endowed with tender instincts, who have not allowed self-love to smother their humanity, who are guilty only of striving to attain some lofty, unselfish object in life, are thwarted and repressed, balked and confounded at every turn. This is particularly interesting in view of his latter-day exhortations to men, on the duty of toiling for others, sacrificing everything for others. Nevertheless, it must stand as a monument to the fidelity of his powers of analysis of life in general, and of the individual characters in whose lot he demonstrates his theory.

This contrast between the two conflicting principles, a haughty individualism and peaceable submission to a higher power, of which the concrete representative is the mass of the population, is set forth with especial clearness in "War and Peace," where the two principal heroes, Prince Andréi Bolkónsky and Pierre Bezúkoff, represent individualism.

In "Anna Karénin," in the person of his favorite hero, Konstantín Levín, Tolstóy first enunciates the doctrine of moral regeneration acquired by means of physical labor, and his later philosophical doctrines are the direct development of the views there set forth. He had represented a hero of much earlier days, Prince Nekhliúdoff, in "The Morning of a Landed Proprietor," as convinced that he should make himself of use to his peasants; and he had set forth the result of those efforts in terms which tally wonderfully well with his direct personal comments in "My Confession," of a date long posterior to "Anna Karénin." "Have my peasants become any the richer?" he writes; "have they been educated or developed morally? Not in the slightest degree. They are no better off, and my heart grows more heavy with every passing day. If I could but perceive any success in my undertaking; if I could descry any gratitude—but no; I see false routine, vice, distrust, helplessness! I am wasting the best years of my life in vain."

But Nekhliúdoff—Tolstóy was not alone in devoting himself to his peasants; before he withdrew to the country he had led a gay life in St. Petersburg, after resigning from the army, and in writing his fine peasant story,

"Polikúshka," setting up peasant-schools on his estate, and the like, he was merely paying his tribute to the spirit of the time (which reached him even in his seclusion), and imitating the innumerable village schools and Sunday schools in the capitals (for secular instruction of the laboring classes who were too busy for education during the week) in which the aristocratic and educated classes in general took a lively interest.* But the leisure afforded by country life enabled him to compose his masterpieces. "War and Peace," which was begun in 1864, was published serially in "The Russian Messenger," beginning in 1865, and in book form in 1869, and "Anna Karénin," which was published serially in the same journal, in 1875–1876. His style is not to be compared to that of Turgéneff, with its exquisite harmony, art, and sense of proportion. Tolstóy writes carelessly, frequently repeats himself, not infrequently expresses himself ambiguously or obscurely. But the supreme effect is produced, nevertheless.

At last came the diametrical change of views, apparently, which led to this supreme artist's discarding his art, and devoting himself to religious and philosophical writings for which neither nature nor his training had fitted him. He himself dates this change from the middle of the '70's, and it must be noted that precisely at this period that strong movement called "going to the people," i. e., devoting one's self to the welfare of the peasants, became epidemic in Russian society. Again, as fifteen or twenty years previously, Count Tolstóy was merely swept onward by the popular current. But his first pamphlet on his new

* At this period, also, the peasant costume became the fashion in the higher circles. Count Tolstóy is generally (out of Russia) assumed to be the first and only wearer of such garments.

propaganda is ten years later than the date he assigns to
the change. Thereafter for many years he devoted his
chief efforts to this new class of work, "Life," "What
Is to Be Done?" "My Confession," and so forth, being
the more bulky outcome. Some of the stories, written
for the people during this interval, are delightful, both in
tone and artistic qualities. Others are surcharged with
"morals," which in many cases either directly conflict
with the moral of other stories in the same volume, or
even with the secondary moral of the same story. Even
his last work—"in my former style," as he described it—
"Resurrection," has special doctrines and aims too
emphatically insisted upon to permit of the reader deriv-
ing from it the pure literary pleasure afforded by his
masterpieces. In short, with all due respect to the entire
sincerity of this magnificent writer, it must be said that
those who would enjoy and appreciate him rightly, should
ignore his philosophico-religious treatises, which are contradictory and confusing to the last degree. As an illustration, let me cite the case of the famine in Russia of
1891–92. Great sums of money* were sent to Count
Tolstóy, chiefly from America, and were expended by
him in the most practicable and irreproachable manner—
so any one would have supposed—for the relief of the
starving peasants. Count Tolstóy and his assistants lived
the life of the peasants, and underwent severe hardships;
the Count even fell ill, and his wife was obliged to go to
him and nurse him. It would seem that his conscience

* This is a particularly interesting example to the people of America and
to me. I sent to Count Tolstóy over seven thousand dollars which people
throughout the length and breadth of the land had forwarded to me for that
purpose, and I turned thousands more in his direction. His conscience is as
uneasy and as fitful and illogical in pretty nearly all other matters, which is
a pity, because it is both lively and sincere, though mistaken.

had no cause for reproach, and that the situation was an ideal one for him. But before that famine was well over, or the funds expended, he wrote a letter to a London newspaper, in which he declared that helping people by means of money was all wrong—positively a sin. He felt that collecting and distributing money was not the best thing of which he was capable, and called it "making a pipe of one's self," personal service with brains, heart, and muscles being the only right service for God or man. This service he certainly rendered, and without the money he could not have rendered it.

Nothing could more perfectly illustrate this point of view than the following little story, written in 1881, called "The Two Brothers and the Gold."

"In ancient times there lived not far from Jerusalem two brothers, the elder Afanásy, the younger Ioánn. They dwelt on a hill not far from the town, and subsisted on what people gave them. Every day the brothers spent in work. They did not toil at their own work, but at the work of the poor. Wherever there were men overwhelmed with work, wherever there were sick people, orphans and widows, thither went the brothers, and there they toiled and nursed the people, accepting no remuneration. In this wise did the brothers pass the whole week apart, and met only on Saturday evening in their abode. Only on Sunday did they remain at home, praying and chatting together. And the angel of the Lord descended to them and blessed them. On Monday they parted and each went his way. Thus the two brothers lived for many years, and every week the angel of the Lord came down and blessed them.

One Monday as the brothers were starting out to work, and had already separated, going in different directions, Afanásy felt sorry to part with his beloved brother, and halted and glanced back. Ioánn was walking, with head bowed, in his own direction, and did not look back. But all of a sudden, Ioánn also halted, and as though catching sight of something, began to gaze intently in that direction, shading his eyes with his hand. Then he approached what he had espied there, suddenly leaped to one side, and without looking behind him fled down the hill and up the hill, away from the spot, as though a fierce wild beast were pursuing him. Afanásy was amazed and went back to the place in order to find out what had so frightened his brother. As he came near he beheld something gleaming in the sunlight. He approached closer. On the grass, as though poured out of a measure, lay a heap of gold. . . . . And Afanàsy was the more amazed, both at the gold, and at his brother's leap.

"What was he frightened at, and what did he flee from?" said Afanásy to himself. "There is no sin in gold, the sin is in man. One can do evil with gold, but one can also do good with it. How many orphans and widows can be fed, how many naked men clothed, how many poor and sick healed with this gold. We now serve people, but our service is small, according to the smallness of our strength, but with this gold we can serve people more." Afanásy reasoned thus with himself, and wished to tell it all to his brother, but Ioánn had gone off out of earshot, and was now visible on the opposite mountain, no bigger than a beetle.

And Afanásy took of his garment, raked into it as much gold as he was able to carry, flung it on his shoulders and carried it to the city. He came to the inn, gave the gold over to the innkeeper, and went back after the remainder. And when he had brought all the gold he went to the merchants, bought land in the town, bought stone and timber, hired workmen, and began to build three houses. And Afanásy dwelt three months in the town and built three houses in the town, one house, an asylum for widows and orphans, another house, a hospital for the sick and the needy, a third house for pilgrims and paupers. And Afanásy sought out three pious old men, and he placed one over the asylum, another over the hospital, and the third over the hostelry for pilgrims. And Afanásy had three thousand gold pieces left. And he gave a thousand to each old man to distribute to the poor. And people began to fill all three houses, and men began to laud Afanásy for what he had done. And Afanásy rejoiced thereat so that he did not wish to leave the city. But Afanásy loved his brother, and bidding the people farewell, and keeping not a single gold piece for himself, he went back to his abode in the same old garment in which he had quitted it.

Afanásy came to his mountain and said to himself, "My brother judged wrongly when he sprang away from the gold and fled from it. Have not I done better?"

And no sooner had Afanàsy thought this, than suddenly he beheld, standing in his path and gazing sternly at him, that angel who had been wont to bless them. And Afanásy was stupefied with amazement and could utter only, "Why is this, Lord?" And the angel opened his mouth and said, "Get thee hence! Thou art not worthy to dwell with thy brother. Thy brother's one leap is more precious than all the deeds which thou hast done with thy gold."

And Afanásy began to tell of how many paupers and wanderers he had fed, how many orphans he had cared for, and the angel said to him, "That devil who placed the gold there to seduce thee hath also taught thee these words."

And then did Afanásy's conscience convict him, and he understood that he had not done his deeds for the sake of God, and he fell to weeping, and began to repent. Then the angel stepped aside, and left open to him the way, on which Ioánn was already standing awaiting his brother, and from that time forth Afanásy yielded no more to the temptation of the devil who had poured out the gold, and knew that not by gold, but only by labor, can one serve God and men.

And the brothers began to live as before.*

Unfortunately, the best of Tolstóy's peasant stories, such as "Polikúshka," "Two Old Men" (the latter belonging to the recent hortatory period), and the like, are too long for reproduction here. But the moral of the following, "Little Girls Wiser than Old Men," is irre-

* It was to this sort of story that Count Tolstóy referred, when he told me that Lyeskóff had spoiled his talent of recent years by imitating him, Tolstóy.

proachable, and the style is the same as in the more important of those written expressly for the people.

Easter fell early that year. People had only just ceased to use sledges. The snow still lay in the cottage yards, but rivulets were flowing through the village; a big puddle had formed between the cottages, from the dung-heaps, and two little girls, from different cottages, met by this puddle—one younger, the other older. Both little girls had been dressed in new frocks by their mothers. The little one's frock was blue, the big one's yellow, with a flowered pattern. Both had red kerchiefs bound about their heads. The little girls came out to the puddle, after the morning service in church, displayed their clothes to each other, and began to play. And the fancy seized them to paddle in the water. The younger girl was on the point of wading into the pool with her shoes on, but the elder girl says, "Don't go Malásha, thy mother will scold. Come, I'll take off my shoes, and do thou take off thine." The little lasses took off their shoes, tucked up their frocks and waded into the puddle, to meet each other. Malásha went in up to her knees, and says, "It's deep, Akuliushka—I'm afraid" "Never mind," says she; "it won't get any deeper. Come straight towards me." They began to approach each other, and Akúlka says, "Look out, Malásha, don't splash, but walk quietly." No sooner had she spoken, than Malásha set her foot down with a bang in the water, and a splash fell straight on Akúlka's frock. The sarafán was splashed, and some of it fell on her nose and in her eyes as well. Akúlka saw the spot on her frock, got angry at Malásha, stormed, ran after her, and wanted to beat her. Malásha was frightened when she saw the mischief she had done, leaped out of the puddle, and ran home. Akúlka's mother came along, espied the splashed frock and spattered chemise on her daughter. "Where didst thou soil thyself, thou hussy?" "Malásha splashed me on purpose." Akúlka's mother seized Malásha, and struck her on the nape of the neck. Malásha shrieked so that the whole street heard her. Malásha's mother came out. "What art thou beating my child for?" The neighbor began to rail. One word led to another, the women scolded each other. The peasant men ran forth, a big crowd assembled in the street. Everybody shouted, nobody listened to anybody else. They scolded and scolded, One gave another a punch, and a regular fight was imminent, when an old woman, Akúlka's grandmother, interposed. She advanced into the midst of the peasants, and began to argue with them. "What are you about, my good men? Is this the season for such things? We ought to be joyful, but you have brought about a great sin." They paid no heed to the old woman, and almost knocked one another down, and the old woman would not have been able to dissuade them had it not been for Akúlka and Malásha. While the women were wrangling, Akúlka wiped off her frock, and went out again to the puddle in the space between the cottages. She picked up a small stone and began to dig the earth out at the edge of the puddle, so as to let the water out into the street. While she was digging away, Malásha came up also, and began to help her by drawing the water down the ditch with a chip. The peasant men had just come to blows, when the little girls had got the water along the ditch to the street, directly at the spot where the old woman was parting the men.

The little girls came running up, one on one side, the other on the other side of the rivulet. "Hold on, Malásha, hold on!" cried Akúlka. Malásha also tried to say something, but could not speak for laughing.

The little girls ran thus, laughing at the chip, as it floated down the stream. And they ran straight into the midst of the peasant men. The old woman perceived them, and said to the men, "Fear God! Here you have begun to fight over these same little girls, and they have forgotten all about it long ago. and are playing together again in love—the dear little things. They are wiser than you!"

The men looked at the little girls, and felt ashamed of themselves; and then the peasants began to laugh at themselves, and went off to their houses.

"Except ye become as little children, ye shall not enter the kingdom of heaven."

It is a pity that Count Tolstóy, the greatest literary genius of his time, should put his immense talent to such a use as to provoke, on his contradictions of himself, comment like the following, which is quoted from a work by V. S. Soloviéff, an essayist and argumentative writer, who quotes some one on this subject, to this effect:

"Sometimes we hear that the most important truth is in the Sermon on the Mount; then again, we are told that we must till the soil in the sweat of our brows, though there is nothing about that in the Gospels, but in Genesis—in the same place where giving birth in pain is mentioned, but that is no commandment at all, only a sad fate; sometimes we are told that we ought to give everything away to the poor; and then again, that we never ought to give anything to anybody, as money is an evil, and one ought not to harm other people, but only one's self and one's family, but that we ought to work for others; sometimes we are told that the vocation of women is to bear as many healthy children as possible, and then, the celibate ideal is held up for men and women; then again, eating no meat is the first step towards self-perfection, though why no one knows; then something is said against liquor and tobacco, then against pancakes, then against military service as if it were the worst thing on earth, and as if the primary duty of a Christian were to refuse to be a soldier, which would prove that he who is not taken into service, for any reason, is already holy enough."

This may be a trifle exaggerated, but it indicates clearly enough the utter confusion which the teachings of Count Tolstóy produce on ordinary, rational, well-meaning persons.*   In short, he should be judged in his proper sphere as one of the most gifted authors of any age or country, and judged by his legitimate works in his legitimate province, the novel, as exemplified by "War and Peace" and "Anna Karénin."

* I have stated my own theory as to Count Tolstóy's incessant changes of view, and his puzzling inconsistencies, in my "Russian Rambles." It is not necessary or fitting that I should repeat it here.

The reform movement of the '60's of the nineteenth century ended in a reaction which took possession of society as a whole during the '70's. Apathy, dejection, disenchantment superseded the previous exultation and enthusiastic impulse to push forward in all directions. Dull discontent and irritation reigned in all classes of society and in all parties. Some were discontented with the reforms, regarding them as premature, and even ruinous; others, on the contrary, deemed them insufficient, curtailed, only half-satisfactory to the needs of the country, and merely exasperating to the public demands.

These conditions created a special sort of literary school, which made its appearance in the middle of the '70's, and attained its complete development in the middle of the '80's. We have seen that the same sort of thing had taken place with every previous change in the public sentiment. The first thing which impresses one in this school is the resurrection of artistic feeling, a passion for beauty of imagery and forms, a careful and extremely elegant polish imparted to literary productions in technique. None of the authoritative and influential critics preached the cult of pure art. Yet Gárshin, the most promising of the young authors of the day, who was the very last person to be suspected of that cult, finished his works with the utmost care, so that in elegance of form and language they offer an example of faultless perfection. There can be no doubt that this renaissance of the artistic element of poetry, of beauty, was closely connected with the subsidence of the flood-tide of public excitement and agitation, which up to that time had carried writers along with it into its whirlpools, and granted them neither the time nor the desire to polish and adorn their works, and revel in beauty of forms.

Vsévolod Mikháilovitch Gárshin, the son of a petty landed proprietor in the south of Russia, was born in 1855. Despite his repeated attacks of profound melancl olia, which sometimes passed into actual insanity, and despite the brevity of his career (he flung himself down stairs in a fit of this sort and died, in 1889), he made a distinct and brilliant mark in Russian literature.

Gárshin's view of people in general was thus expressed: "All the people whom I have known," he says, "are divided (along with other divisions of which, of course, there are many: the clever men and the fools, the Hamlets and the Don Quixotes, the lazy and the active, and so forth) into two categories, or to speak more accurately, they are distributed between two extremes: some are endowed, so to speak, with a good self-consciousness, while the others have a bad self-consciousness. One man lives and enjoys all his sensations; if he eats he rejoices, if he looks at the sky he rejoices. In short, for such a man, the mere process of living is happiness. But it is quite the reverse with the other sort of man; you may plate him with gold, and he will continue to grumble; nothing satisfies him; success in life affords him no pleasure, even if it be perfectly self-evident. The man simply is incapable of experiencing satisfaction; he is incapable, and that is the end of the matter." And in view of his personal disabilities, it is not remarkable that all his heroes should have belonged to the latter category, in a greater or less degree, some of the incidents narrated being drawn directly from his own experiences. Such are "The Red Flower," his best story, which presents the hallucinations of a madman, "The Coward," "Night," "Attalea Princeps," and "That Which Never Happened." On the other hand, the following have no personal element: "The Meeting," "The Orderly and the Officer," "The Diary of Soldier Ivánoff," "The Bears," "Nadézhda Nikoláevna," and "Proud Aggei."

Another writer who has won some fame, especially by his charming sketches of Siberian life, written during his exile in Siberia, is Grigóry Alexándrovitch Matchtet, born in 1852. These sketches, such as "The Second Truth," "We Have Conquered," "A Worldly Affair," are both true to nature and artistic, and produce a deep impression.

Much more talented and famous is Vladímir Galaktiónovitch Korolénko (1853), also the author of fascinating Siberian sketches, and of a more ambitious work, "The Blind Musician." One point to be noted about Korolénko is that he never joined the pessimists, or the party which professed pseudo-peasant tendencies, and followed Count L. N. Tolstóy's ideas, but has always preserved his independence. His first work, a delightful fantasy, entitled "Makár's Dream," appeared in 1885. Korolénko has been sent to Siberia several times, but now lives in Russia proper,* and publishes a high-class monthly journal.

Until quite recently opinion was divided as to whether Korolénko or Tchékoff was the more talented, and the coming "great author." As we shall see presently, that question seems to have been settled, and in part by Korolénko's friendly aid, in favor of quite another person.

* I tried to see him in Nízhni Nóvgorod, but although he was still under police surveillance, the police could not tell me where to find him, and I obtained the information from a photographer friend of his. Unfortunately, he was then in the Crimea, gathering " material."

Antón Pávlovitch Tchékoff (pseudonym "Tchek-honte," 1860) is the descendant of a serf father and grandfather. His volumes of short stories, "Humorous Tales," "In the Gloaming," "Surly People," are full of humor and of brilliant wit. His more ambitious efforts, as to length and artistic qualities, the productions of his matured talent, are "The Steppe," "Fires," "A Tiresome History," "Notes of an Unknown," "The Peasant," and so forth.

Still another extremely talented writer, who, unfortunately, has begun to produce too rapidly for his own interest, is Ignáty Nikoláevitch Potápenko (1856), the son of an officer in a Uhlan regiment, and of a Little Russian peasant mother. His father afterwards became a priest—a very unusual change of vocation and class—and the future writer acquired intimate knowledge of views and customs in ecclesiastical circles, which he put to brilliant use later on. A delicate humor is the characteristic feature of his work, as can be seen in his best writings, such as "On Active Service" * and "The Secretary of His Grace (the Bishop)."

The former is the story of a talented and devoted young priest, who might have obtained an easy position in the town, among the bishop's officials, with certain prospect of swift promotion. He resolutely declines this position, and requests that he may be assigned to a village parish, where he can be "on active service." Every one regards the request as a sign of an unsettled mind. After much argument he prevails on his betrothed bride's parents to permit the marriage (he cannot be ordained until he is

* Translated into English under the title " A Russian Priest." Another volume contains two charming stories from the same circle, " A Father of Six" and " An Occasional Holiday."

married), and hopes to find a helpmeet in her. The rest of the story deals with his experiences in the unenviable position of a village priest, where he has to contend not only with the displeasure of his young wife, but with the avarice of his church staff, the defects of the peasants, the excess of attention of the local gentlewoman, and financial problems of the most trying description. It ends in his wife abandoning him, and returning with her child to her father's house, while he insists on remaining at his post, where, as events have abundantly proved, the ministrations of a truly disinterested, devout priest are most sadly needed. It is impossible to convey by description the charm and gentle humor of this book.

But acclaimed on all sides, by all classes of society, as the most talented writer of the present day, is the young man who writes under the name of Maxím Górky (Bitter). The majority of the critics confidently predict that he is the long-expected successor of Count L. N. Tolstóy. This gifted man, who at one stroke, conquered for himself all Russia which reads, whose books sell with unprecedented rapidity, whose name passes from mouth to mouth of millions, wherever intellectual life glows, and has won an unnumbered host of enthusiastic admirers all over the world, came up from the depths of the populace.

"Górky" Alexéi Maxímovitch Pyeshkóff was born in Nízhni Nóvgorod in 1868 or 1869. Socially, he belongs to the petty burgher class, but his grandfather, on the paternal side, was reduced from an officer to the ranks, by the Emperor Nicholas I., for harsh treatment of the soldiers under his command. He was such a rough character that his son (the author's father) ran away from home five times in the course of seven years, and definitively

parted from his uncongenial family at the age of seventeen, when he went afoot from Tobólsk to Nízhni Nóvgorod, where he apprenticed himself to a paper-hanger.
Later on he became the office-manager of a steamer company in Ástrakhan. His mother was the daughter of a
man who began his career as a bargee on the Volga, one
of the lowest class of men who, before the advent of
steam, hauled the merchandise-laden barks from Ástrakhan
to Nízhni Nóvgorod, against the current. Afterwards he
became a dyer of yarns, and eventually established a thriv-
ing dyeing establishment in Nízhni.

Górky's father died of cholera at Ástrakhan when the
lad was four years old. His mother soon married again,
and gave the boy to his grandfather, who had him taught
to read and write, and then sent him to school, where he
remained only five months. At the end of that time he
caught smallpox, and his studies were never renewed.
Meanwhile his mother died, and his grandfather was
ruined financially, so Górky, at nine years of age, became
the "boy" in a shoeshop, where he spent two months,
scalded his hands with cabbage soup, and was sent back
to his grandfather. His relations treated him with hostility or indifference, and on his recovery, apprenticed him
to a draftsman, from whose harshness he promptly fled,
and entered the shop of a painter of holy pictures. Next
he became scullion on a river steamer, and the cook was
the first to inculcate in him a love of reading and of good
literature. Next he became gardener's boy; then tried
to get an education at Kazán University, under the mistaken impression that education was free. To keep from
starving he became assistant in a bakery at three rubles a
month; "the hardest work I ever tried," he says; sawed

wood, carried heavy burdens, peddled apples on the wharf, and tried to commit suicide out of sheer want and misery.* "Konováloff" and "Men with Pasts" † would seem to represent some of the experiences of this period, "Konováloff" being regarded as one of his best stories. Then he went to Tzarítzyn, where he obtained employment as watchman on a railway, was called back to Nízhni Nóvgorod for the conscription, but was not accepted as a soldier, such "holy" men not being wanted. He became a peddler of beer, then secretary to a lawyer, who exercised great influence on his education. But he felt out of place, and in 1890 went back to Tzarítzyn, then to the Don Province (of the Kazáks), to the Ukráina and Bessarábia, back along the southern shore of the Crimea to the Kubán, and thence to the Caucasus. The reader of his inimitable short stories can trace these peregrinations and the adventures incident to them. In Tiflís he worked in the railway shops, and in 1892 printed his first literary effort, "Makár Tchúdra," in a local newspaper, the "Kavkáz." In the following year, in Nízhni Nóvgorod, he made acquaintance with Korolénko, to whom he is indebted for getting into "great literature," and for sympathy and advice. When he published "Tchelkásh," in 1893, his fate was settled. It is regarded as one of the purest gems of Russian literature. He immediately rose to honor, and all his writings since that time have appeared in the leading publications. Moreover, he is the most "fashionable" writer in the country. But he enjoys something more than mere popularity; he is deeply loved.

---

* He must have been at Kazán about the time I was there; and I have often wondered if I saw him on the wharf, where I passed weary hours waiting for the steamer.

† See "Orlóff and His Wife," in my translation, 1891.

This is the result of the young artist's remarkable talent for painting absolutely living pictures of both persons and things. The many-sidedness of his genius—for he has more than talent—is shown, among other things, by the fact that he depicts with equal success landscapes, *genre* scenes, portraits of women. His episode of the singers in "Fomá Gordyéeff" (pp. 217–227) is regarded by Russian critics as fully worthy of being compared with the scenes for which Turgéneff is renowned. His landscape pictures are so beautiful that they cause a throb of pain. But, as is almost inevitable under the circumstances, most of his stories have an element of coarseness, which sometimes repels.

In general, his subject is "the uneasy man," who is striving after absolute freedom, after light and a lofty ideal, of which he can perceive the existence somewhere, though with all his efforts he cannot grasp it. We may assume that in this they represent Górky himself. But although all his heroes are seeking the meaning of life, no two of them are alike. His characters, like his landscapes, grip the heart, and once known, leave an ineffaceable imprint. Although he propounds problems of life among various classes, he differs from the majority of people, in not regarding a full stomach as the panacea for the poor man. On the contrary (as in "Fomá Gordyéeff," his most ambitious effort), he seems to regard precisely this as the cause of more ruin than the life of "the barefoot brigade," the tramps and stepchildren of Dame Fortune, with whom he principally deals. His motto seems to be "Man shall not live by bread alone." And because Górky bears this thought ever with him, in brain and heart, in nerves and his very marrow, his work possesses a strength which is almost terrifying, combined with a beauty as terrifying in its way. If he will but develop his immense genius instead of meddling with social and political questions, and getting into prison on that score with disheartening regularity, something incalculably great may be the outcome. It is said that he is now banished in polite exile to the Crimea. If he can be kept there or elsewhere out of mischief, the Russian government will again render the literature of its own country and of the world as great a service as it has already more than once rendered in the past, by similar means.

In the '70's and '80's Russian society was seized with a mania for writing poetry, and a countless throng of young poets made their appearance. No book sold so rapidly as a volume of verses. But very few of these aspirants to fame possessed any originality or serious worth. Poetry had advanced not a single step since the days of Nekrásoff and Shevtchénko, so far as national independence was concerned.

The most talented of the young poets of this period was Semén Yakóvlevitch Nádson (1862–1887). His grandfather, a Jew who had joined the Russian Church, lived in Kíeff. His father, a gifted man and a fine musician, died young. His mother, a Russian gentlewoman, died at the age of thirty-one, of consumption. At the age of sixteen, Nádson fell in love with a young girl, and began to write poetry. She died of quick consumption shortly afterwards. This grief affected the young man's whole career, and many of his poems were inspired by it. He began to publish his poems while still in school, being already threatened with pulmonary trouble, on account of which he had been sent to the Caucasus at the expense of the government, where he spent a year. In 1882 he graduated from the military school, and was appointed an officer in a regiment stationed at Kronstádt. There he lived for two years, and some of his best poems belong to this epoch: "No, Easier 'Tis for Me to Think that Thou Art Dead," "Herostrat," "Dreams," "The Brilliant Hall Has Silent Grown," "All Hath Come to Pass," and so forth. He retired from the military service in 1883, being already in the grasp of consumption. His poems ran through ten editions during the five years which followed his death, and still continue to sell with equal rapidity, so remarkable is their popularity. He was an ideally poetical figure; moreover, he charms by his flowing, musical verse, by the enthralling elegance and grace of his poetical imagery, and genuine lyric inspiration. All his poetry is filled with quiet, meditative sadness. It is by the music of his verse and the tender tears of his feminine lyrism that Nádson penetrates the hearts of his readers. His masterpiece is "My Friend, My Brother," and this reflects the sentiment of all his work.* Here is the first verse:

> My friend, my brother, weary, suffering brother,
> Whoever thou may'st be, let not thy spirit fail;
> Let evil and injustice reign with sway supreme
> O'er all the tear-washed earth.
> Let the sacred ideal be shattered and dishonored;
> Let innocent blood flow in stream—
> Believe me, there cometh a time when Baal shall perish
> And love shall return to earth.

Another very sincere, sympathetic, and genuine, though not great poet, also of Jewish race, is Semén Grigórie-

---

* I do not attempt a metrical translation. Lines 1-3, 2-4, 5-7, 6-8, rhyme in pairs.

vitch Frug (1860–1866), the son of a member of the Jewish agricultural colony in the government of Khersón. He, like Nádson, believes that good will triumph in the end, and is not in the least a pessimist.

Quite the reverse are Nikolái Maxímovitch Vilénkin (who is better known by his pseudonym of "Mínsky" from his native government), and Dmítry Sergiéevitch Merezhkóvsky (1865) who, as a poet, is generally bombastic. His novels are better.

There are many other good, though not great, contemporary writers in Russia, including several women. But they hardly come within the scope of this work (which does not aim at being encyclopedic), as neither their work nor their fame is likely to make its way to foreign readers who are unacquainted with the Russian language. For those who do read Russian there are several good handbooks of contemporary literature which will furnish all necessary information.

QUESTIONS FOR REVIEW

1. How was Russia influenced by the romantic movement in western Europe?

2. Describe the character of the romances of the first period of the fifties.

3. What important historical works appeared at this time?

4. What popular novels were written by Danilévsky?

5. What were the chief works of Mélnikoff, and why are they not likely to be translated into English?

6. Describe the career and influence of Lyeskóff.

7. Why was the fame of Markóvitch's work short-lived?

8. What difficulties did Uspénsky encounter in his early attempts at writing?

9. Describe the effect produced by his "Hard Labor" and "An Eccentric Master."

10. What views of society did Zlatovrátsky express in his writings?

11. Why did Ryeshétnikoff's "The Inhabitants of Podlípovo" become widely popular?

12. Give an account of the experiences of Saltykóff.

13. How did he make use of the material gathered during his exile?

14. How did his writings contribute some new words to the Russian language?

15. What qualities does he show in "The Story of How One Peasant Maintained Two Generals"?

16. Give the chief events in the life of Tolstóy.

17. What characteristics of style did he show in his earliest writings?

18. How is he "subjective" in delineating his characters?

19. Why was his genius not at first appreciated?

20. What was his theory of life?

21. What change came into his life in the seventies?

22. How did this affect his writings?

23. How did his experience with famine sufferers affect his views?

24. What were Gárshin's views of people in general?

25. How do his books bear out his theories?

26. What facts in Korolénko's life have influenced his literary development?

27. What characteristics does Tchékoff show in his short stories?

28. What is the story of Potápenko's "On Active Service"?

29. Give the leading events of Górky's career.

30. How is his many-sided genius shown?

31. What ideals are expressed in his work?

32. Why has Nádson's poetry such a firm hold on the popular mind?

BIBLIOGRAPHY

Danilévsky: *Mirovitch. The Princess Tarakanova.*
Potápenko: *A Russian Priest. A Father of Six. An Occasional Holiday.*

Maxim Górky: *Orloff and His Wife. Foma Gordyéeff.* (Translated by I. F. Hapgood.)

L. N. Tolstóy: All of his works are available in English translations. There are several collections of his short stories. *The Humor of Russia.* (Selections.) E. L. Voynich.

D. S. Merezhkovsky: *The Death of the Gods.* This is the first part of a trilogy, and is an historical novel of the time of Julian the Apostate. The other parts (announced for publication) are: *Resurrection* (time of Leonardo da Vinci) and *The Anti-Christ* (time of Peter the Great.)

INDEX